Management Development and Training

A TQM Approach

Management Development and Training

A TQM Approach

HARRY COSTIN

International Organization New Acropolis
Universidad San Jorge

THE DRYDEN PRESS
Harcourt Brace College Publishers

Fort Worth   Philadelphia   San Diego   New York   Orlando   Austin   San Antonio
Toronto   Montreal   London   Sydney   Tokyo

Acquisitions Editor: Ruth Rominger
Developmental Editor: Dona Hightower
Project Editor: Jim Patterson
Art Director: Brian Salisbury
Production Manager: Eddie Dawson
Permissions Editor: Adele Krause
Product Manager: Lisé W. Johnson
Marketing Coordinator: Sam Stubblefield
Electronic Publishing Coordinator: Kathi Embry

Copy Editor: Karen Pflaumer
Indexer: Sylvia Coates
Text Type: Meridien

Address for orders:
The Dryden Press
6277 Sea Harbor Drive
Orlando, FL 32887-6777
1-800-782-4479, or 1-800-433-0001 (in Florida)

Address for editorial correspondence:
The Dryden Press
301 Commerce Street, Suite 3700
Fort Worth, TX 76102

ISBN: 0-03-015348-4

Library of Congress Catalog Number: 94-62120

Printed in the United States of America

5   6   7   8   0   1   2   3   4   067   9 8 7 6 5 4 3 2 1

The Dryden Press
Harcourt Brace College Publishers

THE DRYDEN PRESS SERIES IN MANAGEMENT

Kirkpatrick and Lewis
Effective Supervision:
Preparing for the 21st Century

Kuehl and Lambing
Small Business:
Planning and Management
Third Edition

Kuratko and Hodgetts
Entrepreneurship:
A Contemporary Approach
Third Edition

Kuratko and Welsch
Entrepreneurial Strategy:
Text and Cases

Lee
Introduction to Management
Science
Second Edition

Lengnick-Hall, Cynthia, and Hartman
Experiencing Quality

Lewis
Io Enterprises Simulation

Long and Arnold
The Power of Environmental
Partnerships

McMullen and Long
Developing New Ventures:
The Entrepreneurial Option

Matsuura
International Business: A New Era

Montanari, Morgan, and Bracker
Strategic Management: A Choice
Approach

Morgan
Managing for Success

Northcraft and Neale
Organizational Behavior: A
Management Challenge
Second Edition

Penderghast
Entrepreneurial Simulation
Program

Ryan, Eckert, and Ray
Small Business:
An Entrepreneur's Plan
Fourth Edition

Sandburg
Career Design Software

Shipley and Ruthstrom
Cases in Operations Management

Sower, Motwani, and Savoie
Classic Readings in Operations
Management

Van Matre
Foundations of TQM: A Readings
Book

Vecchio
Organizational Behavior
Third Edition

Walton
Corporate Encounters: Law, Ethics,
and the Business Environment

Zikmund
Business Research Methods
Fourth Edition

THE HARCOURT BRACE
COLLEGE OUTLINE SERIES

Pentico
Management Science

Pierson
Introduction to Business
Information Systems

Sigband
Business Communication

The Dryden Press will provide complimentary ancillaries or ancillary packages to those qualified adopters under our adoption policy. Based on our adoption policy, please contact your sales representative if you would like to know if or how you may qualify. If the adopter or potential user does not use or will not be needing any of the materials received, please return materials to your representative or send them to:

Attn: Returns Department
Troy Warehouse
465 South Lincoln Drive
Troy, Mo 63379

Introduction

This book addresses training, management development, and problem solving from a Total Quality Management perspective. It also includes approaches to organizational redesign, such as systems thinking and reengineering. The book is based on the premise, eloquently supported by Stanford's Jeffrey Pfeffer, that people are the most important source of sustainable competitive advantage for organizations.

Since the popularization of the Total Quality movement in the 1980s, it has been fashionable for top managers to be people-oriented. However, sympathetic discussions about the needs of employees have contrasted sharply with the newly trimmed, "lean and mean" organizations and the massive layoffs of the early 1990s.

Today, sadly, real commitment to the workforce remains the exception rather than the rule. It is true that global recession in the early 1990s brought about the need to restructure organizations. However, layoffs, the most commonly chosen means of change, have too often been a convenient way to cut costs in the short run, boost quarterly profits, and project the illusion of some new form of efficient management. It is also unfortunate that radical process redesign approaches such as reengineering have been used to justify layoffs in the name of efficiency.

The rapid growth of the contingent workforce is a symptom of increasing social instability. Contingent workers appear as a convenient choice, as their deployment is flexible, and savings may be obtained through decreased benefit costs. However, contingent workers do not owe an allegiance to the companies they work for, nor do they participate in regular on-the-job training.

In contrast, the permanent workforce is committed to its organization, and should be treated with equal commitment in return. A company's commitment to its employees goes beyond benefit plans and a safe and pleasant work environment. A further measure that clearly signals organizational commitment to its employees is allocation of resources for ongoing training.

Ongoing training is the most obvious form of commitment to a workforce that increasingly requires more complex skills, as most jobs are related, in one way or another, to new technologies such as electronic information processing. Also, in case of layoffs, a better trained workforce will find it much easier to transfer to other, high paying jobs. A further advantage of this form of commitment is its ease of measurement, consisting of annual per employee hours and financial resources devoted to training.

It should be noted that it is useful to establish unambiguous standards for each level in the organization (all too often, only management and professional staff benefit from ongoing training), as well as benchmarks for aggregate resources to be devoted to training, such as percentage of the annual payroll and annual working hours.

TQM TRAINING

There are different approaches to the implementation of TQM in organizations. They differ in approach and method, but all of them have in common a set of values that emphasizes respect for people and encouragement of individual creativity and teamwork. These desirable goals are not easily achieved. On the contrary, they require a nurturing environment and ongoing training for staff at all levels of the organization.

Training is at the core of TQM implementation programs and commonly involves the learning of the quality control and the management and planning tools for the purpose of team-based problem solving. This process attempts to solve root causes of problems, and thereby to institutionalize continuous improvement. This process is also referred to as the PDCA cycle (Plan-Do-Check-Act), the basic Total Quality Management model.

The readings included in the book illustrate diverse approaches to TQM training, management development, and team-based problem solving. Further, the specific training needs of individuals and groups, from line workers to top management, are covered extensively. Finally, other well-known approaches to organizational and process redesign, such as systems thinking and reengineering, are described for the purposes of comparison and conceptual enrichment.

ABOUT THE STRUCTURE OF THE BOOK

The book complements the previous *Readings in Total Quality Management* by the same editor and publisher, which provided a broad overview of topics relevant to TQM in its original sources. This volume takes a complementary approach by focusing on the *people* dimension of TQM implementation efforts.

Part 1 provides an overview of Total Quality Management concepts and models and discusses implementation issues. It also focuses on building dynamic learning systems and recognizing a well-trained workforce as the most important source of sustainable competitive advantage.

Part 2 provides an overview of different approaches to problem solving and process redesign, including continuous improvement and reengineering. It also introduces the so-called New TQM Tools, referred to in the text as "Decision and Planning Tools." The "Old Tools," also known as "Seven Quality Control Tools," are covered at length in the companion *Readings* book.

Part 3 addresses specific concerns related to training at different levels of the organization. Training for first-line supervisors is covered in length, because as coaches and team leaders they are called upon to bear the heaviest burden of TQM implementation. Included in this section are also many suggestions for activities and exercises to be used for actual training.

Appendix A provides useful guidance for on-line research of TQM topics. **Appendix B** includes a database of all participating authors who contributed original chapters to the book. They will be happy to hear from you.

ACKNOWLEDGEMENTS

I am indebted to Katherine Kominis, Nancy Mc K. Rees and Nicolas Flattes, who provided significant help editing the manuscript.

Contents

PART 1

IMPLEMENTING TOTAL QUALITY MANAGEMENT AND BUILDING LEARNING SYSTEMS

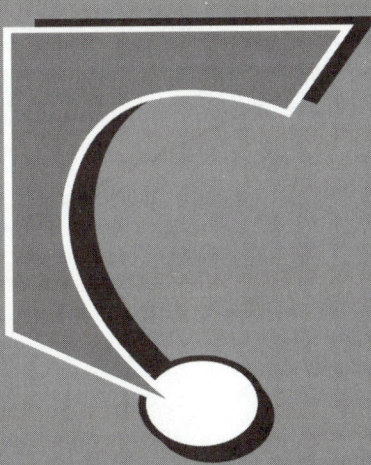

Exploring the Concepts Underlying Total Quality Management

BY HARRY COSTIN

The purpose of this paper is to offer a brief overview of the key concepts underlying the management approach that has come to be known as "Total Quality Management" or until recently as "Total Quality Control." The main themes of the quality literature will be presented in a historically significant sequence followed by an analysis of a few predominant models. Finally, suggestions will be offered for a conceptual enrichment of the field.

KEY TOTAL QUALITY MANAGEMENT CONCEPTS

Although there is no perfect consensus in terms of what all the key concepts of Total Quality Management are, the following themes pervade the literature (most of the following have been suggested by Marchese [1991] as core ideas of the TQM movement):

1. Excellence is ascribed to customer-driven organizations that systematically integrate customer feedback into their strategic planning and delivery of products and services.
2. Customer-driven organizations have a strong focus on quality, with quality being defined as both the measurable dimensions of products and services and the perceptions of internal and external customers.
3. Continuous improvement is the result of a focus on quality.
4. Improvement means making processes work better.
5. There is a strong need to extend the existing mind-set and shift to paradigms that see organizational and individual success as a result of collaboration rather than cutthroat competition.
6. Decisions should be data driven. Previous experience needs to be systematically documented and analyzed to achieve continuous improvement.

7. Teamwork is the practical application of "collaboration." In order to be effective, teams need to be trained in creative and analytical problem-solving techniques.

8. People should be empowered, that is, have real input and decision-making power in job design and organizational policies that affect them.

9. Training and recognition are essential (according to Ishikawa TQM begins and ends with education).

10. A vision (what Senge has termed a "shared vision," which needs to be known and shared by all employees and managers) is the key to give any organization a unified direction and avoid wasteful duplication of efforts and infighting.

11. Organizational change is only possible through effective leadership by example. Empty promises and speeches only make existing problems worse.

HISTORICAL FOUNDATIONS

This management approach and theory has been strongly influenced by the ideas of a few American and Japanese scholars and practitioners. Among the most widely credited "founding fathers" of the so-called TQM (Total Quality Management) movement we find Feigenbaum, Deming, Juran, Crosby, Ishikawa, Kano, Imai, Mizuno, and others. The core concepts of TQM can be found in the writings of these thinkers, who have made a lasting contribution to management theory and practice worldwide.

The term *Total Quality Control* was first introduced by Armand Feigenbaum in the November-December 1956 issue of *Harvard Business Review*. His original exploration of what he referred to as a "way out of the dilemma imposed on businessmen by increasingly demanding customers and by ever-spiraling costs of quality,… a new kind of quality control, which might be called **total quality control**" already integrated some of the key concepts of what today is known as TQM. Quoting Feigenbaum, Ishikawa defined "total quality control" as

> an effective system for integrating the quality development, quality maintenance, and quality improvement efforts of the various groups in an organization so as to enable production and service at the most economic levels which allow for full customer satisfaction. (1985, 90)

Further, for Ishikawa "TQC requires participation of all divisions, including the divisions of marketing, design, manufacturing, inspection, and shipping." This integration was explained by Feigenbaum in the 1956 Havard Business Review article in the following terms:

> The underlying principle of this total quality view—and its basic difference from all other concepts—is that, to provide genuine effectiveness, control must start with the design of the product and end only when the product has been placed in the hands of a customer who remains satisfied.
> The reason for this breadth of scope is that the quality of any product is affected at many stages of the industrial cycle:

1. Marketing evaluates the level of quality customers want and for which they are willing to pay.

2. Engineering reduces this marketing evaluation to exact specifications.
3. Purchasing chooses, contracts with, and retains vendors for parts and materials.
4. Manufacturing engineering selects the jigs, tools, and processes for relay production.
5. Manufacturing supervision and shop operators exert a major quality influence during parts making, subassembly, and final assembly.
6. Mechanical inspection and functional tests check conformance to specifications.
7. Shipping influences the caliber of the packaging and transportation.

In other words, the determination both of quality and of quality costs actually takes place throughout the entire industrial cycle. This is the reason why real quality control cannot be accomplished by concentrating on inspection alone, or design alone, or reject trouble-shooting alone, or operator education alone, or statistical analysis alone—important as each of these individual elements is.

The breadth of the job makes quality control a new and important business management function. Just as the theme of the historical inspection activity was "they (that is, parts) shall not pass," the theme of this new approach is "make them right the first time." Emphasis is on defect prevention so that routine inspection will not be needed to as large an extent. The burden of quality proof rests, not with inspection, but with the maker of the part—machinist, assembly foreman, vendor, as the case may be. (1956, 94)

What Feigenbaum calls the "industrial cycle" was popularized in the business literature of the 1980s as the "value chain" by Porter (1985). In hindsight, the principles expounded by Feigenbaum may not appear as revolutionary, since today they are part of mainstream thinking. But in an era obsessed by "control" and mass production using Frederick Taylor's management approach, they were.

Some of the key concepts that can be recognized in Feigenbaum's early writings that have profoundly influenced the TQM movement are:

- To define the production process (and later, service delivery) as an integrated system that originates with the customer (what the customer wants) and ends with the customer (customer satisfaction).
- The need to redefine the role of the inspection function (defect prevention and line workers' responsibility for quality in order to reduce the need for inspection), the consequent reduction in costs of quality by building quality into the product ("quality by design"), and the usefulness of statistical quality tools ("Statistical Process Control").

The idea of translating customer demands and needs and chosen quality levels into a product "by design" is the basic underlying concept of what is likely the second most widely used TQM process after SPC (Statistical Process Control): Quality Function Deployment, or QFD for short. This is a product or service design process using cross-functional teams that often include customers, marketing and purchasing representatives, and design and manufacturing engineers.

- To define quality as a management function, Deming and Juran elaborated further on this concept by assigning responsibility for quality to everybody in the organization.
- The purchasing function plays an important role in the industrial cycle (or value chain). In modern industrial applications, companies implementing TQM

programs favor the introduction of "vendor partnership programs" whereby the vendors commit to the delivery of consistent quality (for example, implementing SPC processes), thus reducing the need for incoming inspection (Just-in-Time systems).

TQM AS A MANAGEMENT SYSTEM

Dr. W. Edwards Deming, the best-known father of the quality movement, is widely credited with extending the quality concerns to management practice as a whole rather than simply considering them a domain of action of "quality engineers." Two key concepts developed by Dr. Deming, management responsibility and intrinsic motivation of workers and their relationship to statistical process control, deserve attention:

> Competent men in every position, from top management to the humblest worker, if they are doing their best, know all there is to know about their work **except how to improve it**. Help toward improvement can come **only from some other kind of knowledge**. Help may come from outside the company, or from better use of knowledge and skills already within the company, or both. (1975, 6)

According to Dr. Deming, only management has the power to change "systems," which are responsible for 85 percent of all defects:

> Another roadblock is management's supposition that the production workers are responsible for all trouble: that there would be no problems in production or in service if only the workers would do their jobs in the way they were taught. Pleasant dreams. The workers are handicapped by the system.

Using statistical terminology, he makes further reference to management's responsibility in the reduction of variation:

> It is good management to reduce the variation of any quality characteristic. . . . Reduction in variation means greater uniformity and dependability of product, greater output per hour, greater output per unit of raw material, and better competitive position.
>
> Causes of variation and of high cost, with loss of competitive position, may be usefully subsumed under two categories:
>
> •**Faults of the system (common or environmental causes) 85 percent:**
> These faults stay in the system until reduced by management. Their combined effect is usually easy to measure. Some individual causes must be isolated by judgment. Others may be identified by experiment: some by records on operations and materials suspected of being offenders.
> •**Special causes 15 percent:**
> These causes are specific to a certain worker or to a machine. A statistical signal detects the existence of a special cause, which the worker can usually identify and correct. (1975, 6)

Statistical tools allow workers to keep the process in control, once management has provided them with a system capable of running in control. Management's responsibility is to provide adequate training and to continuously strive to improve the existing systems. Supervision and inspection is thereby replaced by training and education.

Dr. Deming is also a firm believer in the workers' intrinsic motivation in a job well done. His "14 points" call for an "elimination of numerical quotas," and throughout his writings he further advocates the need for an educational system that from childhood fosters collaboration rather than competition.

An example of his clearly defined position on this issue can be found in his introduction to Peter Senge's book on the learning organization, *The Fifth Discipline:*

> The prevailing system of management has destroyed our people. People are born with intrinsic motivation, self-esteem, dignity, curiosity to learn, joy in learning. The forces of destruction begin with the toddlers—a prize for the best Halloween costume, grades at school, gold stars—and on up through the university. On the job, people, teams, divisions are ranked—reward for the one at the top, punishment for the one at the bottom.

JURAN'S QUALITY TRILOGY

Dr. J. M. Juran, whose impact on the quality movement in Japan was second only to Deming's, developed a useful framework for what he referred to as "a universal thought process—a universal way of thinking about quality, which fits all functions, all levels, all product lines." He called it the "quality trilogy": (1986)

> The underlying concept of the quality trilogy is that managing for quality consists of three basic quality-oriented processes:
>
> - Quality planning
> - Quality control
> - Quality improvement
>
> The starting point is quality planning—creating a process that will be able to meet established goals and do so under operating conditions. . . . Following the planning, the process is turned over to the operating forces. Their responsibility is to run the process at optimal effectiveness [this includes corrective action]. . .the zone defined by the "quality control" limits.

Finally, quality improvement is "the process for breaking through to unprecedented levels of performance." But quality improvement

> does not happen of its own accord. It results from purposeful action taken by upper management to introduce a new managerial process into the system of managers' responsibilities—the quality improvement process. This quality improvement process is superimposed on the quality control process—a process implemented in addition to quality control, not instead of it.

Juran's approach is essentially the same as Deming's. Quality is a management responsibility that needs to be performed systematically to achieve "continuous improvement" (when it is performed over time).

This is the same basic idea behind the so-called PDCA or Shewhart cycle, known in Japan as the Deming cycle, considered to be the essence of the Japanese approach to Total Quality Control:

Plan: The basic planning process described by Juran.
Do: The implementation of the plan.
Check: Evaluation of performance according to critical measures.
Act: Quality improvement efforts based on the lessons learned from experience. These experiences feed into the new plan, since PDCA is a cyclical process.

DEFINING QUALITY

One of the most widely used terms and concepts in the quality literature is, of course, *quality*. Definitions of quality range from narrowly defined, "primary operating characteristics" of a manufactured product (for example, acceleration or cruising speed for a car) to customer-defined quality (emphasized as "core" definition of quality by most writers in the field, that is, it is the customer who defines what quality is).

Ishikawa, one of the best known Japanese pioneers of the quality movement, makes a distinction between a narrow and a broad definition of quality:

Narrowly interpreted, quality means quality of product. Broadly interpreted, quality means quality of work, quality of service, quality of information, quality of process, quality of division, quality of people, including workers, engineers, managers, and executives, quality of system, quality of company, quality of objectives, etc. (1985, 45)

Garvin (1988) has identified eight dimensions or categories of quality that apply for the most part to manufactured products:

- *Performance* The primary operating characteristics of a product (like clarity, color, and the ability to receive distant stations on a color television set).
- *Features* The "bells and whistles" of a product (like a remote control for the television set).
- *Reliability* The probability of a product's malfunctioning or failing within a specific period of time.
- *Conformance* The degree to which a product's design and operating characteristics meet preestablished standards (a definition of quality often used by Phil Crosby, one of the best known U.S. "quality gurus").
- *Durability* A measure of product life that has both economic and technical dimensions.
- *Serviceability* The speed, courtesy, competence, and ease of repair. Attempts have been made to identify "measurable" characteristics of serviceability (like speed of response) as opposed to the more elusive elements of customer satisfaction.
- *Aesthetics* A user defined, subjective set of attributes, based on individual preferences, of a product—how a product looks, feels, sounds, tastes, or smells according to the customer.

- *Perceived quality* "Consumers do not always possess complete information about a product or a service's attributes. Frequently, indirect measures are the only basis for comparing brands. A product's durability, for example, can seldom be observed directly; it usually must be inferred from various tangible and intangible aspects of a product."

Juran defined quality as "fitness to use," that is, the users of a product or service should be able to count on it for what they needed or wanted to do with it (March 1986). He further identifies five dimensions of fitness for use: quality of design, quality of conformance, availability, safety, and field use.

A narrower approach to defining quality is used by Crosby:

Requirements must be clearly stated so that they cannot be misunderstood. Measurements are then taken continually to determine conformance to those requirements. Any nonconformance detected is the absence of quality. Quality problems become nonconformance problems; and quality becomes definable. . . . If a Cadillac conforms to all the requirements of a Cadillac then it is a quality car. If a Pinto conforms to all the requirements of a Pinto, then it is a quality car. Luxury or its absence is spelled out in specific requirements, such as carpeting or rubber mats. (1980, 15)

Crosby also popularized the concept of *zero defects*, a further definition of quality to be found in the literature, and the ultimate goal of quality improvement efforts. Zero defects were to be achieved through prevention rather than after-the-fact inspection.

It is evident from these definitions that most of them refer to tangible manufactured products. Definitions of service quality have been mostly derived from definitions of product quality, with specific emphasis on measurable attributes and the translation of vague customer-based notions of service quality into terms that can be expressed through sophisticated instruments of market research, like scales of customer satisfaction that compare consumer perceptions of competing products.

Even though specific attempts are made to render quality measurable, it is ultimately the customer who defines what it is and what it is not. In the TQM literature, the concept of *customer* embraces both the *internal* and the *external* customers. Internal customers are the next process in the manufacturing or service delivery value-added chain. External customers include the end user (the "key" customer), suppliers, and even society at large. Many uses of the word *customer* in the TQM literature make us think of the concept of *stakeholders*, commonly found in the management policy literature. In a broad sense, customers are all those affected by what we do.

EVOLUTION OF THE QUALITY MOVEMENT

The evolution of quality concepts, including the development of the concept of quality from a narrowly defined set of product attributes to the nearly all-embracing modern definitions of quality, is closely related to the different eras of the modern quality movement.

Garvin has attempted to map the evolution of the quality movement in the United States and described it in terms of four distinct "quality eras": Inspection, Statistical Quality Control, Quality Assurance, and Strategic Quality Management.

The first stage, the introduction of formal inspection in the industrial process, was the necessary consequence of mass production in the early nineteenth century, while the second stage, Quality Control, can be traced back to the early twentieth century:

> Inspection activities were linked more formally to quality control in 1922 with the publication of G. S. Radford's *The Control of Quality in Manufacturing.* For the first time quality was viewed as a distinct management responsibility and as an independent function. (1988, 5)

During the Quality Control era the essential mathematical and statistical tools of the quality movement were developed. These included the Shewhart cycle and analysis of variability, statistical sampling techniques, and Statistical Process Control (SPC). SPC was used extensively during World War II with phenomenal results (this is one of the reasons why it was so well received in Japan in the 1950s) but came into disuse after the war ended.

The third era, Quality Assurance, includes, according to Garvin, the Total Quality Control approach initiated by Feigenbaum:

> During the period of quality assurance, quality evolved from a narrow, manufacturing-based discipline to one with broader implication for management. Problem prevention remained the primary goal, but the profession's tools expanded far beyond statistics. Four separate elements were involved: quantifying the costs of quality, total quality control, reliability engineering, and zero defects. (12)

The fourth era, Strategic Quality Management, implies a new emerging "vision":

> It embodies a dramatic shift in perspective. For the first time, top managers at the levels of the presidents and chief executive officers have expressed an interest in quality. They have linked it with profitability, defined it from the customer's point of view, and required its inclusion in the strategic planning process. In the most radical departure of all, many have insisted that quality be viewed as an aggressive competitive weapon. (21)

This author disagrees with Garvin's contention that this is new, at least conceptually. Garvin's description adequately defines the key elements of the modern Total Quality Management movement, but the basic underlying concepts can be traced back to the original writings of the founders of the movement, including Deming, Feigenbaum, and Juran. Nevertheless, it is true that the implementation of the strategic perspective to quality is recent, particularly the integration of quality principles and strategic planning in the United States. In Japan, this integration began in 1962 at Bridgestone Tire (Akao 1991) and is known as **Hoshin Kanri** or "Policy Deployment."

Another interpretation of the role of the quality movement in the context of management and organizational theory has been advanced by Senge (1992):

I believe that the quality movement as we have known it up to now in the United States is in fact the first wave in building "learning organizations"—organizations that continually expand their ability to shape the future.

The roots of the quality movement lie in assumptions about people, organizations, and management that have one unifying theme: to make continual learning a way of organizational life, especially improving the performance of the organization as a total system. This can only be achieved by breaking with the traditional authoritarian command and control hierarchy where the top thinks and the local acts to merge thinking and acting at all levels.

This represents a profound re-orientation in the concerns of management—a shift from a predominant concern with controlling to a predominant concern with learning.

Senge further recognizes three waves in the evolution of learning organizations. While the United States is in the first wave (the quality movement as we have known it), Japan has moved on to the second:

In the first wave, the primary focus of change was frontline workers. Management's job was to

- Champion continual improvement.
- Remove impediments (like quality control experts and unnecessary bureaucracy) that disempower local personnel.
- Support new practices like quality training and competitive benchmarking that drive process improvement.

In the second wave, the focus shifts from improving work processes to improving how we work—fostering ways of thinking and interacting conducive to continual learning about the dynamic, complex, conflictual issues that determine system wide performance. In the second wave, the primary focus of change is the managers themselves.

The third wave of quality... These two ways of thinking will, I believe, gradually merge into a third, in which learning becomes "institutionalized" as an inescapable way of life for managers and workers alike (if we even bother maintaining that distinction).

Senge's analysis is useful to understand potential conceptual shortcomings of existing TQM models and possible ways to enrich them. We will explore three models that are representative of current approaches to Total Quality Management: the TQM Wheel Model, the Baldrige Award Criteria, and the European Model for Quality.

THE TQM WHEEL MODEL

The Wheel Model (Exhibit 1) was developed by researchers of GOAL/QPC, a leading research and publishing organization in the field of Total Quality Management with significant input from representatives of large organizations implementing TQM, like GM, Ford, and Hewlett Packard. It represents a systematic effort to integrate all dimensions and processes of TQM around a "Customer-Driven Master Plan" (Moran et al., 1991):

EXHIBIT 1   *The GOAL/QPC TQM Wheel Model*

The Total Quality Management Wheel, shown below, was developed by GOAL/QPC as a holistic model to illustrate the elements of TQM. It depicts the orientation of TQM—customers and the interrelationship among systems, people, and tools within an organization implementing TQM.

Looking at the top of the wheel, unit optimization is used to describe the "who, what, and how" of daily management. The term encompasses the concept of continuous improvement, the individuals and teams who are involved, and the methods or tools that can be used most effectively. Unit optimization is typically the first phase of TQM implementation, and it refers to the identification, measurement, improvement, and standardization of the processes that make up daily work. This initial step, often summarized by the Deming or Shewhart cycle (Plan-Do-Check-Act), involves a variety of individuals, working singly and in teams, in using the Seven Basic Quality Control Tools to manage their day-to-day responsibilities.

Moving clockwise on the wheel, the TQM practitioner next focuses on the vertical alignment phase of TQM implementation. *Vertical alignment* is a term used to describe the "who, what, and how" of Hoshin Planning. Hoshin Planning is a method used to ensure that the mission, vision, goals, and annual objectives of an organization are communicated to and implemented by everyone, from the executive level to the "frontline" level. Senior managers use the Seven Management and Planning Tools to facilitate the sharing of critical information among all members of the organization and to assist in the organizational planning process.

After making gains in Daily Management and Hoshin Planning, senior managers generally face the need for Cross-Functional Management, which requires an integration of quality improvement efforts across the functional areas of an organization. Top-level managers use the advanced TQM tool, Quality Function Deployment (QFD) to elicit the involvement of customer/supplier teams. QFD is a method for integrating the "voice of the customer" into the design of services, and provides the means to analyze and prioritize customer demands. QFD clarifies the actions that are most important to meeting or exceeding customer demands. QFD may also be used at earlier stages of implementation as needed. Additionally, managers use a variety of audit tools to assess how well the organization has incorporated TQM principles and broken down departmental barriers. Strategic information systems can be helpful at this phase to integrate all useful data in the effort to improve quality, cost, delivery, and employee morale.

The Customer-Driven Total Quality Master Plan begins by involving all employees in an organization with the identifications of their customers' needs. . . . Total Quality Management begins with a long-term plan (commitment) rooted in the organization's customers. This plan emphasizes thorough understanding of the customers and their needs along with continual improvement of customer satisfaction.

The implementation of the plan occurs along three dimensions or Macroprocesses: Daily Management (elsewhere called a "bottom up" approach), Cross-Functional Management ("side-by-side") and Hoshin Planning ("top-down").

Most references made to Total Quality (for example, Statistical Process Control and Quality Circles) relate to Daily Management (for example, Kaizen equals

EXHIBIT 1 *continued*

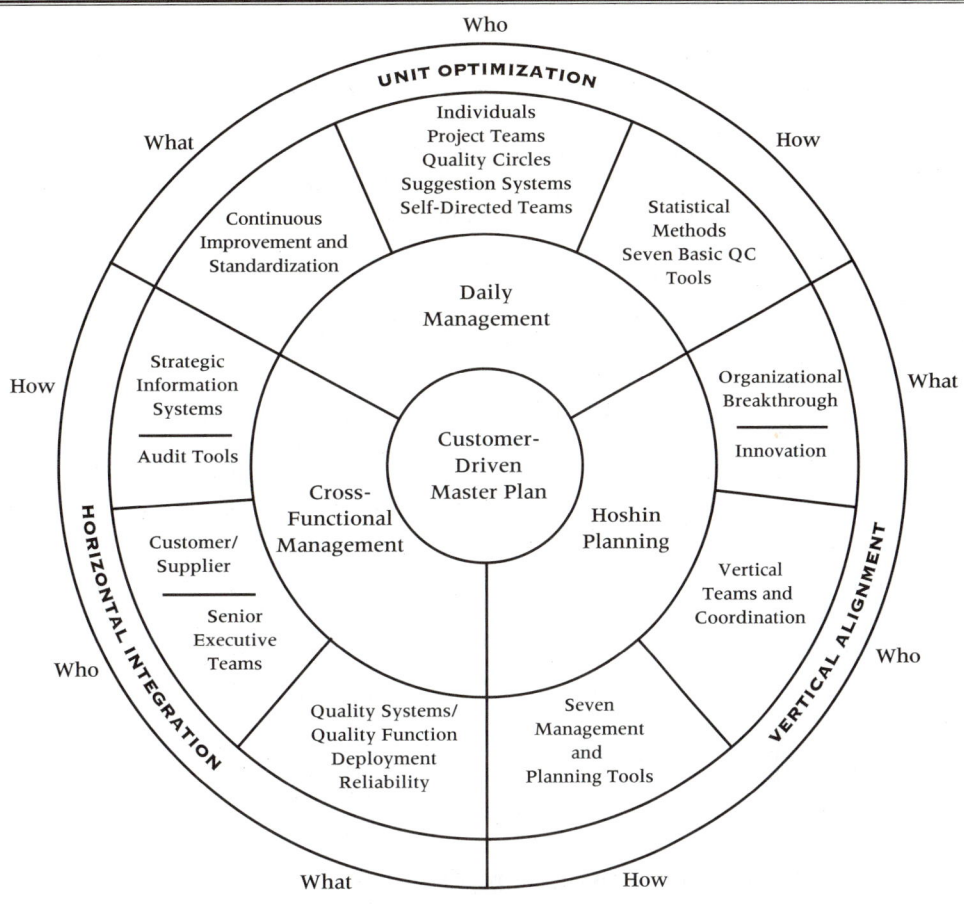

SOURCE: GOAL/QPC TQM in *Health Care Research Report,* 1992.

continuous improvement). Its purpose is the implementation of a daily control, continuous improvement, standardized system of best practices with the direct involvement of line workers working as teams under the "coaching" of their supervisors, or as self-directed teams. Daily Management involves the identification of critical processes and the use of systematic data collection and group problem-solving methods (definition of key indicators and use of the 7 QC Tools equals "Quality Control" tools to do root cause analysis).

The second key element of the wheel model is "Cross-Functional Management":

Whether establishing a Customer-Driven Master Plan, a Daily Management system, or Hoshin Planning, all require horizontal integration of many persons and teams. This integration across the organization is known as Cross-Functional Management.

Cross-Functional Teams have different roles:

> Teams may establish organization-wide quality systems. Another cross-functional sys-
> tem, Quality Function Deployment, helps the organization utilize customer and com-
> petitive data in planning the best possible products and services.

Quality Function Deployment (QFD) has been widely hailed for reducing new
product introduction time, translating customer requirements into actual products, and promoting a dialogue among suppliers, design and manufacturing engineers, and marketing analysts. After SPC and the different types of quality teams
(for example, Quality Circles and Quality Improvement Teams), it is the most popular approach to the implementation of the TQM processes.

The third element of the model is Hoshin Planning, a strategy planning and
implementation process only recently introduced in large U.S. organizations, like
FP&L and Hewlett Packard, but in existence in Japan since the 1970s and pioneered by Bridgestone Tire in 1962:

> When the magnitude of a needed process improvement is widespread and per-
> meates the entire organization, a Daily Management system may not be suffi-
> cient to bring about the needed major improvement. In this case, a 'breakthrough'
> planning system may be needed. One such system, Hoshin Planning, is defined
> as a policy management system. . . . Hoshin Planning is directed by top manage-
> ment but may involve teams throughout the organization. . . . The Hoshin
> Planning system focuses the energy of the entire organization on achieving a
> major improvement in a specific area of critical importance. The improvement
> may be needed to ensure long-term competitiveness or even the survival of the
> organization.

THE MALCOLM BALDRIGE AWARD

A second model, which in this case defines "excellence" in terms of overall quality of an organization (in terms similar to Ishikawa's broad definition of quality),
can be found in the guidelines of the Malcolm Baldrige Award. These guidelines are being used extensively by organizations trying to understand and
implement "quality" as a key internal driving force to achieve competitive
advantage.

The Baldrige Award defines core values and concepts—a "framework" or model
establishing the relationships between the "driver, system, goal, and measures of
progress"—and an implicit hierarchy of priorities and values (points assigned to
each category of the award, which add to a total of 1,000).

The guidelines recognize explicitly the following core values and concepts:

Customer-Driven Quality Quality is judged by the customer. All product and service attributes that contribute value and lead to customer satisfaction and prefer-
ence must be the foundation for a company's quality system. . . . Customer-driven
quality is thus a strategic concept.

Leadership A company's senior leaders must create clear and visible quality values and high expectations. Reinforcement of the values and expectations requires their substantial personal commitment and involvement. The leaders' basic values and commitment need to include areas of public responsibility and corporate citizenship. The leaders must take part in the creation of strategies, systems, and methods for achieving excellence.

Continuous Improvement Achieving the highest levels of quality and competitiveness requires a well-defined and well-executed approach to continuous improvement. The term *continuous improvement* refers to both incremental and "break-through" improvement. A focus on improvement needs to be part of all operations and of all work unit activities of a company.

Employee Participation and Development A company's success in meeting its quality and performance objectives depends increasingly on work force quality and involvement. The close link between employee satisfaction and customer satisfaction creates a "shared fate" relationship between companies and employees. For this reason, employee satisfaction measurement provides an important indicator of the company's efforts to improve customer satisfaction and operating performance. ... Companies need to invest in the development of the work force and to seek new avenues to involve employees in problem solving and decision making.

Fast Response Success in competitive markets increasingly demands ever-shorter cycles for a new or improved product and service introduction. Also, faster and more flexible response to customers is now a more critical requirement of business management.

Design Quality and Prevention Quality systems should place strong emphasis on design quality—problem and waste prevention achieved through building quality into products and services and into the processes through which they are produced.

Long-Range Outlook Achieving quality and market leadership requires a company to have a strong future orientation and a willingness to make long-term commitments to customers, employees, suppliers, stockholders, and the community.

Management by Fact Pursuit of quality and operational performance goals of the company requires that process management be based upon reliable information, data, and analysis. Facts and data needed for quality improvement and quality assessment are of many types, including: customer, product and service performance, operations, market, competitive comparisons, supplier, employee-related, and cost and financial.

Partnership Development Companies should seek to build internal and external partnerships to better accomplish their overall goals. Internal partnerships might include those that promote labor-management cooperation such as agreements

---

EXHIBIT 2   *Baldrige Award Criteria Framework*

The framework has four basic elements:

Driver

Senior executive leadership creates the values, goals, and systems, and guides the sustained pursuit of customer value and company performance improvement.

System

System comprises the set of well-defined and well-designed processes for meeting the company's customer, quality, and performance requirements.

Goal

The basic aim of the quality process is the delivery of ever-improving value to customers. The seven criteria categories shown in the figure are subdivided into examination items and areas to address. These are described below.

Examination Items

There are a total of 28 examination items in the seven examination categories. Each item focuses on a major quality system requirement. All information submitted by applicants is in response to the item requirements. Item titles and examination point values are given below.

Areas to Address

Each examination item includes a set of areas to address (areas). The areas serve to illustrate and clarify the intent of the items and to place emphasis on the types and amounts of information the applicant should provide. Areas are not assigned individual point values, because their relative importance depends upon factors such as the applicant's type and size of business and quality system.

Measures of Progress

Measures of progress provide a results-oriented basis for channeling actions to delivering ever-improving customer value and company performance.

---

with unions. . . . Examples of external partnerships include those with customers, suppliers, and education organizations.

Corporate Responsibility and Citizenship   A company's customer requirements and quality system objectives should address corporate responsibility and citizenship. Corporate responsibility refers to basic expectations of the company—business ethics and protection of public health, public safety, and the environment. . . . Corporate citizenship refers to leadership and support—within reasonable limits of the company's resources—of publicly important purposes. . . . Such purposes might include education, resource conservation, community services, improving industry and business practices, and sharing of nonproprietary quality-related information.

These core values and concepts are embodied in the seven categories integrated in the Baldrige Award Criteria Framework (Exhibit 2), which is the quality model of the award:

1.0	Leadership	95 points
2.0	Information and Analysis	75 points
3.0	Strategic Quality Planning	60 points

EXHIBIT 2   *continued*

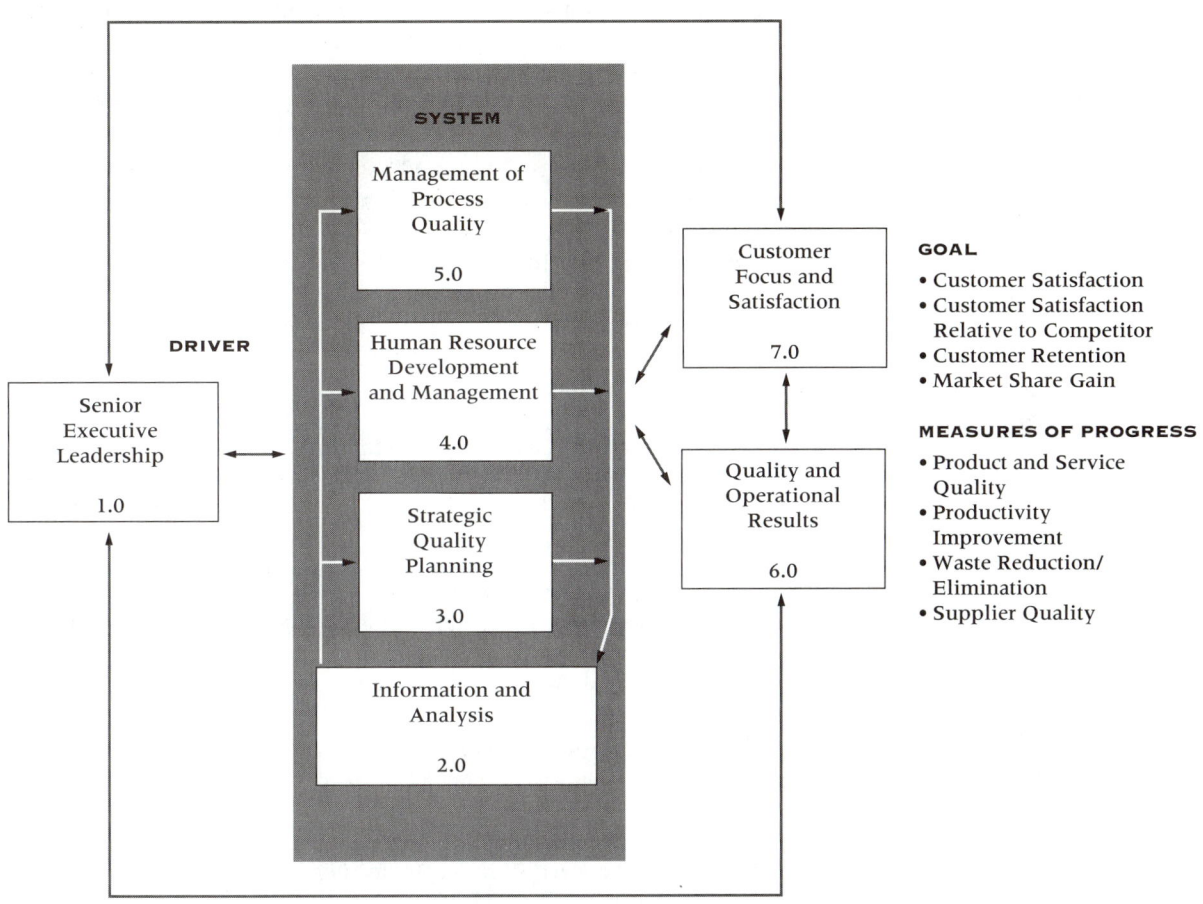

SYSTEM

Management of
Process
Quality

5.0

DRIVER

Human Resource
Development
and Management

4.0

Senior
Executive
Leadership

1.0

Strategic
Quality
Planning

3.0

Information and
Analysis

2.0

Customer
Focus and
Satisfaction

7.0

Quality and
Operational
Results

6.0

GOAL
• Customer Satisfaction
• Customer Satisfaction
  Relative to Competitor
• Customer Retention
• Market Share Gain

MEASURES OF PROGRESS
• Product and Service
  Quality
• Productivity
  Improvement
• Waste Reduction/
  Elimination
• Supplier Quality

SOURCE: U.S. Department of Commerce.

4.0	Human Resource Development and Management	150 points
5.0	Management of Process Quality	140 points
6.0	Quality and Operational Results	180 points
7.0	Customer Focus and Satisfaction	300 points
		1,000 points

The relative number of points assigned to each category establishes a hierarchy of importance of "quality values." It is to be noted that the category with the strongest weight is "Customer Focus and Satisfaction," the key principle to be found throughout the quality literature.

THE EUROPEAN QUALITY AWARD

Based on both the Deming and Baldrige awards, the European Community, under the auspices of the Commission and the European Foundation for Quality Management, have recently instituted The European Quality Award, which was awarded for the first time in October 1992 to companies demonstrating excellence in the implementation of Total Quality Management.

The European model, which "was developed as a framework for the European Quality Award, jointly sponsored by the European Commission, the European Foundation for Quality Management, and the European Organization for Quality" (Exhibit 3) has nine elements that link "enablers" with "results":

> Processes are the means by which the organization harnesses and releases the talents of its people to produce results. In other words, the processes and the people are the ENABLERS which provide RESULTS.

> **People (employee) Satisfaction, Customer Satisfaction** and **Impact on Society** are achieved through **Leadership**, which drives **People Management, Policy and Strategy, Resources** and **Processes** leading ultimately to excellence in **Business Results**.

> Each of the nine elements shown in the model is a criterion that can be used to appraise the organization's progress towards Total Quality Management.
> The Results aspects are concerned with **what** the organization has achieved and is achieving.
> The Enablers are concerned with **how** results are being achieved.

A particular feature of the model is also the integration of "Impact on Society" as one of the nine elements:

> In the 1990s it is vital that the organization achieves positive results in terms of the community at large. The criterion "Impact on Society" is included in the model for this reason.

This element includes explicitly an environmental dimension, "the organization's approach to quality of life, the environment, and...the preservation of global resources," a consideration largely absent in U.S. quality definitions and models.

OPPORTUNITIES FOR CONCEPTUAL ENRICHMENT AND MODEL BUILDING

This paper has explored some of the predominant concepts and models of the quality literature. Many of these concepts are key to rethinking the role of management in the 1990s and to understanding the opportunities for cooperative relationship between management and labor, and businesses and society at large.

As the field evolves, the need for further conceptual clarity and model building becomes evident. In most of the current literature, the following conceptual shortcomings, or rather "opportunities for improvement" by building on paradigms of other fields, can be found:

EXHIBIT 3   *The European Model for Quality*

The European Model

This model was developed as a framework for The European Quality Award, jointly sponsored by the European Commission, the European Foundation for Quality Management, and the European Organization for Quality. Essentially the model tells us that:

People (employee) Satisfaction, Customer Satisfaction, and *Impact on Society** are achieved through *Leadership* which drives *People Management, Policy and Strategy, Resources,* and *Processes,* leading ultimately to excellence in *Business Results.*

Each of the nine elements shown in the model is a criterion that can be used to appraise the organization's progress toward Total Quality Management.

The Results aspects are concerned with *what* the organization has achieved and is achieving.

The Enablers aspects are concerned with *how* results are being achieved.

The objective of a comprehensive quality management self-appraisal and self-improvement program is to regularly review each of these nine criteria and, thereafter, to adopt relevant improvement strategies.

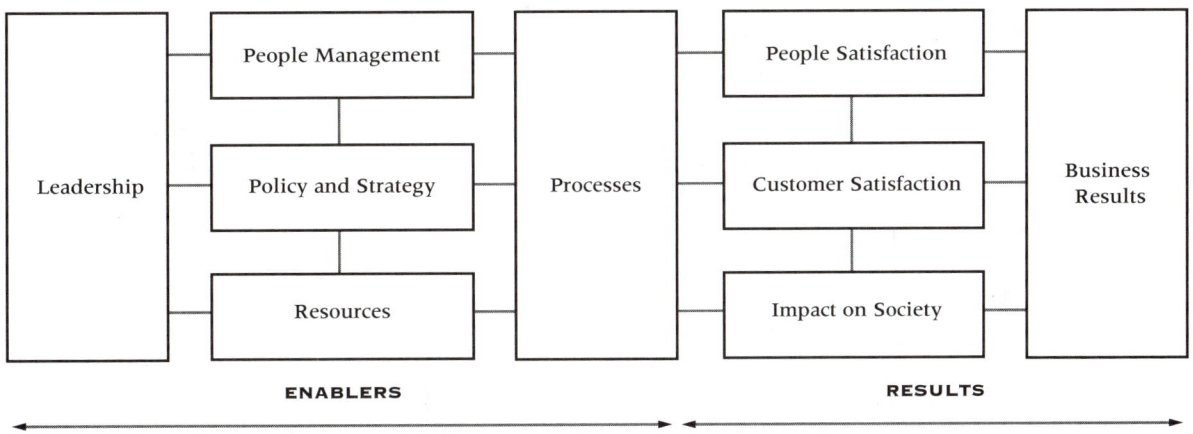

NOTES: *In the 1990s it is vital that the organization achieves positive results in terms of the community at large. The criterion "Impact on Society" is included in the model for this reason.

SOURCE: European Foundation for Quality Management.

---

1. The underlying concept of **organization** is not clearly defined. From a point of view of organizational theory, the organization seems largely conceived as a rational unitary decision maker (organizations that succeed or fail) or as a series of interlocking teams (management team, teams of workers, and so on). What is absent is any systematic exploration of the concept of "informal organization" and its implications for the decision-making process. This key concept was already analyzed by Barnard in the 1940s.

Network theories of organizations would provide useful insights as the quality literature insists on the need to build networks between suppliers, customers, companies, educational institutions, and so on. Applications of TQM, like Just-in-Time, are built on the assumption of efficiently working networks.

2. A second perspective largely absent in the literature are political views of organizations. It is insisted (for example, Baldrige Award) that management and labor should collaborate, but the simple insistence on collaboration does not provide adequate guidance to conflict resolution. U.S. unions have been suspicious of TQM implementation efforts, which they have seen as a clear threat to established labor practices.

   If TQM fails to acknowledge the political realities of organizations and of its models to integrate political concepts, it will continue to provide weak guidelines for implementation in turbulent industrial environments or times of economic distress. Political views of organizations begin addressing questions of values, power, and legitimacy, and at the implementation level, the basic concern expressed by Pfeffer and Salancick in their landmark study on *The External Control of Organizations* (1978): "What matters more to organizational success—efficiency (largely embraced by the quality definitions) or effectiveness (the political maneuvers to co-opt collaboration and resources from the external environment)?"

3. One of the key contributions of the writings of quality gurus like Deming and Ishikawa may also constitute one of the potential shortcomings of the literature—the normative approach to management theory of these writings, that is, the insistence on value-driven management practices (empowerment, teamwork, and so on). The attempt to construct organizational reality may lead to ignoring reality as it is, a key problem during implementation of TQM programs. We are reminded of Mintzberg (1973), who decided to research what managers "actually do" rather than "what they are supposed to do." The richness of well-designed case analysis may be a prerequisite to design the value-driven organizations hailed in the quality literature.

CONCLUSION

The concepts on which Total Quality thinking is based imply basic values of respect for the individual and a sense of social responsibility. Efficiency is seen as a natural result of our intrinsic motivation and desire to learn. Continuous improvement based on collaboration is a never-ending process to be expanded to all facets of individual life and societal action.

It is the responsibility of all to make these noble desires a reality, but this can only be achieved through the clear understanding of the complexities inherent in the activities of individuals, groups, and organizations and their interactions in society at large.

BIBLIOGRAPHY

Akao, Yoki, ed. *Hoshin Kanri: Policy Deployment for Successful TQM.* Cambridge, MA: Productivity Press, 1991.

————. *Quality Function Deployment: Integrating Customer Requirements into Product Design.* Cambridge. MA: Productivity Press. 1990.

Barnard, Chester. *The Functions of the Executive.* Cambridge. MA: Harvard University Press, 1968.

Crosby, Philip. *Quality Is Free.* New York: Mentor Books, 1980.

Deming, W. Edwards, "On Some Statistical Aids Toward Economic Production," *Interface* 3, 4 (August 1975).

————. *Out of the Crisis.* Cambridge, MA: MIT Press, 1982.

U.S. Department of Commerce. *Malcolm Baldrige National Quality Award: 1993 Award Criteria.*

Dertouzos, et al. *Made in America.* Cambridge, MA: MIT Press, 1989.

Ernst & Young and American Quality Foundation. *International Quality Study* 1991.

European Foundation for Quality Management. *Total Quality Management: The European Model for Self-Appraisal 1992.* Eindhoven, Netherlands, 1992.

Feigenbaum, Armand V. "Total Quality Control." *Harvard Business Review* 34, 6 (November-December 1956).

————. "Total Quality Control & Customer Satisfaction." *Performance Management* (Fall/Winter, 1984).

Garvin, David A. *Managing Quality: The Strategic and Competitive Edge.* New York: The Free Press, 1988.

Hosotani, Katsuya. *Japanese Quality Concepts: An Overview.* New York: Quality Resources, 1992.

Ishikawa, Kaoru. *What Is Total Quality Management?: The Japanese Way.* Englewood Cliffs, NJ: Prentice Hall, 1985.

Juran, J. M. "The Quality Trilogy." *Quality Progress* (August 1986): 19–24.

King, Bob. *Better Designs in Half the Time: Implementing QFD in America.* Methuen, MA: GOAL QPC, 1989.

March, Artemis. "A Note on Quality: The Views of Deming, Juran and Crosby." Note 9.687-011. Harvard Business School. Cambridge, MA, 1986.

Marchese, Ted. "TQM Reaches the Academy." *American Association for Higher Education Bulletin* (November 1991): 13–18.

Mintzberg, Henry. *The Nature of Managerial Work.* New York: Harper & Row, 1973.

Mizuno, Shigeru, ed. *Management for Quality Improvement: The Seven New QC Tools.* Cambridge, MA: Productivity Press, 1988.

Moran, Jack, et al. *Daily Management.* Methuen, MA: GOAL QPC, 1990.

Morgan, Gareth. *Images of Organization.* Newbury Park, CA: Sage Publications, 1986.

Neave, Henry R. *The Deming Dimension.* Knoxville, TN: SPC Press, 1990.

Nemoto, Masao. *Total Quality Control for Management: Strategies and Techniques from Toyota and Toyoda Gosei.* Englewood Cliffs, NJ: Prentice Hall, 1987.

Perrow, Charles. *Complex Organizations.* 3d. ed. New York: Random House, 1986.

Pfeffer, Jeffrey, and Gerald Salanzick. *The External Control of Organizations.* New York: Harper & Row, 1978.

Porter, Michael. *Competitive Advantage: Creating and Sustaining Superior Performance.* New York: The Free Press, 1985.

Reich, Robert B. *Tales of a New America.* New York: Times Books, 1987.

Schoenberger, Richard J. "Is Strategy Strategic? Impact of Total Quality Management on Strategy." *The Executive* 6, 3 (August 1992).

Senge, Peter M. *The Fifth Discipline: The Art and Practice of the Learning Organization.* New York: Doubleday Currency, 1990.

————. "Building Learning Organizations." *Journal for Quality and Participation* (March 1992).

Smircich, Linda, et al., eds. "New Intellectual Currents in Organization and Management Theory." Theory Development Forum. Special Issue. *Academy of Management Review* (July 1992).

Thompson James. *Organizations in Action.* New York: McGraw-Hill, 1967.

Young, S. Mark. "A Framework for Successful Adoption and Performance of Japanese Manufacturing Practices in the United States." *Academy of Management Review* 17, 4 (October 1992): 647–676.

Implementing Total Quality Management

BY HARRY COSTIN

The first reading in this introductory section provides an overview of how the quality movement has developed, and a description of several well-known TQM models, including the Baldrige Award Model and the European Model for Total Quality Management among others.

These models illustrate processes and relationships among many organizational variables and are useful in describing the integration of systems advocated by TQM. However, their complexity makes it difficult to tailor them to specific action plans for organizational change.

This second introductory reading takes a less systematic approach than the first. It discusses issues that relate to TQM implementation and describes a model I developed for the purposes of organizational assessment and for use as a framework to tie together different implementation approaches.

My understanding of TQM implementation has evolved with my personal experiences as researcher, trainer, and consultant. Working from conceptualization to implementation, I have seen the need to modify existing implementation models, such as the Baldrige, according to variables such as the size of an organization and the industry it belongs to (govermnent versus private, manufacturing versus service, highly versus not highly regulated, etc.).

As a consultant, I have to provide results in a cost- and time-efficient manner. This process involves making a preliminary organizational assessment, developing an implementation program, and describing the rationale for my analysis to top management. During past consulting projects, I benefited from insights provided by existing TQM models. However, as existing models could not be applied in all organizations, I developed what might be called a "contingency approach" to organizational change. I found that no single model or implementation approach represented a magic solution to all, or most, organizational problems. Organizational restructuring, team-based problem solving, reengineering, and other similar approaches all had their place, but could not be applied in every organization to bring about positive change.

This contingency approach to TQM implementation appears to be a characteristic difference between American and Japanese TQM models. American models, such as the Baldrige, strive to be all-encompassing. Japanese models, by contrast, focus on the basics, such as the PDCA cycle. Cha Nakui, a Japanese consultant with GOAL/QPC, when asked about the Japanese approach to TQM implementation, invariably provided the same answer: "It is a case-by-case approach." This apparently simple, but truly profound insight, has been confirmed by my own experience, and also provides a powerful reminder when I feel tempted to use a "one-size-fits-all" approach during my own consulting projects.

THE SEARCH FOR AN IMPLEMENTATION MODEL

As a consultant, my first step is to gain some preliminary understanding of the status quo of the organization I am working with. Trying to make sense of organizational dynamics is difficult, especially after only limited exposure to the organization, since many organizational variables such as structure, size, communication systems, and delegation of the power to decide interact in complex ways.

Since I am called on to make recommendations based on my assessment of the company's needs, I use a framework for evaluation that can also serve as a guide to the implementation of a program for organizational change. I find it useful to integrate into one model both organizational assessment and implementation of organizational change programs. This approach allows for every problem to be translated directly into a remedial action plan. Such a model must:

• Be sophisticated enough to explain complex organizational reality.
• Be flexible enough for use in many different organizational settings.
• Be simple enough to be easily described and implemented.

In other words, the model must provide the analyst with the means of understanding the status quo of an organization, of identifying existing problems, of developing potential solutions, and of communicating the consultant's assessment of the situation and recommended course of action to top management.

As I attempted to develop such an implementation model, I found it useful to keep separate three different, problem-solving related issues. First, it is necessary to develop a basic typology of organizational issues or types of problems to be dealt with. Obsolete technologies, inefficient processes, and lack of motivation, to mention some common problems found in organizations, are all important and need to be addressed. However, these problems belong to different categories or domains. I will refer again to the concept of *problem domain,* outlining how different issues are dealt with at different levels of the organization. Commonly, so-called strategic problems are dealt with by top management, while day-to-day issues are handled by line managers.

Second, addressing problems belonging to different domains is an issue separate from using diverse approaches to find solutions to a problem belonging to a specific domain. For example, one of the most frequently asked questions in organizations concerns process efficiency, that is the effort to maximize output and quality while minimizing resource input. The question of efficiency is dealt with differently in continuous improvement and reengineering models. In continuous improvement models, small, ongoing efforts are viewed as adding up to significant improvements over time. Reengineering, by contrast, starts from the assumption that most critical processes in organizations are outdated (for such reasons as the development of new technologies) and need to be redesigned from scratch.

Third, different "languages," such as relevant statistics or charts illustrating trends in a graphic form, can be used to describe problems and potential solutions. The language issue is critical, and personal preferences can be ascribed to training and familiarity with a specific form of expression and also to individual learning styles. Misunderstandings regarding what is being said are one of the most frequently found causes of conflict in organizations.

The use of a common language is critical to the improvement of vertical and horizontal communication in organizations. In TQM implementation efforts, the "tools" (Quality Control Tools and Management and Planning Tools) are largely seen as an answer to this problem. These tools are powerful instruments that allow for the graphic representation of large amounts of data and are drawn from areas as diverse as engineering and anthropology.

DEFINING GENERIC ORGANIZATIONAL DOMAINS

There are many different ways to map organizational domains. All of them relate to forms in which organizations are conceived in the first place, that is, to organizational theory. The field of organizational theory is complex and includes abstract concepts such as hierarchies, networks, and systems. All these notions are powerful frameworks for research, but difficult to translate into implementation programs that are easy to understand and communicate.

A relatively simple conception of an organization includes the notion of a legal entity, with a clearly defined purpose (profit or nonprofit), offering products and services, in the context of a competitive environment to customers. This definition of an organization is not intended to be all-encompassing, but practical and understandable.

In order to describe domains, the three organizational elements to be highlighted are:

1. The relationship between the organization and its environment (that is, customers and competitors).
2. The processes by which inputs are translated into products and services for specific customer segments.
3. The people, that is, management and employees, who do the planning and perform day-to-day operations.

THE FIRST DOMAIN: STRATEGY

The first domain is the stated or implied strategy of an organization that determines the relationship between the organization, its competitors, and its customers. At a practical level, the purpose of an organizational strategy has to do with the bottom line, that is, maximizing shareholder return on investment. In the marketplace, strategy includes the following steps:

1. Select the right business to be in.
2. Know and anticipate future customer needs and wants. Focus on customer-based value. You need to understand that it is your customer who will define what quality is and is not.
3. Offer a bundle of products and services your customers need and want (or will want once they see them!).
4. Build a basis of "sustainable" competitive advantage. It is not enough to be ahead of your competition at some point in time; you also need to stay ahead.
5. Be flexible!

TQM models recognize other strategic goals besides profits. These include the impact on society of organizational activities (for example, job creation or minimizing harm to the environment) and employee satisfaction.

THE SECOND DOMAIN: OPERATIONS

Operations are the specific value-adding activities related to the delivery of products and services to customers. Sometimes they are also referred to as "processes." However, these concepts are not synonymous, since strategic decision making is also a process.

Operations are the processes or individual links of the customer-defined value chain. They must be updated periodically, due to factors such as the emergence of new technologies or shifting customer demands. Such a redefinition is the focus of reengineering.

The difference between "strategic" and "operational" decisions is not always evident and depends upon factors such as company size and industrial sector. For a large organization, a $1 million annual investment in information processing equipment may be routine and part of the established budget, that is, an operational decision made by line managers. By contrast, for a small company, a $100,000 expenditure may be strategic, because of the sizable impact upon cash flow.

THE THIRD DOMAIN: PEOPLE

People make the organizational wheels turn. Individually, and also in groups, they make decisions, perform routine operations, solve problems, and innovate. People are not replaceable gears but the very heart of organizations.

People are the most valuable resource of any organization, and at the same time the most difficult to understand and manage. It is out of sheer frustration that this dimension of organizational life is so often ignored in organizational change programs.

People participate in organizational activities as individuals and also as members of diverse formal and informal groups. Their feelings and behaviors are quite different in these varied and shifting contexts.

INTEGRATING THE THREE DOMAINS

The three domains previously described coexist and interact in all organizations, and we must deal with them simultaneously for the purposes of TQM implementation.

I have come to understand TQM as the point of interaction and synthesis of the three domains (Figure 1). This simple model is also accurate from a historical point of view. The quality movement originally focused on efficiency goals through a process design to ensure quality (Quality Assurance), then on teamwork for quality (Quality Circles), and finally, as explained by Garvin (1988, see bibliography for Reading 1), on the strategic dimension of quality, that is, quality as a source of sustainable competitive advantage.

This model has been useful as an explanatory tool to relate the different aspects of TQM implementation programs. The concepts of the three domains or perspectives have been well received by groups of managers, as a pragmatic synthesis with which to address related, but different, organizational issues. The model has also provided me with a template for organizational assessment, which I use before I suggest a particular implementation approach to an organization.

FIGURE 1

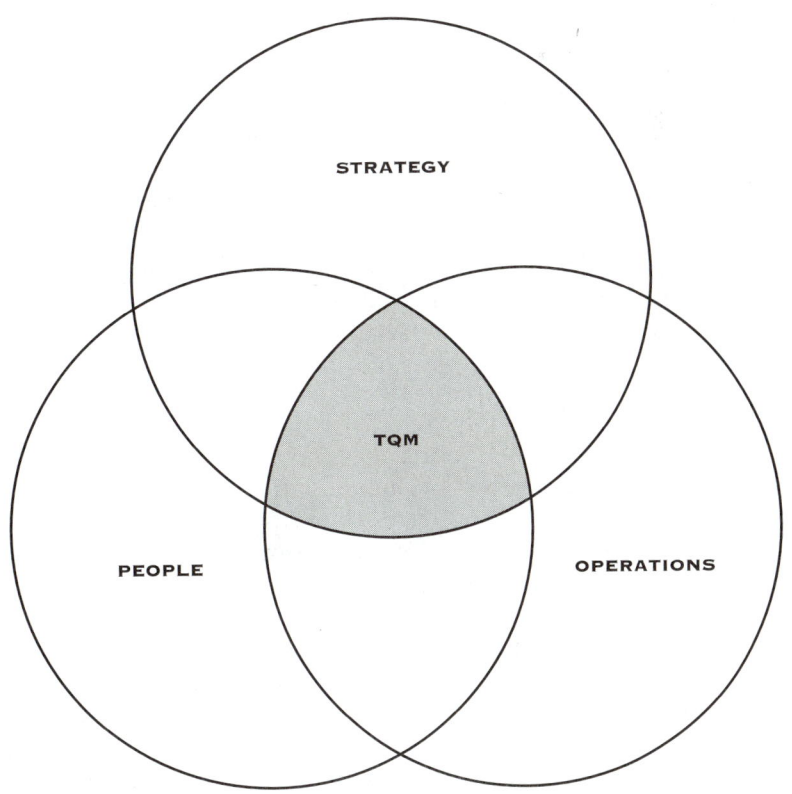

DEFINING ORGANIZATIONAL GOALS: A TQM PERSPECTIVE

If TQM is the meeting point of the three domains, specific goals pertinent to each domain need to be pursued simultaneously. This is what is unique about TQM. An organization implementing TQM needs to be effective, efficient, and to demonstrate commitment to its workforce in practical ways. This is no easy task but is critical for survival and long-term growth.

STRATEGY

The main strategic goal is *effectiveness,* that is, to be in the right business at the right time, offering products and services customers need and/or want, and to achieve sustainable competitive advantage over existing and potential competitors. Effectiveness cannot be achieved by simply improving process efficiency.

For example, a transportation company with which I consulted was experiencing, like all its competitors, severe losses as freight rates fell by approximately 50 percent over a 3–5 year period, while costs were rising due to necessary investments in new technology. In this case, marginal improvements in productivity could not solve a basic structural problem. Excess capacity in shrinking markets represented an insurmountable obstacle in the short- and medium-term. This is a clear example of "being in the wrong business."

OPERATIONS

The main operational goal is *efficiency,* that is, producing the maximum output, at the highest quality, with a minimal amount of resources. Most TQM processes, such as Statistical Process Control (SPC), focus on the efficiency goal and bring about continuous improvement over time. Process reengineering also focuses on efficiency and may bring about significant results in the short term, in cases where existing processes have become outdated and do not take advantage of state-of-the-art technologies.

PEOPLE

The most important goal of every organization is a *motivated* workforce. People are the heart of any organization, and according to Stanford's Jeffrey Pfeffer, the most important source of sustainable competitive advantage.

Frameworks such as Senge's *learning organization* go beyond the goal of a motivated workforce. Senge advocates the need to integrate personal mastery and two types of learning: team and organizational. Models such as Senge's are powerful normative frameworks but, for the purposes of our synthetic implementation model, too complex and abstract. It is easy to get lost in esoteric discussions regarding organizations as systems or complex models with many variables that are attractive to top managers, who like to be seen as representatives of state-of-the-art thinking. However, when it comes to implementation, people-related problems in organizations need to be solved at a more basic level. The immediate needs that organizations need to address are respect (which these days includes clear guidelines for a job environment free of sexual harassment), job security, flexible benefit plans, ongoing training, and opportunities to participate in decision making. The goals of the learning organization can become a reality only in organizations that optimally fill the basic needs of their employees.

The "people" dimension is the most difficult to manage, particularly in times of cutthroat competition and shrinking markets, when layoffs seem inevitable. In practice, few organizations measure up to the lofty goals advocated in models such as the Baldrige.

In assessing how well an organization treats its employees as part of TQM implementation, there are two indicators that measure how much an organization values its workforce: resources devoted to ongoing training (time and money) and personnel procedures such as layoffs.

ORGANIZATIONAL ASSESSMENT AND TQM IMPLEMENTATION

A TQM consultant usually begins a relationship with a specific organization by interacting with its top managers. This interaction takes the form of interviews and TQM overviews (1/2 to 2 days in length). During these early interactions with decision makers, I have found it useful to address basic strategic questions, since, among other reasons: 1) there are strategic problems that cannot be solved through process improvement; 2) it helps the interaction and team building of top managers; and 3) it provides a necessary reality check for further implementation of a process improvement program.

In most organizations, I have found it beneficial to have area managers talk about the reality of their areas and have the top management team do a preliminary competitive analysis using tools such as a SWOT (Strengths-Weaknesses-Opportunities-Threats) analysis or matrices of products/market segments/competitors. I suggest this initial step to help top management develop a pragmatic, reality-based assessment of the company's situation in the marketplace. I am aware that other consultants prefer to focus first on the development of a common "Vision," that is, the desired future state of the company, but I have found the initial reality check to be a more useful learning tool for top managers.

Once there is basic agreement regarding the current situation of the firm, it is highly desirable to define the Mission, (what business are we in, who are our key customers, and what are our organizational values) and if radical organizational change is intended, to create a Vision (how we see our company in the future). With the Vision as our starting point, we continue the planning process, using a simplified Hoshin-type process to define critical breakthrough goals and plan implementation projects to achieve them.

After Strategy, Mission, and Vision are defined, the focus shifts to specific processes to be improved. This may be done with teams at different levels of the organization. At this stage, it is possible to integrate the goals of *efficiency* and *motivation*.

Efficiency is achieved through systematic problem solving. Problem solving skills should not be taken for granted. They require significant amounts of well planned and delivered training. This training is an important source of motivation for people at all levels, because it demonstrates to staff that their company is investing resources in their skills. Also, to have managers present at training meetings, or conducting training, carries the clear message that they care about their staff.

I am a strong believer in a train-as-needed approach, rather than intensive training up front. The length and frequency of training sessions are also critical. It is useless to have people sit through an 8-hour training session and expect them to make sense of, and retain, everything they hear. Smaller modules of training, followed up by practical and useful applications of the tools to be learned, take more time, but bring about the desired learning and do much more to motivate people.

During training, I find it useless to preach the prerequisite of a personal shift of paradigms. Practical examples that people can relate to are usually more powerful catalysts for change. For example, everybody can relate to the need to "walk the walk," since we all sense hypocrisy in empty slogans.

The approach described in this section can be summarized in the following way:

Strategy
- Do a preliminary assessment of the firm's competitive position, including the following aspects:

  Portfolio of products/services

  Key customers and their needs

  Real and potential competitors

  Sources of sustainable competitive advantage

- Define the Mission and Vision of the organization.
- Describe the core values and culture of the organization.
- Select one or more achievable breakthrough objectives.

Operations
- Define critical processes.
- Flow chart critical processes. Simplify and document critical processes.
- Implement systematic problem solving.
- Do process reengineering where needed.
- Institutionalize PDCA. Implement continuous improvement processes, such as Daily Management and Statistical Process Control.

People
- Provide training in problem-solving techniques. Follow up demonstrations of each tool and technique with practical applications.

- Form teams as needed to work on real problems.
- Institutionalize training.

OTHER APPROACHES TO IMPLEMENTATION

There are many other approaches to TQM implementation. One I have also found extremely effective is the implementation of an ISO 9000 compliant quality assurance system. It is effective because:

- ISO 9000 is commonly externally driven (demanded by customers or regulatory agencies) and therefore a strategic priority for top management.
- ISO 9000 implementation is a project that has a clear, measurable goal (certification by an external registrar). The process of achieving certification usually requires 1–2 years.
- ISO 9000 is an excellent platform for TQM. When implemented appropriately it can result in a "map" of documented procedures of all critical processes in the organization.
- Resources for training are more easily justified, since ISO 9000 certification is seen as a strategic goal by top management.

CONCLUSION

This reading is intended to illustrate the thought processes that translate TQM concepts and models into specific implementation efforts. The TQM model that I have suggested integrates strategic, operational, and human concerns. It has also provided me with a useful tool to assess organizations and to explain to management the systemic nature of TQM and, at a more practical level, to develop implementation plans.

The Leader's New Work: Building Learning Organizations

By Peter M. Senge
MIT Sloan School of Management

MOVING TOWARD LEARNING ORGANIZATIONS

Human beings are designed for learning. No one has to teach an infant to walk, or talk, or master the spatial relationships needed to stack eight building blocks that don't topple. Children come fully equipped with an insatiable drive to explore and experiment. Unfortunately, the primary institutions of our society are oriented predominantly toward controlling rather than learning, rewarding individuals for performing for others rather than for cultivating their natural curiosity and impulse to learn. The young child entering school discovers quickly that the name of the game is getting the right answer and avoiding mistakes—a mandate no less compelling to the aspiring manager.

"Our prevailing system of management has destroyed our people," writes W. Edwards Deming, leader in the quality movement.[1] "People are born with intrinsic motivations, self-esteem, dignity, curiosity to learn, joy in learning. The forces of destruction begin with toddlers—a prize for the best Halloween costume, grades at school, gold stars—and on up through the university. On the job, people, teams, divisions are ranked—reward for the one at the top, punishment at the bottom. MBO, quotas, incentive pay, business plans, put together separately, division by division, cause further loss, unknown and unknowable."

Ironically, by focusing on performing for someone else's approval, corporations create the very conditions that predestine them to mediocre performance. Over the long run, superior performance depends on superior learning. A Shell study showed that, according to former planning director Arie de Geus, "a full one-third of the Fortune '500' industrials listed in 1970 had vanished by 1983."[2]

Today, the average lifetime of the largest industrial enterprises is probably less than *half* the average lifetime of a person in an industrial society. On the other hand, de Geus and his colleagues at Shell also found a small number of companies that survived for seventy-five years or longer. Interestingly, the key to their survival was the ability to run "experiments in the margin," to continually explore new business and organizational opportunities that create potential new sources of growth.

If anything, the need for understanding how organizations learn and accelerating that learning is greater today than ever before. The old days when a Henry Ford, Alfred Sloan, or Tom Watson *learned for the organization* are gone. In an increasingly dynamic, interdependent, and unpredictable world, it is simply no longer possible for anyone to "figure it all out at the top." The old model, "the top thinks and the local acts," must now give way to integrating thinking and acting at all levels. While the challenge is great, so is the potential payoff. "The person who figures out how to harness the collective genius of the people in his or her organization" according to former Citibank CEO Walter Wriston, "is going to blow the competition away."

ADAPTIVE LEARNING AND GENERATIVE LEARNING

The prevailing view of learning organizations emphasizes increased adaptability. Given the accelerating pace of change, or so the standard view goes, "the most successful corporation of the 1990s," according to *Fortune* magazine, "will be something called a learning organization, a consummately adaptive enterprise."[3] As the Shell study shows, examples of traditional authoritarian bureaucracies that responded too slowly to survive in changing business environments are legion.

But increasing adaptiveness is only the first stage in moving toward learning organizations. The impulse to learn in children goes deeper than desires to respond and adapt more effectively to environmental change. The impulse to learn, at its heart, is an impulse to be generative, to expand our capability. This is why leading corporations are focusing on *generative* learning, which is about creating, as well as *adaptive* learning, which is about coping.[4]

The total quality movement in Japan illustrates the evolution from adaptive to generative learning. With its emphasis on continuous experimentation and feedback, the total quality movement has been the first wave in building learning organizations. But Japanese firms' view of serving the customer has evolved. In the early years of total quality, the focus was on "fitness to standard," making a product reliably so that it would do what its designers intended it to do and what the firm told its customers it would do. Then came a focus on "fitness to need," understanding better what the customer wanted and then providing products that reliably met those needs. Today, leading edge firms seek to understand and meet the "latent need" of the customer—what customers might truly value but have never experienced or would never think to ask for. As one Detroit executive commented recently, "You could never produce the Mazda Miata solely from market research. It required a leap of imagination to see what the customer *might* want."[5]

Generative learning, unlike adaptive learning, requires new ways of looking at the world, whether in understanding customers or in understanding how to better manage a business. For years, U.S. manufacturers sought competitive advantage in aggressive controls on inventories, incentives against overproduction, and rigid adherence to production forecasts. Despite these incentives, their performance was eventually eclipsed by Japanese firms who saw the challenges of manufacturing differently. They realized that eliminating delays in the production process was the key to reducing instability and improving cost, productivity, and service. They worked to build networks of relationships with trusted suppliers and to redesign physical production processes so as to reduce delays in materials procurement, production set up, and in-process inventory—a much higher-leverage approach to improving both cost and customer loyalty.

As Boston Consulting Group's George Stalk has observed, the Japanese saw the significance of delays because they saw the process of order entry, production scheduling, materials procurement production, and distribution *as an integrated system.* "What distorts the system so badly is time," observed Stalk—the multiple delays between events and responses. "These distortions reverberate throughout the system, producing disruptions, waste, and inefficiency."[6] Generative learning requires seeing the systems that control events. When we fail to grasp the systemic source of problems, we are left to "push on" symptoms rather than, eliminate underlying causes. The best we can ever do is adaptive learning.

THE LEADER'S NEW WORK

"I talk with people all over the country about learning organizations, and the response is always very positive," says William O'Brien, CEO of the Hanover Insurance companies. "If this type of organization is so widely preferred, why don't people create such organizations? I think the answer is leadership. People have no real comprehension of the type of commitment it requires to build such an organization."[7]

Our traditional view of leaders—as special people who set the direction, make the key decisions, and energize the troops—is deeply rooted in an individualistic and nonsystemic worldview. Especially in the West, leaders are *heroes*—great men (and occasionally women) who rise to the fore in times of crisis. So long as such myths prevail, they reinforce a focus on short-term events and charismatic heroes rather than on systemic forces and collective learning.

Leadership in learning organizations centers on subtler and ultimately more important work. In a learning organization, leaders' roles differ dramatically from that of the charismatic decision maker. Leaders are designers, teachers, and stewards. These roles require new skills: the ability to build shared vision, to bring to the surface and challenge prevailing mental models, and to foster more systemic patterns of thinking. In short, leaders in learning organizations are responsible for *building organizations* where people are continually expanding their capabilities to shape their future—that is, leaders are responsible for learning.

CREATIVE TENSION: THE INTEGRATING PRINCIPLE

Leadership in a learning organization starts with the principle of creative tension.[8] Creative tension comes from seeing clearly where we want to be, our "vision," and telling the truth about where we are, our "current reality." The gap between the two generates a natural tension (see Figure 1).

Creative tension can be resolved in two basic ways: by raising current reality toward the vision, or by lowering the vision toward current reality. Individuals, groups, and organizations who learn how to work with creative tension learn how to use the energy it generates to move reality more reliably toward their visions.

The principle of creative tension has long been recognized by leaders. Martin Luther King, Jr., once said, "Just as Socrates felt that it was necessary to create a tension in the mind, so that individuals could rise from the bondage of myths and half truths. . . so must we. . . create the kind of tension in society that will help men rise from the dark depths of prejudice and racism."[9]

Without vision there is no creative tension. Creative tension cannot be generated from current reality alone. All the analysis in the world will never generate a vision. Many who are otherwise qualified to lead fail to do so because they try to substitute analysis for vision. They believe that, if only people understood current reality, they would surely feel the motivation to change. They are then

---

FIGURE 1   *The Principle of Creative Tension*

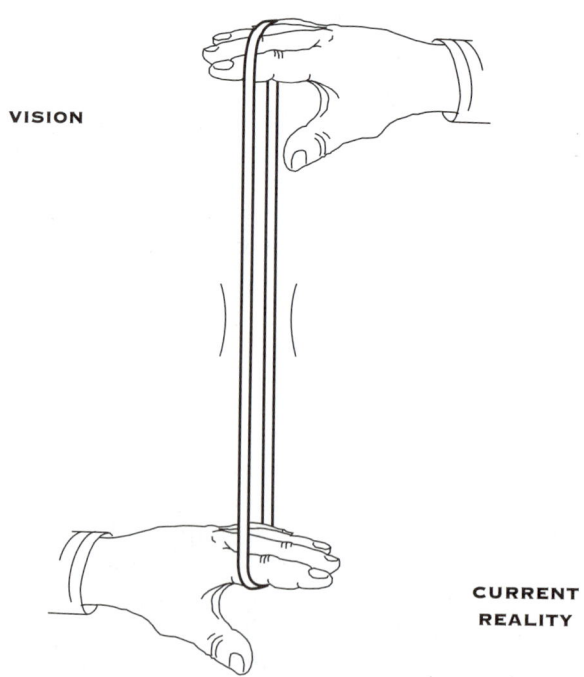

VISION

CURRENT
REALITY

disappointed to discover that people "resist" the personal and organizational changes that must be made to alter reality. What they never grasp is that the natural energy for changing reality comes from holding a picture of what might be that is more important to people than what is.

But creative tension cannot be generated from vision alone; it demands an accurate picture of current reality as well. Just as King had a dream, so too did he continually strive to "dramatize the shameful conditions" of racism and prejudice so that they could no longer be ignored. Vision without an understanding of current reality will more likely foster cynicism than creativity. The principle of creative tension teaches that *an accurate picture of current reality is just as important as a compelling picture of a desired future.*

Leading through creative tension is different than solving problems. In problem solving, the energy for change comes from attempting to get away from an aspect of current reality that is undesirable. With creative tension, the energy for change comes from the vision, from what we want to create, juxtaposed with current reality. While the distinction may seem small, the consequences are not. Many people and organizations find themselves motivated to change only when their problems are bad enough to cause them to change. This works for a while, but the change process runs out of steam as soon as the problems driving the change become less pressing. With problem solving, the motivation for change is extrinsic. With creative tension, the motivation is intrinsic. This distinction mirrors the distinction between adaptive and generative learning.

NEW ROLES

The traditional authoritarian image of the leader as "the boss calling the shots" has been recognized as oversimplified and inadequate for some time. According to Edgar Schein, "Leadership is intertwined with culture formation." Building an organization's culture and shaping its evolution is the "unique and essential function" of leadership.[10] In a learning organization, the critical roles of leadership—designer, teacher, and steward—have antecedents in the ways leaders have contributed to building organizations in the past. But each role takes on new meaning in the learning organization and, as will be seen in the following sections, demands new skills and tools.

LEADER AS DESIGNER

Imagine that your organization is an ocean liner and that you are "the leader." What is your role?

I have asked this question of groups of managers many times. The most common answer, not surprisingly, is "The captain." Others say, "The navigator, setting the direction." Still others say, "The helmsman, actually controlling the direction," or, "The engineer down there stoking the fire, providing energy," or, "The social director, making sure everybody's enrolled, involved, and communicating." While these are legitimate leadership roles, there is another which, in many ways, eclipses them all in importance. Yet rarely does anyone mention it.

The neglected leadership role is the *designer* of the ship. No one has a more sweeping influence than the designer. What good does it do for the captain to say, "Turn starboard 30 degrees," when the designer has built a rudder that will only turn to port, or which takes six hours to turn to starboard? It's fruitless to be the leader in an organization that is poorly designed.

The functions of design, or what some have called "social architecture" are rarely visible; they take place behind the scenes. The consequences that appear today are the result of work done long in the past, and work today will show its benefits far in the future. Those who aspire to lead out of a desire to control, or gain fame, or simply to be at the center of the action, will find little to attract them to the quiet design work of leadership.

But what, specifically, is involved in organizational design? "Organization design is widely misconstrued as moving around boxes and lines," says Hanover's O'Brien. "The first task of organization design concerns designing the governing ideas of purpose, vision, and core values by which people will live." Few acts of leadership have a more enduring impact on an organization than building a foundation of purpose and core values.

In 1982, Johnson & Johnson found itself facing a corporate nightmare when bottles of its best-selling Tylenol were tampered with, resulting in several deaths. The corporation's immediate response was to pull all Tylenol off the shelves of retail outlets. Thirty-one million capsules were destroyed, even though they were tested and found safe. Although the immediate cost was significant, no other action was possible given the firm's credo. Authored almost forty years earlier by president Robert Wood Johnson, Johnson & Johnson's credo states that permanent success is possible only when modern industry realizes that:

- service to its customers comes first;
- service to its employees and management comes second;
- service to the community comes third; and
- service to its stockholders, last.

Such statements might seem like motherhood and apple pie to those who have not seen the way a clear sense of purpose and values can affect key business decisions. Johnson & Johnson's crisis management in this case was based on that credo. It was simple, it was right, and it worked.

If governing ideas constitute the first design task of leadership, the second design task involves the policies, strategies, and structures that translate guiding ideas into business decisions. Leadership theorist Philip Selznick calls policy and structure the "institutional embodiment of purpose."[11] "Policy making (the rules that guide decisions) ought to be separated from decision making," says Jay Forrester.[12] "Otherwise, short-term pressures will usurp time from policy creation."

Traditionally, writers like Selznick and Forrester have tended to see policy making and implementation as the work of a small number of senior managers. But that view is changing. Both the dynamic business environment and the mandate of the learning organization to engage people at all levels now make it clear that this second design task is more subtle. Henry Mintzberg has argued that strategy is less a rational plan arrived at in the abstract and implemented throughout the organization than an "emergent phenomenon." Successful organizations "craft strategy" according to Mintzberg, as they continually learn about shifting business conditions and balance what is desired and what is possible.[13] The key is not getting the right strategy but fostering strategic thinking. "The choice of individual action is only part of. . . the policymaker's need, according to Mason and Mitroff.[14] "More important is the need to achieve insight into the nature of the complexity and to formulate concepts and world views for coping with it."

Behind appropriate policies, strategies, and structures are effective learning processes; their creation is the third key design responsibility in learning organizations. This does not absolve senior managers of their strategic responsibilities. Actually, it deepens and extends those responsibilities. Now, they are not only responsible for ensuring that an organization have well-developed strategies and policies, but also for ensuring that processes exist whereby these are continually improved.

In the early 1970s, Shell was the weakest of the big seven oil companies. Today, Shell and Exxon are arguably the strongest, both in size and financial health. Shell's ascendance began with frustration. Around 1971 members of Shell's "Group Planning" in London began to foresee dramatic change and unpredictability in world oil markets. However, it proved impossible to persuade managers that the stable world of steady growth in oil demand and supply they had known for twenty years was about to change. Despite brilliant analysis and artful presentation, Shell's planners realized, in the words of Pierre Wack, that they "had failed to change behavior in much of the Shell organization."[15] Progress would probably have ended there, had the frustration not given way to a radically new view of corporate planning.

As they pondered this failure, the planners' view of their basic task shifted: "We no longer saw our task as producing a documented view of the future business environment five or ten years ahead. Our real target was the microcosm (the 'mental model') of our decision makers." Only when the planners reconceptualized their basic task as fostering learning rather than devising plans did their insights begin to have an impact. The initial tool used was "scenario analysis," through which planners encouraged operating managers to think through how they would manage in the future under different possible scenarios. It mattered not that the managers believed the planners' scenarios absolutely, only that they became engaged in ferreting out the implications. In this way, Shell's planners conditioned managers to be mentally prepared for a shift from low prices to high prices and from stability to instability. The results were significant. When OPEC became a reality, Shell quickly responded by increasing local operating company control (to enhance maneuverability in the new political environment), building buffer stocks, and accelerating development of non-OPEC sources—actions that its competitors took much more slowly or not at all.

Somewhat inadvertently, Shell planners had discovered the leverage of designing institutional learning processes, whereby, in the words of former planning director de Geus, "Management teams change their shared mental models of their company, their markets, and their competitors."[16] Since then, "planning as learning" has become a byword at Shell, and Group Planning has continually sought out new learning tools that can be integrated into the planning process. Some of these are described below.

LEADER AS TEACHER

"The first responsibility of a leader" writes retired Herman Miller CEO Max de Pree, "is to define reality."[17] Much of the leverage leaders can actually exert lies in helping people achieve more accurate, more insightful, and more *empowering* views of reality.

Leader as teacher does *not* mean leader as authoritarian expert whose job it is to teach people the "correct" view of reality. Rather, it is about helping everyone in the organization, oneself included, to gain more insightful views of current reality. This is in line with a popular emerging view of leaders as coaches, guides, or facilitators.[18] In learning organizations, this teaching role is developed further by virtue of explicit attention to people's mental models and by the influence of the systems perspective.

The role of leader as teacher starts with bringing to the surface people's mental models of important issues. No one carries an organization, a market, or a state of technology in his or her head. What we carry in our heads are assumptions. These mental pictures of how the world works have a significant influence on how we perceive problems and opportunities, identify courses of action, and make choices.

One reason that mental models are so deeply entrenched is that they are largely tacit. Ian Mitroff, in his study of General Motors, argues that an assumption that prevailed for years was that, in the United States, "Cars are status symbols. Styling is therefore more important than quality."[19] The Detroit automakers didn't say, "We have a mental model that all people care about is styling." Few actual managers would even say publicly that all people care about is styling. So long as the view remained unexpressed, there was little possibility of challenging its validity or forming more accurate assumptions.

But working with mental models goes beyond revealing hidden assumptions. "Reality," as perceived by most people in most organizations, means pressures that must be borne, crises that must be reacted to, and limitations that must be accepted. Leaders as teachers help people *restructure their views of reality* to see beyond the superficial conditions and events into the underlying causes of problems and therefore to see new possibilities for shaping the future.

Specifically, leaders can influence people to view reality at three distinct levels: events, patterns of behavior, and systemic structure.

Systemic Structure
(Generative)
↓
Patterns of Behavior
(Responsive)
↓
Events
(Reactive)

The key question becomes *where do leaders predominantly focus their own and their organization's attention?*

Contemporary society focuses predominantly on events. The media reinforces this perspective, with almost exclusive attention to short-term, dramatic events. This focus leads naturally to explaining what happens in terms of those events: "The Dow Jones average went up sixteen points because high fourth-quarter profits were announced yesterday."

Pattern-of-behavior explanations are rarer, in contemporary culture, than event explanations, but they do occur. "Trend analysis" is an example of seeing patterns of behavior. A good editorial that interprets a set of current events in the context of long-term historical changes is another example. Systemic, structural explanations go even further by addressing the question, "What causes the patterns of behavior?"

In some sense, all three levels of explanation are equally true. But their usefulness is quite different. Event explanations—who did what to whom—doom their holders to a reactive stance toward change. Pattern-of-behavior explanations focus on identifying long-term trends and assessing their implications. They at least suggest how, over time, we can respond to shifting conditions. Structural explanations are the most powerful. Only they address the underlying causes of behavior at a level such that patterns of behavior can be changed.

By and large, leaders of our current institutions focus their attention on events and patterns of behavior, and, under their influence, their organizations do likewise. That is why contemporary organizations are predominantly reactive, or at best responsive—rarely generative. On the other hand, leaders in learning organizations pay attention to all three levels, but focus especially on systemic structure; largely by example, they teach people throughout the organization to do likewise.

LEADER AS STEWARD

This is the subtlest role of leadership. Unlike the roles of designer and teacher, it is almost solely a matter of attitude. It is an attitude critical to learning organizations.

While stewardship has long been recognized as an aspect of leadership, its source is still not widely understood. I believe Robert Greenleaf came closest to explaining real stewardship, in his seminal book *Servant Leadership*.[20] There, Greenleaf argues that "The servant leader *is* servant first. . . It begins with the natural feeling that one wants to serve, to serve *first*. This conscious choice brings one to aspire to lead. That person is sharply different from one who is leader first, perhaps because of the need to assuage an unusual power drive or to acquire material possessions."

Leaders' sense of stewardship operates on two levels: stewardship for the people they lead and stewardship for the larger purpose or mission that underlies the enterprise. The first type arises from a keen appreciation of the impact one's leadership can have on others. People can suffer economically, emotionally, and spiritually under inept leadership. If anything, people in a learning organization are more vulnerable because of their commitment and sense of shared ownership. Appreciating this naturally instills a sense of responsibility in leaders. The second type of stewardship arises from a leader's sense of personal purpose and commitment to the organization's larger mission. People's natural impulse to learn is unleashed when they are engaged in an endeavor they consider worthy of their fullest commitment. Or, as Lawrence Miller puts it, "Achieving return on equity does not, as a goal, mobilize the most noble forces of our soul."[21]

Leaders engaged in building learning organizations naturally feel part of a larger purpose that goes beyond their organization. They are part of changing the way businesses operate, not from a vague philanthropic urge, but from a conviction that their efforts will produce more productive organizations, capable of achieving higher levels of organizational success and personal satisfaction than more traditional organizations. Their sense of stewardship was succinctly captured by George Bernard Shaw when he said,

> This is the true joy in life, the being used for a purpose you consider a mighty one, the being a force of nature rather than a feverish, selfish clod of ailments and grievances complaining that the world will not devote itself to making you happy.

NEW SKILLS

New leadership roles require new leadership skills. These skills can only be developed, in my judgment, through a lifelong commitment. It is not enough for one or two individuals to develop these skills. They must be distributed widely throughout the organization. This is one reason that understanding the *disciplines* of a learning organization is so important. These disciplines embody the principles and practices that can widely foster leadership development.

Three critical areas of skills (disciplines) are building shared vision, surfacing and challenging mental models, and engaging in systems thinking.[22]

BUILDING SHARED VISION

How do individual visions come together to create shared visions? A useful metaphor is the hologram, the three-dimensional image created by interacting light sources.

If you cut a photograph in half, each half shows only part of the whole image. But if you divide a hologram, each part, no mater how small, shows the whole image intact. Likewise, when a group of people come to share a vision for an organization, each person sees an individual picture of the organization at its best. Each shares responsibility for the whole, not just for one piece. But the component pieces of the hologram are not identical. Each represents the whole image from a different point of view. It's something like poking holes in a window shade; each hole offers a unique angle for viewing the whole image. So, too, is each individual's vision unique.

When you add up the pieces of a hologram, something interesting happens. The image becomes more intense, more lifelike. When more people come to share a vision, the vision becomes more real in the sense of a mental reality that people can truly imagine achieving. They now have partners, co-creators; the vision no longer rests on their shoulders alone. Early on, when they are nurturing an individual vision, people may say it is "my vision." But, as the shared vision develops, it becomes both "my vision" and "our vision."

The skills involved in building shared vision include the following:

Encouraging Personal Vision Shared visions emerge from personal visions. It is not that people only care about their own self-interest—in fact, people's values usually include dimensions that concern family, organization, community, and even the world. Rather, it is that people's capacity for caring is *personal.*

Communicating and Asking for Support Leaders must be willing to continually share their own vision, rather than being the official representative of the corporate vision. They also must be prepared to ask, "Is this vision worthy of your commitment?" This can be difficult for a person used to setting goals and presuming compliance.

Visioning as an Ongoing Process   Building shared vision is a never-ending process. At any one point there will be a particular image of the future that is predominant, but that image will evolve. Today, too many managers want to dispense with the "vision business" by going off and writing the Official Vision Statement. Such statements almost always lack the vitality, freshness, and excitement of a genuine vision that comes from people asking, "What do we really want to achieve?"

Blending Extrinsic and Intrinsic Visions Many energizing visions are extrinsic—that is, they focus on achieving something relative to an outsider, such as a competitor. But a goal that is limited to defeating an opponent can, once the vision is achieved, easily become a defensive posture. In contrast, intrinsic goals like creating a new type of product, taking an established product to a new level, or setting a new standard for customer satisfaction can call forth a new level of creativity and innovation. Intrinsic and extrinsic visions need to coexist; a vision solely predicated on defeating an adversary will eventually weaken an organization.

Distinguishing Positive from Negative Visions Many organizations only truly pull together when their survival is threatened. Similarly, most social movements aim at eliminating what people don't want: for example, anti-drugs, anti-smoking, or anti-nuclear arms movements. Negative visions carry a subtle message of powerlessness: people will only pull together when there is sufficient threat. Negative visions also tend to be short term. Two fundamental sources of energy can motivate organizations: fear and aspiration. Fear, the energy source behind negative visions, can produce extraordinary changes in short periods, but aspiration endures as a continuing source of learning and growth.

SURFACING AND TESTING MENTAL MODELS

Many of the best ideas in organizations never get put into practice. One reason is that new insights and initiatives often conflict with established mental models. The leadership task of challenging assumptions without invoking defensiveness requires reflection and inquiry skills possessed by few leaders in traditional controlling organizations.[23]

Seeing Leaps of Abstraction Our minds literally move at lightning speed. Ironically, this often slows our learning, because we leap to generalizations so quickly that we never think to test them. We then confuse our generalizations with the observable data upon which they are based, treating the generalizations *as if they were data*. The frustrated sales rep reports to the home office that "customers don't really care about quality, price is what matters," when what actually happened was that three consecutive large customers refused to place an order unless a larger discount was offered. The sales rep treats her generalization, "customers care only about price," as if it were absolute fact rather than an assumption (very likely an assumption reflecting her own views of customers and the market). This thwarts future learning because she starts to focus on how to offer attractive discounts rather than probing behind the customers' statements. For example, the customers may have been so disgruntled with the firm's delivery or customer service that they are unwilling to purchase again without larger discounts.

Balancing Inquiry and Advocacy Most managers are skilled at articulating their views and presenting them persuasively. While important, advocacy skills can become counterproductive as managers rise in responsibility and confront increasingly complex issues that require collaborative learning among different, equally knowledgeable people. Leaders in learning organizations need to have both inquiry *and* advocacy skills.[24]

Specifically, when advocating a view, they need to be able to:

- explain the reasoning and data that led to their view;
- encourage others to test their view (e.g., Do you see gaps in my reasoning? Do you disagree with the data upon which my view is based?); and
- encourage others to provide different views (e.g., Do you have either different data, different conclusions, or both?).

When inquiring into another's views, they need to:

- actively seek to understand the other's view, rather than simply restating their own view and how it differs from the other's view; and
- make their attributions about the other and the other's view explicit (e.g., Based on your statement that . . . ; I am assuming that you believe . . . ; Am I representing your views fairly?).

If they reach an impasse (others no longer appear open to inquiry), they need to:

- ask what data or logic might unfreeze the impasse, or if an experiment (or some other inquiry) might be designed to provide new information.

Distinguishing Espoused Theory from Theory in Use We all like to think that we hold certain views, but often our actions reveal deeper views. For example, I may proclaim that people are trustworthy, but never lend friends money and jealously guard my possessions. Obviously, my deeper mental model (my theory in use), differs from my espoused theory. Recognizing gaps between espoused views and theories in use (which often requires the help of others) can be pivotal to deeper learning.

Recognizing and Defusing Defensive Routines As one CEO in our research program puts it, "Nobody ever talks about an issue at the 8:00 business meeting exactly the same way they talk about it at home that evening or over drinks at the end of the day." The reason is what Chris Argyris calls "defensive routines," entrenched habits used to protect ourselves from the embarrassment and threat that come with exposing our thinking. For most of us, such defenses began to build early in life in response to pressures to have the right answers in school or at home. Organizations add new levels of performance anxiety and thereby amplify and exacerbate this defensiveness. Ironically, this makes it even more difficult to expose hidden mental models, and thereby lessens learning.

The first challenge is to recognize defensive routines, then to inquire into their operation. Those who are best at revealing and defusing defensive routines operate with a high degree of self-disclosure regarding their own defensiveness (e.g., I notice that I am feeling uneasy about how this conversation is going. Perhaps I don't understand it or it is threatening to me in ways I don't yet see. Can you help me see this better?)

SYSTEMS THINKING

We all know that leaders should help people see the big picture. But the actual skills whereby leaders are supposed to achieve this are not well understood. In my experience, successful leaders often *are* "systems thinkers" to a considerable extent. They focus less on day-to-day events and more on underlying trends and forces of change. But they do this almost completely intuitively. The consequence is that they are often unable to explain their intuitions to others and feel frustrated that others cannot see the world the way they do.

One of the most significant developments in management science today is the gradual coalescence of managerial systems thinking as a field of study and practice. This field suggests some key skills for future leaders:

Seeing Interrelationships, Not Things, and Processes, Not Snapshots Most of us have been conditioned throughout our lives to focus on things and to see the world in static images. This leads us to linear explanations of systemic phenomenon. For instance, in an arms race each party is convinced that the other is *the cause* of problems. They react to each new move as an isolated event, not as part of a process. So long as they fail to see the interrelationships of these actions, they are trapped.

Moving beyond Blame We tend to blame each other or outside circumstances for our problems. But it is poorly designed systems, not incompetent or unmotivated individuals, that cause most organizational problems. Systems thinking shows us that there is no outside—that you and the cause of your problems are part of a single system.

Distinguishing Detail Complexity from Dynamic Complexity Some types of complexity are more important strategically than others. Detail complexity arises when there are many variables. Dynamic complexity arises when cause and effect are distant in time and space, and when the consequences over time of interventions are subtle and not obvious to many participants in the system. The leverage in most management situations lies in understanding dynamic complexity, not detail complexity.

Focusing on Areas of High Leverage Some have called systems thinking the "new dismal science" because it teaches that most obvious solutions don't work—at best, they improve matters in the short run, only to make things worse in the long run. But there is another side to the story. Systems thinking also shows that small, well-focused actions can produce significant, enduring improvements, if they are in the right place. Systems thinkers refer to this idea as the principle of "leverage." Tackling a difficult problem is often a matter of seeing where the high leverage lies, where a change—with a minimum of effort—would lead to lasting, significant improvement.

Avoiding Symptomatic Solutions The pressures to intervene in management systems that are going awry can be overwhelming. Unfortunately, given the linear thinking that predominates in most organizations, interventions usually focus on symptomatic fixes, not underlying causes. This results in only temporary relief, and it tends to create still more pressures later on for further, low-leverage intervention. If leaders acquiesce to these pressures, they can be sucked into an endless spiral of increasing intervention. Sometimes the most difficult leadership acts are to refrain from intervening through popular quick fixes and to keep the pressure on everyone to identify more enduring solutions.

While leaders who can articulate systemic explanations are rare, those who *can* will leave their stamp on an organization. One person who had this gift was Bill Gore, the founder and long-time CEO of W.L. Gore and Associates (makers of Gore-Tex and other synthetic fiber products). Bill Gore was adept at telling stories that showed how the organization's core values of freedom and individual responsibility required particular operating policies. He was proud of his egalitarian organization, in which there were (and still are) no "employees," only "associates," all of whom own shares in the company and participate in its management. At one talk, he explained the company's policy of controlled growth: "Our limitation is not financial resources. Our limitation is the rate at which we can bring in new associates. Our experience has been that if we try to bring in more than a 25 percent per year increase, we begin to bog down. Twenty-five percent per year growth is a real limitation; you can do much better than that with an authoritarian organization." As Gore tells the story, one of the associates, Esther Baum, went home after this talk and reported the limitation to her husband. As it happened, he was an astronomer and mathematician at Lowell Observatory. He said, "That's a very interesting figure." He took out a pencil and paper and calculated and said, "Do you realize that in only fifty-seven and a half years, everyone in the world will be working for Gore?"

Through this story, Gore explains the systemic rationale behind a key policy, limited growth rate—a policy that undoubtedly caused a lot of stress in the organization. He suggests that, at larger rates of growth, the adverse effects of attempting to integrate too many new people too rapidly would begin to dominate. (This is the "limits to growth" systems archetype explained below.) The story also reaffirms the organization's commitment to creating a unique environment for its associates and illustrates the types of sacrifices that the firm is prepared to make in order to remain true to its vision. The last part of the story shows that, despite the self-imposed limit, the company is still very much a growth company.

The consequences of leaders who lack systems thinking skills can be devastating. Many charismatic leaders manage almost exclusively at the level of events. They deal in visions and in crises, and little in between. Under their leadership, an organization hurtles from crisis to crisis. Eventually, the worldview of people in the organization becomes dominated by events and reactiveness. Many, especially those who are deeply committed, become burned out. Eventually, cynicism comes to pervade the organization. People have no control over their time, let alone their destiny.

Similar problems arise with the "visionary strategist," the leader with vision who sees both patterns of change and events. This leader is better prepared to manage change. He or she can explain strategies in terms of emerging trends, and thereby foster a climate that is less reactive. But such leaders still impart a responsive orientation rather than a generative one.

Many talented leaders have rich, highly systemic intuitions but cannot explain those intuitions to others. Ironically, they often end up being authoritarian leaders, even if they don't want to, because only they see the decisions that need to be made. They are unable to conceptualize their strategic insights so that these can become public knowledge, open to challenge and further improvement.

NEW TOOLS

Developing the skills described above requires new tools—tools that will enhance leaders' conceptual abilities and foster communication and collaborative inquiry. What follows is a sampling of tools starting to find use in learning organizations.

SYSTEMS ARCHETYPES

One of the insights of the budding, managerial systems-thinking field is that certain types of systemic structures recur again and again. Countless systems grow for a period, then encounter problems and cease to grow (or even collapse) well before they have reached intrinsic limits to growth. Many other systems get locked in runaway vicious spirals where every actor has to run faster and faster to stay in the same place. Still others lure individual actors into doing what seems right locally, yet which eventually causes suffering for all.[25]

Some of the system archetypes that have the broadest relevance include:

Balancing Process with Delay In this archetype, decision makers fail to appreciate the time delays involved as they move toward a goal. As a result, they overshoot the goal and may even produce recurring cycles. Classic example: Real estate developers who keep starting new projects until the market has gone soft, by which time an eventual glut is guaranteed by the properties still under construction.

Limits to Growth A reinforcing cycle of growth grinds to a halt, and may even reverse itself, as limits are approached. The limits can be resource constraints, or external or internal responses to growth. Classic examples: Product life cycles that peak prematurely due to poor quality or service, the growth and decline of communication in a management team, and the spread of a new movement.

Shifting the Burden A short-term "solution" is used to correct a problem, with seemingly happy immediate results. As this correction is used more and more, fundamental long-term corrective measures are used less. Over time, the mechanisms of the fundamental solution may atrophy or become disabled, leading to even greater reliance on the symptomatic solution. Classic example: Using corporate human resource staff to solve local personnel problems, thereby keeping managers from developing their own interpersonal skills.

Eroding Goals When all else fails, lower your standards. This is like "shifting the burden" except that the short-term solution involves letting a fundamental goal, such as quality standards or employee morale standards, atrophy. Classic example: A company that responds to delivery problems by continually upping its quoted delivery times.

Escalation Two people or two organizations, who each see their welfare as depending on a relative advantage over the other, continually react to the other's advances. Whenever one side gets ahead, the other is threatened, leading it to act more aggressively to reestablish its advantage, which threatens the first, and so on. Classic examples: Arms race, gang warfare, price wars.

Tragedy of the Commons[26] Individuals keep intensifying their use of a commonly available but limited resource until all individuals start to experience severely diminishing returns. Classic examples: Sheepherders who keep increasing their flocks until they overgraze the common pasture; divisions in a firm that share a common salesforce and compete for the use of sales reps by upping their sales targets, until the salesforce burns out from overextension.

Growth and Underinvestment Rapid growth approaches a limit that could be eliminated or pushed into the future, but only by aggressive investment in physical and human capacity. Eroding goals or standards cause investment that is too weak, or too slow, and customers get increasingly unhappy, slowing demand growth and thereby making the needed investment (apparently) unnecessary or

---

FIGURE 2   *"Shifting the Burden" Archetype Template*

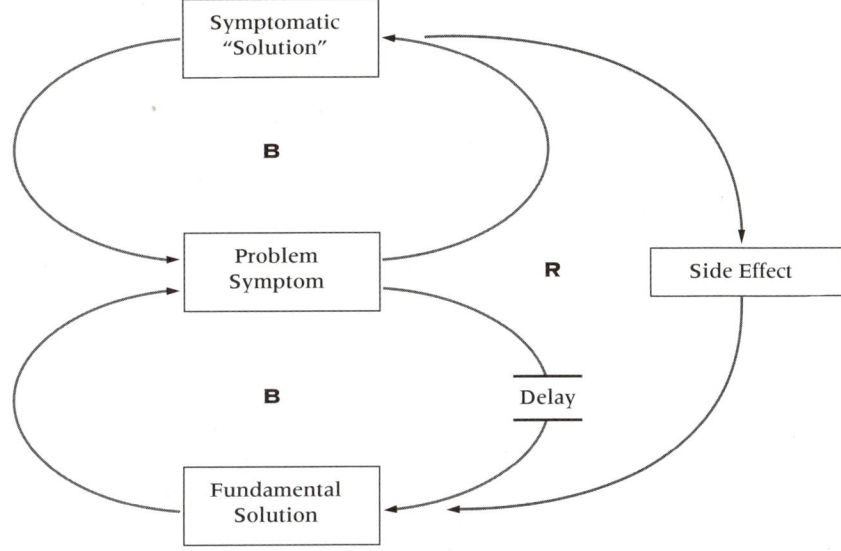

In the "shifting the burden" template, two balancing processes (B) compete for control of a problem symptom. Both solutions affect the symptom, but only the fundamental solution treats the cause. The symptomatic "solution" creates the additional side effect (R) of deferring the fundamental solution, making it harder and harder to achieve.

---

impossible. Classic example: Countless once-successful growth firms that allowed product or service quality to erode, and were unable to generate enough revenues to invest in remedies.

The Archetype template is a specific tool that is helping managers identify archetypes operating in their own strategic areas (see Figure 2).[27] The template shows the basic structural form of the archetype but lets managers fill in the variables of their own situation. For example, the shifting the burden template involves two balancing processes ("B") that compete for control of a problem symptom. The upper, symptomatic solution provides a short-term fix that will make the problem symptom go away for a while. The lower, fundamental solution provides a more enduring solution. The side effect feedback ("R") around the outside of the diagram identifies unintended exacerbating effects of the symptomatic solution, which, over time, make it more and more difficult to invoke the fundamental solution.

Several years ago, a team of managers from a leading consumer goods producer used the shifting the burden archetype in a revealing way. The problem they focused on was financial stress, which could be dealt with in two different ways: by running marketing promotions (the symptomatic solution) or by product innovation (the fundamental solution). Marketing promotions were fast. The company was expert in their design and implementation. The results were highly predictable. Product innovation was slow and much less predictable, and the company had a history over the past ten years of product-innovation mismanagement. Yet only through innovation could they retain a leadership position in their industry, which had slid over the past ten to twenty years. What the managers saw clearly was that the more skillful they became at promotions, the more they shifted the burden away from product innovation. But what really struck home was when one member identified the unintended side effect: the last three CEOs had all come from advertising function, which had become the politically dominant function in the corporation, thereby institutionalizing the symptomatic solution. Unless the political values shifted back toward product and process innovation, the managers realized, the firm's decline would accelerate—which is just the shift that has happened over the past several years.

CHARTING STRATEGIC DILEMMAS

Management teams typically come unglued when confronted with core dilemmas. A classic example was the way U.S. manufacturers faced the low cost–high quality choice. For years, most assumed that it was necessary to choose between the two. Not surprisingly, given the short-term pressures perceived by most managements, the prevailing choice was low cost. Firms that chose high quality usually perceived themselves as aiming exclusively for a high quality, high price market niche. The consequences of this perceived either-or choice have been disastrous, even fatal, as U.S. manufacturers have encountered increasing international competition from firms that have chosen to consistently improve quality *and* cost.

In a recent book, Charles Hampden-Turner presented a variety of tools for helping management teams confront strategic dilemmas creatively.[28] He summarizes the process in seven steps:

- **Eliciting the Dilemmas.** Identifying the opposed values that form the "horns" of the dilemma, for example, cost as opposed to quality, or local initiative as opposed to central coordination and control. Hampden-Turner suggests that humor can be a distinct asset in this process since "the admission that dilemmas even exist tends to be difficult for some companies."
- **Mapping.** Locating the opposing values as two axes and helping managers identify where they see themselves, or their organization, along the axes.
- **Processing.** Getting rid of nouns to describe the axes of the dilemma. Present participles formed by adding "ing" convert rigid nouns into processes that imply movement. For example, central control versus local control becomes "strengthening national office" and "growing local initiatives." This loosens the bond of implied opposition between the two values. For example, it becomes possible to think of "strengthening national services from which local branches can benefit."
- **Framing/Contextualizing.** Further softening the adversarial structure among different values by letting "each side in turn be the frame or context for the other." This shifting of the "figure-ground" relationship undermines any implicit attempts to hold one value as intrinsically superior to the other, and thereby to become mentally closed to creative strategies for continuous improvement of both.

- **Sequencing.** Breaking the hold of static thinking. Very often, values like low cost and high quality appear to be in opposition because we think in terms of a point in time, not in terms of an ongoing process. For example, a strategy of investing in new process technology and developing a new production-floor culture of worker responsibility may take time and money in the near term, yet reap significant long-term financial rewards.
- **Waving/Cycling.** Sometimes the strategic path toward improving both values involves cycles where both values will get "worse" for a time. Yet, at a deeper level, learning is occurring that will cause the next cycle to be at a higher plateau for both values.
- **Synergizing.** Achieving synergy where significant improvement is occurring along all axes of all relevant dilemmas. (This is the ultimate goal, of course.) Synergy, as Hampden-Turner points out, is a uniquely systemic notion, coming from the Greek *syn-ergo* or "work together."

"THE LEFT-HAND COLUMN": SURFACING MENTAL MODELS

The idea that mental models can dominate business decisions and that these models are often tacit and even contradictory to what people espouse can be very threatening to managers who pride themselves on rationality and judicious decision making. It is important to have tools to help managers discover for themselves how their mental models operate to undermine their own intentions.

One tool that has worked consistently to help managers see their own mental models in action is the "left-hand column" exercise developed by Chris Argyris and his colleagues. This tool is especially helpful in showing how we leap from data to generalization without testing the validity of our generalizations.

When working with managers, I start this exercise by selecting a specific situation in which I am interacting with other people in a way that is not working, that is not producing the learning that is needed. I write out a sample of the exchange, with the script on the right-hand side of the page. On the left-hand side, I write what I am thinking but not saying at each stage in the exchange (see box titled "The Left-Hand Column: An Exercise").

The left-hand column exercise not only brings hidden assumptions to the surface, it shows how they influence behavior. In the example, I make two key assumptions about Bill: he lacks confidence and he lacks initiative. Neither may be literally true, but both are evident in my internal dialogue, and both influence the way I handle the situation. Believing that he lacks confidence, I skirt the fact that I've heard the presentation was a bomb. I'm afraid that if I say it directly, he will lose what little confidence he has, or he will see me as unsupportive. So I bring up the subject of the presentation obliquely. When I ask Bill what we should do next, he gives no specific course of action. Believing he lacks initiative, I take this as evidence of his laziness; he is content to do nothing when action is definitely required. I conclude that I will have to manufacture some form of pressure to motivate him, or else I will simply have to take matters into my own hands.

The exercise reveals the elaborate webs of assumptions we weave, within which we become our own victims. Rather than dealing directly with my assumptions about Bill and the situation, we talk around the subject. The reasons for my avoidance are self-evident: I assume that if I raised my doubts, I would provoke a defensive reaction

THE LEFT-HAND COLUMN: AN EXERCISE

Imagine my exchange with a colleague, Bill, after he made a big presentation to our boss on a project we are doing together. I had to miss the presentation, but I've heard that it was poorly received.

Me: How did the presentation go?
Bill: Well, I don't know. It's really too early to say. Besides, we're breaking new ground here.
Me: Well, what do you think we should do? I believe that the issues you were raising are important.
Bill: I'm not so sure. Let's just wait and see what happens.
Me: You may be right, but I think we may need to do more than just wait.

Now, here is what the exchange looks like with my "left-hand column":

WHAT I'M THINKING	WHAT IS SAID
Everyone says the presentation was a bomb.	**Me**: How did the presentation go?
Does he really not know how bad it was? Or is he not willing to face up to it?	**Bill**: Well, I don't know. It's too early to say. Besides, we're breaking new ground here.
	Me: Well, what do you think we should do? I believe that the issues you were raising are important.
He really is afraid to see the truth. If he only had more confidence, he could probably learn from a situation like this.	**Bill**: I'm not so sure. Let's just wait and see what happens.
I can't believe he doesn't realize how disastrous that presentation was to our moving ahead.	**Me**: You may be right, but I think we may need to do more than just wait.
I've got to find some way to light a fire under the guy.	

that would only make matters worse. But the price of avoiding the issue is high. Instead of determining how to move forward to resolve our problems, we end our exchange with no clear course of action. My assumptions about Bill's limitations have been reinforced. I resort to a manipulative strategy to move things forward.

The exercise not only reveals the need for skills in surfacing assumptions, but that we are the ones most in need of help. There is no one right way to handle difficult situations like my exchange with Bill, but any productive strategy revolves around a high level of self-disclosure and willingness to have my views challenged. I need to recognize my own leaps of abstraction regarding Bill, share the events and reasoning that are leading to my concern over the project, and be open to Bill's views on both. The skills to carry on such conversations without invoking defensiveness take time to develop. But if both parties in a learning impasse start by doing their own left-hand column exercise and sharing them with each other, it is remarkable how quickly everyone recognizes their contribution to the impasse and progress starts to be made.

LEARNING AT HANOVER INSURANCE

Hanover Insurance has gone from the bottom of the property and liability industry to a position among the top 25 percent of U.S. insurance companies over the past twenty years, largely through the efforts of CEO William O'Brien and his predecessor, Jack Adam. The following comments are excerpted from a series of interviews Senge conducted with O'Brien as background for his book.

Senge: Why do you think there is so much change occurring in management and organizations today? Is it primarily because of increased competitive pressures?

O'Brien: That's a factor, but not the most significant factor. The ferment in management will continue until we find models that are more congruent with human nature.

One of the great insights of modern psychology is the hierarchy of human needs. As Maslow expressed this idea, the most basic needs are food and shelter. Then comes belonging. Once these three basic needs are satisfied, people begin to aspire toward self-respect and esteem, and toward self-actualization—the fourth- and fifth-order needs.

Our traditional hierarchical organizations are designed to provide for the first three levels, but not the fourth and fifth. These first three levels are now widely available to members of industrial society, but our organizations do not offer people sufficient opportunities for growth.

Senge: How would you assess Hanover's progress to date?

O'Brien: We have been on a long journey away from a traditional hierarchical culture. The journey began with everyone understanding some guiding ideas about purpose, vision, and values as a basis for participative management. This is a better way to begin building a participative culture than by simply "letting people in on decision making." Before there can be meaningful participation, people must share certain values and

pictures about where we are trying to go. We discovered that people have a real need to feel that they're part of an enobling mission. But developing shared visions and values is not the end, only the beginning.

Next we had to get beyond mechanical linear thinking. The essence of our jobs as managers is to deal with "divergent" problems—problems that have no simple answer. "Convergent" problems—problems that have a "right" answer—should be solved locally. Yet we are deeply conditioned to see the world in terms of convergent problems. Most managers try to force-fit simplistic solutions and undermine the potential for learning when divergent problems arise. Since everyone handles the linear issues fairly well, companies that learn how to handle divergent issues will have a great advantage.

The next basic stage in our progression was coming to understand inquiry and advocacy. We learned that real openness is rooted in people's ability to continually inquire into their own thinking. This requires exposing yourself to being wrong—not something that most managers are rewarded for. But learning is very difficult if you cannot look for errors or incompleteness in your own ideas.

What all this builds to is the capability throughout an organization to manage mental models. In a locally controlled organization, you have the fundamental challenge of learning how to help people make good decisions without coercing them into making *particular* decisions. By managing mental models, we create "self-concluding" decisions—decisions that people come to themselves—which will result in deeper conviction, better implementation, and the ability to make better adjustments when the situation changes.

continued

Senge: What concrete steps can top managers take to begin moving toward learning organizations?

O'Brien: Look at the signals you send through the organization. For example, one critical signal is how you spend your time. It's hard to build a learning organization if people are unable to take the time to think through important matters. I rarely set up an appointment for less than one hour. If the subject is not worth an hour, it shouldn't be on my calendar.

Senge: Why is this so hard for so many managers?

O'Brien: It comes back to what you believe about the nature of your work. The authoritarian manager has a "chain gang" mental model: "The speed of the boss is the speed of the gang. I've Got to keep things moving fast, because I've got to keep people working." In a learning organization, the manager shoulders an almost sacred responsibility to create conditions that enable people to have happy and productive lives. If you understand the effects the ideas we are discussing can have on the lives of people in your organization, you will take the time.

LEARNING LABORATORIES: PRACTICE FIELDS FOR MANAGEMENT TEAMS

One of the most promising new tools is the learning laboratory or "microworld": constructed microcosms of real-life settings in which management teams can learn how to learn together.

The rationale behind learning laboratories can best be explained by analogy. Although most management teams have great difficulty learning (enhancing their collective intelligence and capacity to create), in other domains team learning is the norm rather than the exception—team sports and the performing arts, for example. Great basketball teams do not start off great. They learn. But the process by which these teams learn is, by and large, absent from modern organizations. The process is a continual movement between practice and performance.

The vision guiding current research in management learning laboratories is to design and construct effective practice fields for management teams. Much remains to be done, but the broad outlines are emerging.

First, since team learning in organizations is an individual-to-individual and individual-to-system phenomenon, learning laboratories must combine meaningful business issues with meaningful interpersonal dynamics. Either alone is incomplete.

Second, the factors that thwart learning about complex business issues must be eliminated in the learning lab. Chief among these is the inability to experience the long-term, systemic consequences of key strategic decisions. We all learn best from experience, but we are unable to experience the consequences of many important organizational decisions. Learning laboratories remove this constraint through system dynamics simulation games that compress time and space.

Third, new learning skills must be developed. One constraint on learning is the inability of managers to reflect insightfully on their assumptions, and to inquire effectively into each other's assumptions. Both skills can be enhanced in a learning laboratory, where people can practice surfacing assumptions in a low-risk setting. A note of caution: It is far easier to design an entertaining learning laboratory than it is to have an impact on real management practices and firm traditions outside the learning lab. Research on management simulations has shown that they often have greater entertainment value than educational value.

One of the reasons appears to be that many simulations do not offer deep insights into systemic structures causing business problems. Another reason is that they do not foster new learning skills. Also, there is no connection between experiments in the learning lab and real life experiments. These are significant problems that research on learning laboratory design is now addressing.

DEVELOPING LEADERS AND LEARNING ORGANIZATIONS

In a recently published retrospective on organization development in the 1980s, Marshall Sashkin and N. Warner Burke observe the return of an emphasis on developing leaders who can develop organizations.[29] They also note Schein's critique that most top executives are not qualified for the task of developing culture.[30] Learning organizations represent a potentially significant evolution of organizational culture. So it should come as no surprise that such organizations will remain a distant vision until the leadership capabilities they demand are developed. "The 1990s may be the period," suggest Sashkin and Burke, "during which organization development and (a new sort of) management development are reconnected."

I believe that this new sort of management development will focus on the roles, skills, and tools for leadership in learning organizations. Undoubtedly, the ideas offered above are only a rough approximation of this new territory. The sooner we begin seriously exploring the territory, the sooner the initial map can be improved—and the sooner we will realize and age-old vision of leadership:

> *The wicked leader is he who the people despise. The good leader is he who the people revere. The great leader is he who the people say, "We did it ourselves."*
>
> –LAO TSU

NOTES

1. P. Senge, *The Fifth Discipline: The Art and Practice of the Learning Organization* (New York: Doubleday/Currency, 1990).
2. A.P. de Geus, "Planing as Learning," *Harvard Business Review,* March-April 1988, pp. 70–74.
3. B. Domain, *Fortune,* 3 July 1989, pp. 48–62.
4. The distinction between adaptive and generative learning has its roots in the distinction between what Argyris and Schon have called their "single-loop" learning, in which individuals or groups adjust their behavior relative to fixed goals, norms, and assumptions, and "double-loop" learning, in which goals, norms, and assumptions, as well as behavior, are open to change (e.g., see C. Argyris and D. Schon, *Organizational Learning: A Theory-in-Action Perspective* (Reading, Massachusetts: Addison-Wesley, 1978)).
5. All unattributed quotes are from personal communications with the author.
6. G. Stalk, Jr., "Time: The Next Source of Competitive Advantage," *Harvard Business Review,* July-August 1988, pp. 41–51.
7. Senge (1990).
8. The principle of creative tension comes from Robert Fritz' work on creativity. See R. Fritz, *The Path of Least Resistance* (New York: Ballantine, 1989) and *Creating* (New York: Ballantine, 1990).

9. M.L. King, Jr, "Letter from Birmingham Jail," *American Visions,* January-February 1986, pp. 52–59.

10. E. Schein, *Organizational Culture and Leadership* (San Francisco: Jossey-Bass, 1985). Similar views have been expressed by many leadership theorists. For example, see: P. Selznick, *Leadership in Administration* (New York: Harper & Row, 1957); W. Bennis and B. Nanus, *Leaders* (New York: Harper & Row, 1985); and N.M. Tichy and M.A. Devanna, *The Transformational Leader* (New York: John Wiley & Sons, 1986).

11. Selznick (1957).

12. J.W. Forrester, "A New Corporate Design," *Sloan Management Review* (formerly *Industrial Management Review*), Fall 1965, pp. 5–17.

13. See, for example, H. Mintzberg, "Crafting Strategy," *Harvard Business Review,* July-August 1987, pp. 66–75.

14. R. Mason and I. Mitroff, *Challenging Strategic Planning Assumptions* (New York: John Wiley & Sons, 1981), p. 16.

15. P. Wack, "Scenarios: Uncharted Waters Ahead," *Harvard Business Review,* September-October 1985, pp. 73–89.

16. de Geus (1988).

17. M. de Pree, *Leadership Is an Art* (New York: Doubleday, 1989), p. 9.

18. For example, see T. Peters and N. Austin, *A Passion for Excellence* (New York: Random House, 1985) and J.M. Kouzes and B.Z. Posner, *The Leadership Challenge* (San Francisco: Jossey-Bass, 1987).

19. I. Mitroff, *Break-Away Thinking* (New York: John Wiley & Sons, 1988), pp. 66–67.

20. R.K. Greenleaf, *Servant Leadership: A Journey into the Nature of Legitimate Power and Greatness* (New York: Paulist Press, 1977).

21. L. Miller, *American Spirit: Visions of a New Corporate Culture* (New York: William Morrow, 1984), p. 15.

22. These points are condensed from the practices of the five disciplines examined in Senge (1990).

23. The ideas below are based to a considerable extent on the work of Chris Argyris, Donald Schon, and their Action Science colleagues: C. Argyris and D. Schon, *Organizational Learning: A Theory-in-Action Perspective* (Reading, Massachusetts: Addison-Wesley, 1978); C. Argyris, R. Putnam, and D. Smith, *Action Science* (San Francisco: Jossey-Bass, 1985); C. Argyris, *Strategy, Change, and Defensive Routines* (Boston: Pitman, 1985); and C. Argyris, *Overcoming Organizational Defenses* (Englewood Cliffs, New Jersey: Prentice-Hall, 1990).

24. I am indebted to Diana Smith for the summary points below.

25. The system archetypes are one of several systems diagraming and communication tools. See D.H. Kim, "Toward Learning Organizations: Integrating Total Quality Control and Systems Thinking" (Cambridge, Massachusetts: MIT Sloan School of Management, Working Paper No. 3037-89-BPS, June 1989).

26. This archetype is closely associated with the work of ecologist Garrett Hardin, who coined its label: G Hardin, "The Tragedy of the Commons," *Science,* 13 December 1968.

27. These templates were originally developed by Jennifer Kemeny, Charles Kiefer, and Michael Goodman of Innovative Associates, Inc, Framingham, Massachusetts.

28. C. Hampden-Turner, *Charting the Corporate Mind* (New York: The Free Press, 1990).

29. M. Sashkin and W.W. Burke, "Organization Development in the 1980s" and "An End-of-the-Eighties Retrospective," in *Advances in Organization Development*, ed. F. Masarik (Norwood, New Jersey: Ablex, 1990).

30. E. Schein (1985).

PART 2

PROBLEM SOLVING, CONTINUOUS IMPROVEMENT, AND REENGINEERING

Solving Problems and Improving Processes: Which Model Shall We Use?

MICHAEL J. BROWER

TQM is, in part, about solving problems in the workplace. This is nothing new, but what TQM adds is an insistence on fixing root causes and not just symptoms, so that we will stop "fixing" the same problem over and over again. To do this, however, requires that we select and follow a rigorous, disciplined model.

We Americans love action. Whenever there is a problem or a crisis, some, perhaps most of us, want to jump to the solution and get moving; never mind talk, data, and analysis. We are likely to say: "We know what the problem is! We know what the solution is! Stop wasting time sitting around and talking. Every hour we sit here talking with the machine (or line, or whatever) down (or not putting out the correct product, or not providing the right service) costs us *x* number of dollars." To deal with this impatience, this bias towards action, this tendency to assume that we know what the real cause is and what the one perfect solution is, requires that we understand and work within a disciplined model.

TQM's main focus, however, is on improving processes, not on problem solving. There are basically three criteria that TQM asks us to apply to a process. One, is the process *stable*, that is, under statistical control, so that it is producing predictable results, with virtually all variation explained by common causes? Two, is the process *capable* of producing results that will meet or exceed the customers' specifications. Three, even after the process is both stable and capable, can we find ways to further improve the process, to reduce its variation and/or make it shorter, simpler, faster, cheaper? So TQM is about continuous improvement in our processes, even after they are brought under control and into capability. We never stop or accept a given performance level as a final, permanent achievement. To do this requires tools, and TQM uses many tools, some of which are mentioned in the following section. However, each of these tools is only part of the whole picture.

Each has its strengths and its limitations. None, used alone, will do the whole job. Each must be used in conjunction with others, as part of a structured problem solving or process improvement model.

The PDCA Plan-Do-Check-Act model is the most fundamental process improvement model. Simple and powerful, it tells us to Plan before we Do; to implement, or Do; to Check after Doing; and then to reflect and Act on what we have learned. But this is very general. Plan What? How? Check what and how? Then what kind of follow-through Action? We need models to guide us with more details within PDCA.

Fortunately, there are good models out there, but perhaps so many as to be confusing. Examples of three kinds of models are presented briefly in Sections I – III: problem solving; process improvement; and hybrid, or mixed models. In section IV we discuss some of the key elements that should be included in whichever model you choose.

I. PROBLEM-SOLVING MODELS

Problem solving models have been around for a long time; they were in use long before TQM became widely known. Drawing from various models, the key elements are:

- identifying and clarifying a problem,
- gathering data,
- brainstorming possible causes of the problem,
- using the data for analysis to determine the root cause(s) of the problem,
- thinking of alternative solutions,
- choosing the best solution (or package of solutions), and
- implementing that solution.

Most models leave out one or more of these steps, or combine several steps into one. Beyond this, a good model should also include:

- an auditing step,
- a follow-through step for making further corrections and for eliminating or reducing the probability of the same problem occurring again, and
- a standardization step.

But many of the models do not. Compare these lists with the steps in the following six basic models.

In the late 1970s a prize winning QC Circle at the Ricoh Company's Numazu plant followed and reported on the following seven activities in their quality story (Imai, 1986, pp. 66–74):

1. Selection of a theme
2. Understanding the situation
3. Setting the target
4. Factors and measures

5. Results
6. Measures to prevent backsliding
7. Insights and future directions

This model is especially strong because it lists Steps 6 and 7, which many U.S. problem solving models, especially at that time, overlooked.

The Juran Institute (1992) uses a six step "Quality Improvement Process." It too is solid, especially in Step 5 by highlighting the importance of "holding the gains" (because if we do not consciously work on this, we will backslide) and in Step 6 by spreading the benefits of the project.

1. Identify a project
2. Establish the project
3. Diagnose the cause
4. Remedy the cause
5. Hold the gains
6. Replicate results and nominate new projects

In the original GOAL/QPC *The Memory Jogger* (Brassard, 1985, p. 6) we find another simple six step model:

1. Decide which problem will be addressed first (or next)
2. Arrive at a statement that describes the problem in terms of what it is specifically, where it occurs, when it happens, and its extent
3. Develop a complete picture of all the possible causes of the problem
4. Agree on the basic cause(s) of the problem
5. Develop an effective and implementable solution and action plan
6. Implement the solution and establish needed monitoring procedures and charts

In addition to reminding us to set up monitoring procedures and charts (to hold the gains), this model is especially strong in guiding us to clearly define the problem, to look for all possible causes, and to zero in on the basic cause(s).

The Miller Consulting Group (Miller, 1991, pp. 151–152) "Six-Step Problem Solving Model" is:

1. Define the problem
2. Brainstorm possible causes
3. Analyze the data
4. Brainstorm possible solutions
5. Reach consensus on solutions
6. Develop the action plan

As you can see, this model is strong on the front end, the "Plan" part, giving us five steps for defining, understanding, and solving the problem. It is, however, weaker than the other models at the end, leaving us with an Action Plan, but no guidance on the "Check" or "Act" steps.

One of the best models overall is the following, highly disciplined, Seven Step Model taught by Dr. Shoji Shiba (Shiba, 1993) of the Center for Quality Management at M.I.T.:

1. Select theme
2. Collect and analyze data
3. Analyze causes
4. Plan and implement solution
5. Evaluate effects/confirm results
6. Standardize solutions
7. Reflect on the process

Notice the balance and symmetry in this model. It starts with selecting a theme, proceeds to two steps of data and cause analysis, includes planning and implementation, and then closes with three steps of follow-through, standardization and reflection.

Imai (1986, page 76) presents a similar seven step "Problem-Solving Cycle" explicitly and graphically built around Plan-Do-Check-Act, as shown in Figure 1.

Whichever problem solving model is used, teams need to learn the importance of root cause analysis (without which we often end up solving only symptoms), of detailed action planning, and of auditing and learning from results. Teams also need to learn how to use each of the main QC problem solving tools, with the help initially of knowledgeable leadership. These tools include:

- Flow charting, both at a general level, and at a level of great detail
- Check sheets for gathering and recording data
- Run Charts for recording, examining, and analyzing data over time
- Histograms for discovering the distribution patterns in data
- Pareto diagrams for showing problems or causes in order of frequency
- Cause-effect diagrams (fishbones) for brainstorming probable causes
- Cost-Benefit analysis for choosing among alternative solutions
- Control charts for discovering whether or not a process is in control and for distinguishing between special and common causes of variations

For more information on these tools, see Costin (1994), Part III; Brassard (1985); Brassard and Ritter (1994); Ishikawa (1976); and Wheeler and Chambers (1986).

II. PROCESS IMPROVEMENT MODELS

There are at least four main limitations to problem solving. One, our attention is not triggered until something breaks, or goes wrong. This may be a single event, such as a machine breaking down, or a series of events leading to performance dropping below an "acceptable" level, such as the infection rate in a hospital operating room or ward. "If it ain't broke, don't fix it" is almost a national slogan that illustrates this limitation.

FIGURE 1

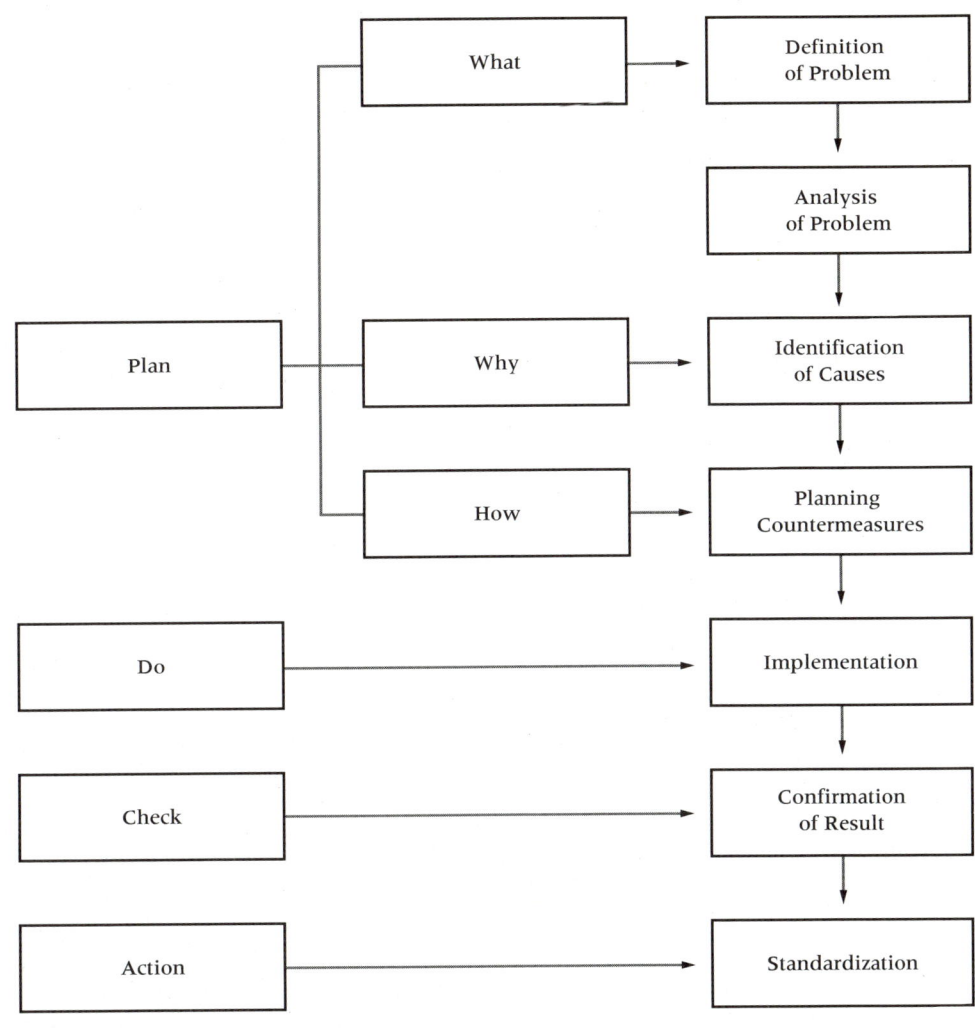

Two, problem solving and its models imply or state that the goal is to get us back to the previous, presumably acceptable, standard or level of performance, even if it involved a few errors in every ten thousand cases, or even worse, a few per hundred. Much better is a mind-set and associated model or models that ask us to repeatedly raise the standard.

Three, problem solving models almost never direct us to find out who are the relevant customers, and what it would take to meet or exceed their requirements. When we do this, we are likely to be more on target for what is important and to continually raise the standard, since customer expectations are dynamic.

Four, problem solving by its very nature implies that what we are facing is a "problem" that can be "solved." In the real world we often actually face a complex situation, or "mess," which we will have to work continuously on improving, since it will never be "solved."

To deal with these limitations, there is a whole separate mind-set and collection of models for process improvement, also called *continuous improvement of processes*. Process improvement does not wait for something to break; it is focused on a process, not events; it determines customer requirements of that process; it works on improving that process, then on standardizing the improvements; and then goes on to seek further improvements. Process improvement calls for a different mentality from problem solving, a different model, and a slogan that might be: "If it ain't broke, improve it anyway."

One of the simplest of such models is the Joiner (Scholtes, 1988, pp. 5–26) Five Stage Model:

1. Understand the process
2. Eliminate errors
3. Remove slack
4. Reduce variation
5. Plan for continuous improvement

Notice how different this model is from the problem solving models in Section I. Notice also that this model still does not explicitly include the customers.

One of the best of the process improvement models is the AT&T (1988) version:

1. Establish process management responsibilities
2. Define process and identify customer requirements
3. Define and establish measures
4. Assess conformance to customer requirements
5. Investigate process to identify improvement opportunities
6. Rank improvement opportunities and set objectives
7. Improve process quality

Notice that this model is very strong on the beginning and middle steps: definitions, customer requirements, measures, alternative improvement opportunities, and objectives. On the other hand, the model ends weakly, closing with only a single, rather vague step of: "Improve process quality." However, when we study the AT&T guide, we find that it emphasizes focusing on "sustained process *improvement*," and "Once process improvement is realized, follow-through is essential to ensure that the results of your improvement efforts do not deteriorate over time" (AT&T, 1988, p.55). Furthermore, the single Step 7 in this model turns out to call for a Quality Improvement Team (QIT) to follow "The AT&T Quality Improvement Cycle" (AT&T, 1988, pp. 60–61), which is itself an eight step model, as follows:

1. Select improvement area
2. Identify outputs and customers
3. Determine customer expectations
4. Describe current processes

5. Focus on improvement opportunities
6. Determine root causes (diagnostic journey)
7. Trial and implement solution (remedial journey)
8. Hold the gains (follow-through)

The reader may notice what appears to be some overlap between these two AT&T models. The authors are explicit about this, and suggest that, if the first model has been already followed by a higher level steering team or committee (AT&T calls these Process Management Teams), some QITs may be able to jump from Step 1 to Step 5. And note here again, the emphasis on customers and on holding the gains. As outsiders, we could only ask if AT&T might want to integrate these two models, eliminating the overlap.

III. COMBINED PROBLEM SOLVING/PROCESS IMPROVEMENT MODELS

A few organizations have recently attempted to include both problem solving and process improvement in a single model. For example, GOAL/QPC (with inputs from a group of us that work at or with GOAL/QPC), working in part from the AT&T model, developed the following "Problem Solving/Process Improvement Model," which is published and illustrated in the new *The Memory Jogger II* (Brassard and Ritter, 1994, pp. 115–131):

PLAN

1. Select the problem/process that will be addressed first (or next) and describe the improvement opportunity.
2. Describe the current process surrounding the improvement opportunity.
3. Describe all of the possible causes of the problem and agree on the root cause(s).
4. Develop an effective and workable solution and action plan, including targets for improvement.

DO

5. Implement the solution or process change.

CHECK

6. Review and evaluate the result of the change.

ACT

7. Reflect and act on learnings.

This model starts with a combined first step, follows with a process improvement step, swings into problem solving in the third and fourth steps, moves back to a combined Step 5 and neutral (very strong) Step 6 and 7. Overall, it is an impressive first effort at combining the two conceptual approaches into a single model. Still missing is an explicit step calling for focus on customers and gathering of information from customers of the process being improved. However, in the text under Step 1 we do find as two sub-steps: "Look for changes in important business indicators" and "Review customer data." Overall, though, I find it confusing to mix the two approaches in a single model since problem solving and process improvement come from very different historical, conceptual, and even ideological, roots. I believe it is preferable to use a strong, clear process improvement model and then use a separate or subsidiary problem solving model when that is the specific, limited need.

IV. KEY ELEMENTS TO INCLUDE IN YOUR PROCESS IMPROVEMENT MODEL

Regardless of which model you are now using, or may use, in your organization, it is important that you use a structured, complete model. And if you are going to go beyond problem solving into the world of TQM, focusing on and continuously improving those processes that determine your quality of customer service, then you will need a process improvement model.

Whichever model you choose, make sure that it includes each of the following elements. They do not necessarily have to be in this exact order. In actually using these models, we often have to double back and recheck or redo some steps anyway. Nor do these all have to be major steps; some can be listed as sub-steps or components. If the model you are using lacks some of these elements, add them as additional steps or sub-steps, or adopt a better model.

1. Issue selection. A thoughtful selection of what to work on, including consideration of which processes are most important to your overall success in serving your customers.
2. Customer interviews. A focus on the customers' relationship to the process you have chosen to improve, and a serious effort to determine what those customers have received in the past (from you and from any real or potential competition), must receive in the present or near future, and would like to receive in the long term.
3. Objectives or vision of the ideal future. A careful definition of what you are trying to accomplish. There should be an option and encouragement to set objectives or a vision that not only reaches, but goes beyond, previous best performance.
4. Process understanding and root causes. Develop a full understanding of the current process, using detailed flow charting and measurements on each key step in the process. On parts of the process that need or may need improvement, apply root cause analysis, using such tools as the cause-effect diagram and the "5 Whys"—the Japanese technique of asking "Why?" five times in a row to get to deeper and deeper causes.
5. Use of measurements, data, and analysis. Make sure that your understanding of the present process; its shortcomings; its time, quality, or money costs; its potential for improvement; and your intended changes are built on solid

measurements and analysis. This may be aided by using such tools as check sheets, run and control charts, Pareto diagrams, and histograms where appropriate.

6. Alternative possible solutions. Do not accept, or let your teams accept, the first solution proposed, or the most popular one, without developing some possible alternatives, using such tools as brainstorming, the affinity diagram, and the cause-effect diagram.

7. Careful selection of which solution(s) to implement. Teams should learn and apply consensus decision making, voting, nominal group technique voting, or some other agreed upon decision process. They should also learn and make use of cost-benefit analysis for those cases where costs and benefits can be reasonably estimated, and decision matrices for use where they cannot be well estimated or where several alternatives should be weighed against multiple, weighted criteria.

8. Action planning. For minor implementation work, teams should use as a minimum an action planning list of questions, such as "Who will do what?," "By when?," and so on. For more complicated changes and projects, the teams will need to use such planning tools as the tree diagram and an assignment matrix that elaborates primary and secondary responsibilities, resources needed, comments, and a time line for each specific action line.

9. Consider objections, restraining forces, and what can go wrong. Any significant change will make somebody's or some department's work more complicated, more difficult, or at least require learning a new way of doing things. It may depend upon some new form of information gathering, analysis, or sharing. Successful change efforts anticipate these difficulties and requirements as much as possible and include the counter measures or reconciling efforts in the original plan. Some tools that are helpful in doing this are the process decision program chart, the two-force force field analysis, and a three force model, which includes the activating and restraining forces of the traditional force field and adds a third reconciling force or viewpoint for anticipating and reconciling restraints.

10. Audit (check). Plan and carry out auditing (checking) on implementation and its results.

11. Reflect and act on learnings. This results in one or more of three things:
    - Going around the model, or part of it, again to achieve further needed gains
    - Standardizing the process improvements to make sure we hold the gains
    - Spreading the learnings to other shifts, lines, departments, plants, and so on

12. Celebrate the successes. Improvement of processes, at least major processes, is hard work. It sometimes fails. It often takes a lot of time in any given week or month, and it may spread out over many months. It can be discouraging and frustrating. For all these reasons, it is very important that managers provide teams with recognition and that they organize celebrations, even for interim and partial successes, along the way.

Of course, choosing a model is just the start. Here are some tips on the rest:

First, training is required to explain the reasons for using the model, the logic of the model, the components of the model, and how to use the model. Managers, supervisors, team leaders, and facilitators will need this training in some depth.

Training for team members can be less intensive, as long as they have well trained leaders and have the chance to learn by using the model.

Next, there is the importance of actually using the model. All the preparation and training will be wasted if the model is not used, over and over again. Team leaders and facilitators will have to be firm and persuasive in getting teams to stick to the model, even when some team members are sure they know the best solution and are vehemently demanding that the team not waste so much time in following some "stupid old model when we know what to do." The model must be used with enough regularity and persistence so that it becomes a powerful vehicle for training teams and their members in logical, disciplined, interactive thinking; thinking that will carry over to everyday work beyond the formal team work on processes or problems.

Make it visible. Creating large storyboards posted on the wall that illustrate each of the model's major steps and sub-steps can be a very useful help in training the teams and in reminding them where they are as they follow the model. These storyboards can then be reproduced and each team can put their own content into each step as they work through the model on their own processes.

Also, the teams need to learn the importance of "managing with facts": of using facts, data, information, and analysis before deciding on causes and solutions.

Finally, do not forget to apply PDCA to the model itself. After the model is used to work on and improve a process, the team should reflect not only on their work, but also on the model and how well it worked for them. After some experience with your model, you will be in a position either to improve the model, or to write your own that will work better for you.

BIBLIOGRAPHY

AT&T Quality Steering Committee. *Process Quality Management & Improvement Guidelines,* Indianapolis: AT&T's Customer Information Center, 1987, 1988, issue 1.1.

Brassard, Michael. *The Memory Jogger.* Methuen, MA: GOAL/QPC, 1985.

———.*The Memory Jogger Plus+®.* Methuen, MA: GOAL/QPC, 1989.

Brassard, Michael, and Diane Ritter. *The Memory Jogger ™II.* Methuen, MA: GOAL/QPC, 1994.

Costin, Harry, *Readings in Total Quality Management,* Fort Worth: The Dryden Press, 1994.

Donnell, Augustus, and Margaret Dellinger, for the AT&T Quality Steering Committee, *Analyzing Business Process Data: The Looking Glass,* Indianapolis: AT&T's Customer Information Center, 1990.

Imai, Masaaki, *Kaizen, The Key to Japan's Competitive Success,* New York: Random House, 1986.

Ishikawa, Kaoru, *Guide to Quality Control,* Tokyo: Asian Productivity Organization, 1976.

Juran Institute, *Quality Improvement, Team Training Workbook,* Wilton, CT: 1992.

Miller, Lawrence M. and Jennifer Howard, *Managing Quality Through Teams,* Atlanta: The Miller Consulting Group, 1991.

Scholtes, Peter R. *The Team Handbook,* Madison: Joiner Associates, 1988.

Shiba, Dr. Shoji, November 15, 1993 talk jointly sponsored by the Merrimack Valley Chapter of the American Society for Quality Control (ASQC) and the Greater Boston Chapter of the Association for Quality and Participation (AQP).

Wheeler, Donald J., and David S. Chambers, *Understanding Statistical Process Control,* Knoxville, TN: Statistical Process Controls, Inc., 1986.

Decision and Planning Tools

BY GLEN D. HOFFHERR AND NORMAN W. YOUNG

In our daily business we face many situations for which we do not have detailed factual information. We are forced to make decisions on what we think rather than on what we know. We then apply the accumulation of our experiences, knowledge, and possibly the recommendations of our associates to make the decision. We are generally thought to have good judgment if the results of our decisions are good for the organization. Decisions that do not bring about the desired results may cause our judgment to be called into question. The tools in this article will help you make better decisions by focusing on the information you have.

There is a group of tools often called the *7 New QC tools,* or the *7 Management and Planning tools.* These names do not describe the power of these tools or who should use them. They would more accurately be called decision and planning tools. This article lists and describes the authors' favorite decision and planning tools. They are used most effectively to make decisions and plans when you do not have hard data or facts. There is no right or wrong way to use any of these tools. Remember that the purpose of any tool is to enable you to make a better decision. These tools are powerful vehicles for gathering, organizing, examining, and presenting the collective judgment(s) of you and your coworkers. They will improve the quality of the decisions you make and increase your success at solving problems and achieving goals.

Many of these tools can be used in multiple ways. Some have facets that predispose them to certain situations. As you work with the tools, you will find that you use some every day and others infrequently. You will develop comfort and expertise with the tools you use most often.

In our zeal to develop the science of leadership and decision making, we often over-use tools and techniques. The result is that we lose sight of the goal that we are trying to accomplish, or miss an opportunity through analysis paralysis. Thus, it is most important to know when not to use tools. When the proper decision is clear to all concerned, when you have adequate resources and everyone is in agreement—ACT! You will, however, want to employ the tools when:

SOURCE: Much of the information contained in this article is taken from *The Toolbook: Decision Making & Planning for Optimum Results* and the courseware that is associated with it. The authors gratefully acknowledge the publisher, Markon Inc. for granting permission to use excerpts from these two works.

- you are having difficulty analyzing complex alternatives,
- you disagree with coworkers and must find a way to come to consensus,
- you need to organize large volumes of data,
- you have limited resources and must set priorities, or
- you want to develop a complete plan including priorities, schedules, and contingency plans.

These tools organize judgmental or soft data into clear pictures that promote effective decision making. Successful decision making begins with the proper mindset. In traditional organizations, we have assumed that one person, the manager, has all the answers. As our world has become more complex, so have the decisions we face. Today everyone in the organization must be able to make good decisions; they must have the appropriate tools to be able to function adequately in their jobs.

Today good decisions involve the consideration of many alternatives. Through the participation of others, we search for every possible option. We try to consider what could go wrong. Our attitudes towards others and the process we use will affect the value we receive. To receive the most benefit from these tools:

- value the differences of others; they can offer a different point of view,
- value the ideas of others; this will keep creative ideas flowing,
- embrace ambiguity; it promotes creativity,
- be flexible; this will lead to more effective planning,
- trust your (and others') initial reactions; it may prevent making fundamental mistakes, and
- use them only when they are needed, not because you think you should.

Each tool is different, but there are some common guidelines that make all the tools more effective.

- Get the right people to form the group—diverse, willing, and skilled.
- Empower the group by defining operating limits, granting the authority to make changes, providing protection, support, and resources, and defining measures of accountability.
- Clearly define the opportunity or goal.
- Allow time to complete the process.
- Include new ideas at any time.
- Make decisions only by consensus. Majority vote creates winners and losers. The time required to reach consensus will be offset by the speed of implementation.
- **Make the tool work for you, do not work for the tool.**

These tools are known by many different names. The name listed first is the authors' choice. The tools that will be covered in this article are brainstorming, forced choice, card sort (affinity diagram), cause & effect map (relationship diagram, ID), selection window, tree diagram, force field analysis, matrices, problem prevention plan (contingency plan, PDPC), and PERT chart (CPM, arrow diagram).

BRAINSTORMING

Brainstorming is the most commonly used method for the generation of a large number of ideas in a group setting. Despite its widespread usage, there remains a body of empirical data that indicates that its use by individuals or nominal groups (groups that never physically meet) may be more effective than its use by people in a meeting-type setting. We think brainstorming is most effective when used by a group of four to nine people.

Like many commonly used tools, there is some confusion regarding the source of brainstorming. Mizuno in the *7 New QC Tools* (1979), indicated that it was introduced to Japan in 1952. Donelson Forsyth in *An Introduction To Group Dynamics* (1983) cites the following version.

> Brainstorming was developed in 1957 by Alex F. Osborne, an advertising executive. He defined four traits which contributed to the generation of new alternatives or ideas. Virtually all brainstorming work today is based on the traits of expressiveness, non-evaluative, quantity, and building as described below.
>
> Osborne recommended:
>
> - recording all of the ideas in full view of participants,
> - stimulating ideas by asking open-ended questions,
> - utilizing a turn-taking procedure if interaction becomes unequal,
> - evaluating ideas at a later session.
>
> In 1974, Rickards added the idea of warm up exercises to 'break the ice' and get discussion started.
>
> Experience has shown that training in brainstorming procedures, practicing brainstorming, and allowing the participants to record their ideas after the brainstorming session improves the group's proficiency.

The cornerstone of judgmental decision making is the generation of creative alternatives. Virtually every decision and planning tool requires such alternatives. As a freewheeling vehicle for getting new ideas, brainstorming can help a group break through existing patterns of thought and generate new options. Often, however, we fail to get the results we need by omitting one of the few **but critical** rules of brainstorming. Remember, creativity is the result of productive controversy. The following rules apply to any type of group creative process, including brainstorming.

1. **Expressiveness.** Each individual in the group must have complete freedom to express any idea that comes to mind, no matter how strange, wild, or fanciful. Freewheeling ideas are encouraged, and constraint is avoided.
2. **Non-evaluative.** Ideas are not to be evaluated in any way during the generation phase. All ideas are valuable, and criticizing another's viewpoint is not allowed. A negative comment can stifle the energy and creativity of a group so that the exercise becomes useless.
3. **Quantity.** The goal of the generation process is to create as many ideas as possible. Even the most unrealistic idea can provide the stimulus or basis for a totally new and valuable idea. Having many new ideas increases the possibility of generating excellent solutions.

4. **Building.** Brainstorming is conducted in a group so that participants can draw from one another. We draw from each other by modifying and adding to our ideas. This will create mental bridges to new opportunities.

To complete a brainstorming session, first select a purpose. Be as specific as possible, but consider the resources available to the group. Be sure everyone in the group fully understands and agrees with the purpose. Next, organize your group. Decide who will write, and where the ideas will be placed for best visibility. Be sure to place only one idea on a card and write clearly so that everyone can read the cards. Be wild! Impossible ideas can stimulate spontaneity and help to suspend critical judgment. Finally, set a time limit. The pressure of a time limit helps to put evaluation on hold. It is the creative, right side of the brain that has the ability to react, while the evaluative left brain requires time to think through any new idea. The output of a typical brainstorming session is shown in Figure 1.

FORCED CHOICE

Forced choice is an adaptation of a forced choice matrix from a training course taught by M. B. Bryce Associates in the late 1960s. It relies on a basic pairwise comparison to aid the user in sorting large lists, or lists where there is little difference

FIGURE 1   *Results of Brainstorming*

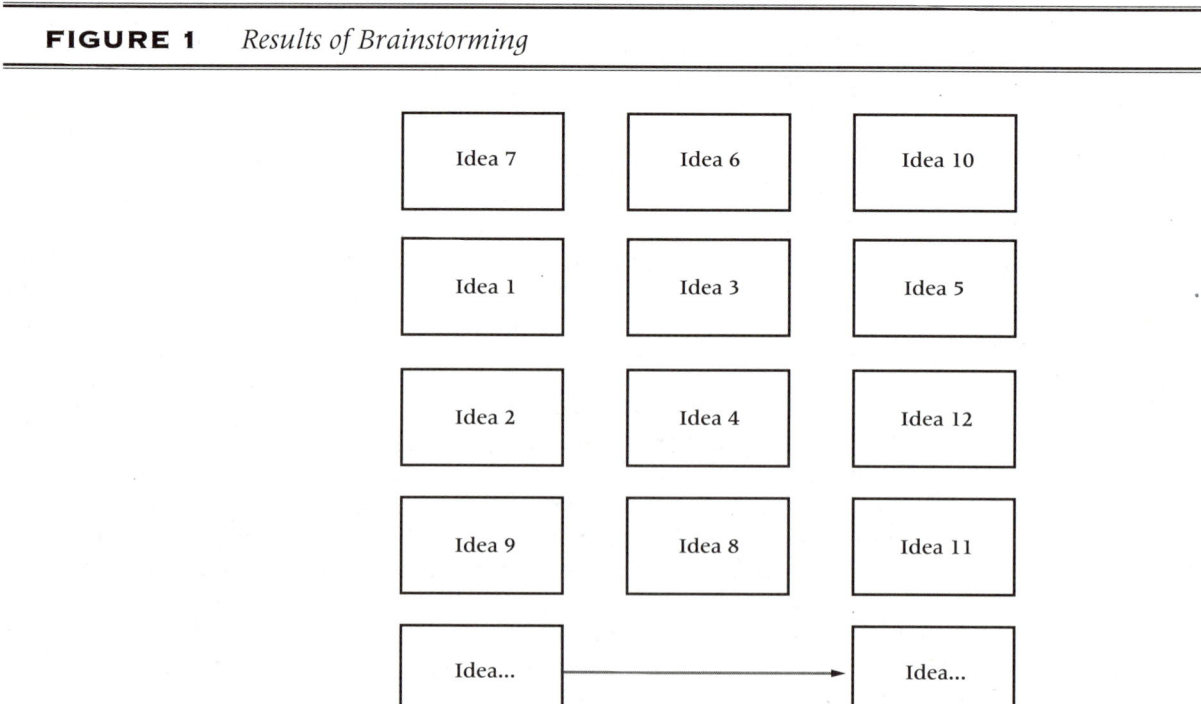

between the options presented. In its matrix form, the forced choice was cumbersome to use and required the use of special preprinted matrix forms.

The free form adaptation described here was developed by N. W. Young in 1981 when he created a list-based pairwise comparison in a basic language computer program. It was further refined for use in a facilitated group setting to aid the group in reaching consensus on the priority of options in a list.

The forced choice requires a list of items or alternatives to be sorted against an agreed-upon standard. Each alternative is measured against the standard. It also requires a method of marking the choices made during a sort. Completing the forced choice can help you make choices in complex situations, as well as to help defuse difficult political situations by helping a group make choices together. It is most effective in defining areas of inconsistency in logic and is easily completed individually or in a group.

To complete a forced choice, select a list to be sorted or ranked. This list can be the product of a creative effort, such as brainstorming or any other situation that produces alternatives to be sorted. Write the list where everyone can see it. Leave a blank area or column to the right. Draw a line to separate the area on the right from the list and additional lines to separate each of the alternatives. This is not required, but it will simplify the necessary record keeping. Now define a standard for the sort. When selecting standards, consider customer impact, satisfaction, time, cost, level of quality, and so on. The standard must be clearly voiced.

Then perform a pairwise comparison to isolate a single choice among many choices. The comparison will focus all resources on the single choice and simplify the process of selection. Since the number of comparisons required to sort or rank a list grows rapidly as the list gets longer, the use of the pairwise comparison is limited only by time. Begin the pairwise comparison of each item in the list with every other item in the list. Form a sentence using the items being compared and the standard of comparison. Make a mark in the right-hand column for the item that wins the comparison. Continue using the same comparison until each possible pairwise comparison has been made once. To ensure that no possible comparisons are missed and none are performed more than once, use the following methodology.

a. Compare the **1st** item with each item below it in the list, that is, compare item 1 with item 2, compare item 1 with item 3, compare item 1 with item 4, and so on until you reach the end of the list.

b. Compare the **2nd** item with each item below it in the list, that is, compare item 2 with item 3, compare item 2 with item 4, and so on until you reach the end.

c. Compare the **nth** item with each item below it in the list, that is, compare item n with item n+1, compare item n with item n+2, and so on.

d. The last comparison will be the next to last item with the last item.

After you have completed all comparisons, summarize and analyze the results by adding the number of marks each item received and writing that number at the end of the row. The item, or option, with the highest number has best met the standard. Those with lower numbers have met the standard to a lesser degree. Understanding of the results will be improved for larger lists by rewriting the list in numerical order from the top to the bottom.

Beware of items that have the same numerical value. This points out areas where the results of your comparisons were inconsistent or circular reasoning was used. Such inconsistencies near the bottom of your list (after reordering) will have little effect on your future efforts. Inconsistencies at or near the top of the reordered list suggest fuzzy comprehension of the most important items. Further discussion and more research may be necessary before you are ready to take action, based on the results of the forced choice. Figure 2 shows how to complete a forced choice.

CARD SORT (AFFINITY DIAGRAM)

The card sort is a generic name for a tool that uses the creativity of a group to organize large amounts of information or complex situations into manageable order. It begins with a clearly defined purpose to keep the group on track. It then uses creative techniques, such as brainstorming or mind mapping, to generate a large volume of ideas. Finally, silent sorting promotes group interaction without criticism.

The card sort has a long history and is known by several other names and variations including the following:

The **person card sort** was used in anthropological work in the 1930s to sort information about artifacts. It was also used to some advantage during the Watergate investigations and to plan the Apollo moon landings.

FIGURE 2   *Forced Choice Using Brainstormed List*

GREATEST IMPACT ON REDUCED SALES		
Out of Control Processes	///	3
Flexibility to Customer Needs	//	2
Customer Communication Difficulties	////	4
Product Quality Is Lacking	/	1
Product Shipping Problems		0

The **KJ Method** ® is the registered trademark of Jiro Kawakita who is credited with creating the card sort as we know it today. In the 1960s this Japanese anthropologist developed the rules that allow us to sift efficiently through large amounts of data and to allow new patterns of information to rise to the surface.

The **affinity diagram** is a variation of the KJ Method first documented in *The 7 New QC Tools* by Shigeru Mizuno.

The **Shiba method** is a creation of Shobi Shiba, a Japanese consultant who was a student of Dr. Kawakita. He uses a new rule set, popularized at the Center for Quality in Boston, Massachusetts, based on logical rather that intuitive methods.

The **whole brain affinity model** was developed by Glen Hoffherr, John Moran, and Richard Talbot and published in GOAL/QPC's *Competitive Times Newsletter*. The whole brain affinity takes the power and strength of the traditional card sort and adds Ned Herrmann's brain dominance model. The Herrmann brain dominance model is a metaphorical interpretation of how we think. This seminal work on problem solving combines the two into a colorful implementation of the card sort that shows the cognitive styles of the participant group.

The card sort combines techniques from the variations to produce an integrated tool that performs the task in a straightforward manner.

The card sort is a technique to bring order and structure to a large number of ideas. It helps a group reach consensus. Its primary strength is that it promotes interaction without criticism and facilitates building a plan. It can provide the synergy to break through old paradigms that might have prevented progress in the past as well as unite a group that has been divided on an issue. The card sort works best with a diverse group of four to nine people that contains at least one content expert. It begins with a clear statement of purpose to focus the group's energy. Materials such as 3" x 5" cards or Post-it® notes to facilitate the gathering and movement of ideas are a must.

To complete a card sort, first select a purpose. Be as specific as possible, but consider the resources available to the group. The purpose may be assigned, result from the use of some other tool or method, or evolve from your current discussion. Be sure the purpose is worded clearly and everyone in the group fully understands and agrees. Write the purpose where it can be clearly seen by the entire group. The more important the purpose, the easier it is to motivate the group to generate ideas.

Headline the purpose and record ideas, leaving ample space to list more ideas. Generate a list of ideas typically through brainstorming. There are a number of other creative techniques, including mind mapping and dialogue, that can help generate the list. (The list may already exist from some other source, in which case simply transfer it to the card sort medium.)

Each idea should be expressed in at least three words, including a noun and a verb. Place only one idea on a card and write clearly. As each idea is placed where everyone can see it, someone should read it aloud. When the group has posted all of the ideas, it is time to begin sorting.

The sorting process is a group activity. The idea cards must be accessible to all members of the group. Sort the cards by picking up a card and placing it next to another card that you feel is related. Cards can be moved several times and put in a new cluster. The sorting is done in silence by all members of the group at the same time. Continue sorting in silence until the sorting visibly slows down. This will normally require about 15 to 20 minutes. Each cluster of cards should contain no more than nine.

The next step is to develop headers. During this part of the card sort, there is opportunity for much interaction and discussion. The group must generate a header for each cluster. The header ideally summarizes and compresses all the ideas of the cards in the cluster. Any card that does not fit within a cluster should be set to the side for later consideration. Each header statement needs at least three words, including a noun and a verb. Headers should be as specific as possible to reduce the chance for misinterpretation. The group reaches consensus on the theme and wording of each header. When a header has been defined and accepted, place it above the cards in the cluster. This header card should be clearly marked to distinguish it from the idea cards. The group may choose to use an idea card as a header. If this is done, be sure it is clearly marked as a header. Each card in a cluster should also be marked with the identification of the header. This can be a letter, number, color, or even a word if the cards are large enough. Figure 3 shows how a completed card sort would appear.

CAUSE & EFFECT MAP (RELATIONSHIP DIAGRAM, ID)

In *The 7 New QC Tools* Shigeru Mizuno describes the "Relations Diagram Method" as having been developed by The Society for QC Technique Development in 1979. It was based on the work of T. Brown in a 1977 paper titled, "Inquiry into the Relation of Cause and Effect," Delmar, New York: Scholar's Facsimiles & Reprints. The method was created to:

• analyze problems with a complex network of causes and effects, and
• view the whole problem from a broad perspective.

Another name for the tool is *interrelationship digraph* or *ID*. The authors have not been able to find any reason for this choice of name and no adequate definition of digraph has been unearthed.

Cause and effect relationships exist when the action of one item determines or creates conditions (effects) in another item. Understanding cause and effect relationships allows groups to focus resources where they are most likely to produce results. They also provide a beginning point for developing the order of tasks and process steps, balancing resource distribution to prevent overloading, and isolating root causes to focus continuous improvement efforts in any planning process. Cause and effect networks are complex sets of relationships.

The cause and effect map is a technique to display graphically this type of relationship, invoking the intuitive right side of the brain. This method helps determine cause and effect relationships by providing a way to visually identify key driving forces as root causes, as well as point out key bottlenecks (major effects). The cause and effect map can help a group effectively analyze situations with a complex network of cause and effect relationships by providing a broad perspective. Key

FIGURE 3   *Card Sort Using Brainstormed List*

HEADER A	HEADER B	HEADER C	HEADER D	HEADER E	HEADER F
Idea 12 A	Idea... B	Idea 8 C	Idea 3 D	Idea 6 E	Idea 10 F
Idea 1 A		Idea 7 C	Idea 5 D	Idea... E	Idea 9 F
Idea 4 A		Idea 11 C		Idea... E	
		Idea 2 C			

drivers are primary, or root causes, that are having the greatest impact on the network. They are often the most effective place to concentrate efforts to resolve the entire situation. Bottlenecks are the restraints in a network. They are effected by the most causes and usually cannot be resolved by themselves. The cause and effect map requires a set of interrelated options, ideas, or issues to be analyzed. It is best completed by a group of four to nine people, drawing the map where everyone can see it.

To complete the cause and effect map, begin by identifying the topic or purpose for the map and putting it at the top of the work area. Now write the options, ideas, or issues to be analyzed in a circular pattern. Write large enough that everyone can read the options. After placing the options around a circular pattern, number them to make the process of comparison easier to track. Numbering is particularly important with larger option lists.

When the options have been placed on the map, it is time to begin the process of pairwise comparisons. Each option must be compared just once with each of the other options to determine if there is a cause and effect relationship. When such a relationship is found, draw a line with an arrow pointing to the effect. If no relationship is found, simply proceed to the next pair. (To keep track of the comparisons, it helps to proceed in an orderly fashion. Compare option one with option two, then option one with option three, and so on until you have traversed the entire circle of options.)

When option one has been compared to each of the others, then start with option two and compare it with option three and all of the other options except option one. The cause and effect relationship between option two and option one was already examined. After completing the option two comparisons, continue around the circle comparing each option with every other option just once until you have a map of options connected by their relationships.

Analyze the map by counting the number of incoming arrows and outgoing arrows for each option and note the numbers for in and out beside the option as shown in Figure 4. The option or options with the highest number of outgoing arrows are the primary drivers or root causes. Changes in these options will affect the majority of the other options. Therefore, resources applied to these areas can produce pronounced change.

The option or options that are receiving the most incoming arrows are key bottlenecks. These outcomes are affected by many other options and may even be inhibiting other options from proceeding as they should. Mark visibly the key drivers and bottlenecks to further clarify your map in complex networks.

Be certain to examine only cause and effect relationships. If the group stays with this criteria, it is probable that only about 50 percent of the relationships will have arrows. In addition, this tool forces a group to make a decision since it does not allow for two-way arrows. Figure 4 shows a completed cause and effect map.

SELECTION WINDOW

A bit of wisdom from a book by Peter Drucker, *The Effective Executive,* taught that effectiveness comes not from doing things well but from "doing the right things." The selection window is a helpful vehicle for choosing the right thing to do. Apart from *The Toolbook,* the authors are unaware of any other sources for this tool. In his national best-seller, *The Seven Habits of Highly Effective People,* Stephen Covey describes a tool he calls "The Time Management Matrix." Using scales of importance and urgency, he teaches us to create the habit of putting first things first, or doing the right thing. The selection window uses a similar rationale but uses the scales of importance and effort. It is designed to integrate your resources and purposes and help you to decide what is the right thing to do.

The selection window is a simple technique to select the right things to do, integrating effort and importance with your purpose. It is a method for deciding when to use groups, as well as a way to evaluate and understand the importance and effort (resources) needed. It requires a clearly defined high-level purpose, a list of options or alternatives to accomplish the purpose, and the time to provide a careful consideration of each option. The selection window can keep you focused on your purpose and aid in short- and long-term projects.

To complete the selection window, begin by identifying your purpose. It helps to write your purpose where it can be a constant reminder. Generate a list of options, alternatives, or opportunities that can help you accomplish your purpose. One list that often benefits by this type of analysis is the "To Do" list.

Begin the selection window by drawing a square containing four equal boxes. The boxes must be large enough to write the opportunities inside. Mark the square with effort on the left and importance on the bottom. Use a numerical scale from a low of 1 to a high of 10. Evaluate each option against the criteria of effort and importance. Now review the selection window and take appropriate action.

FIGURE 4   *Cause & Effect Map Using Card Sort Headers*

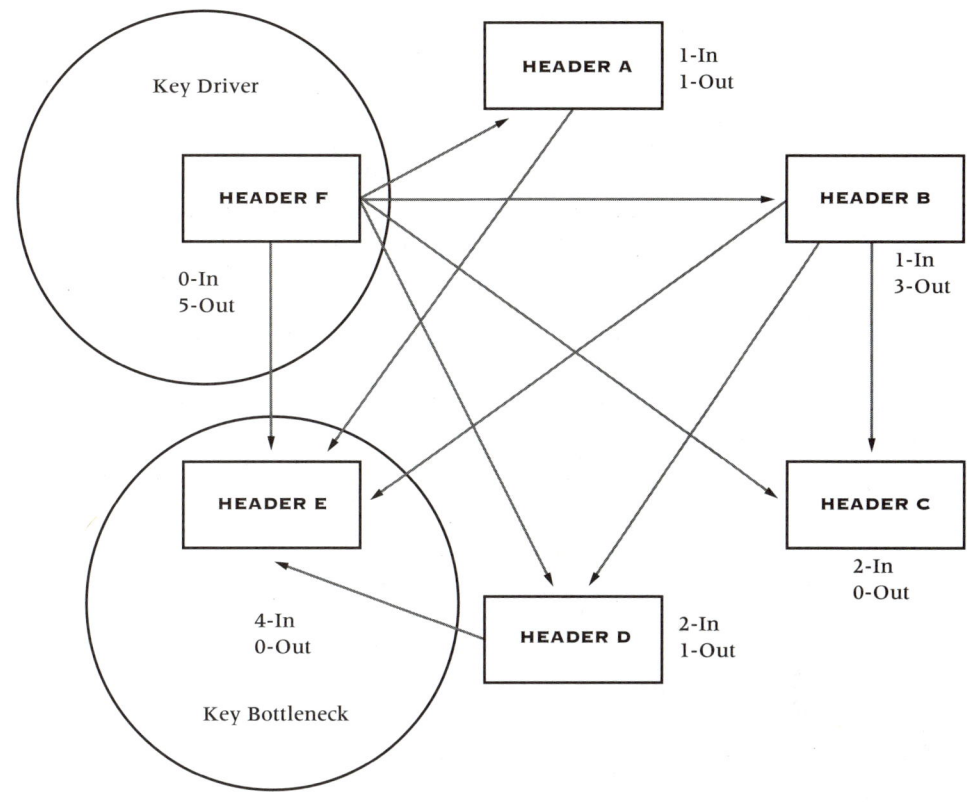

Do Now. Items of high importance, and low effort should be done immediately. These are the "right" things that you have the resources and time to do now. Each will have significant impact on achieving your purpose.

To Do. Items of low importance and low effort should be placed on a "To Do" list. Use these items as fillers. Although they are of low importance (we did not say no importance), they are possibly important enough to justify a small expenditure of resources. Be careful! It may seem unimportant to determine priorities, but these areas can dominate our time to the exclusion of our most important items.

Forget. Items of low importance and high effort do not justify the expenditure of the high level of resources required to complete them.

Groups. Items of high importance and high effort should be the focus of groups. They are important enough to deserve the attention that only a skilled group of people working together effectively can supply. They will determine whether or not you accomplish your purpose.

Figure 5 shows a completed selection window on things that could be done to satisfy a customer in a small office supply company.

TREE DIAGRAM

The concept of using a *tree* or subdividing a subject like branches of a tree is not new. We have all seen tree-type diagrams used to portray the structure and relationships within an organization. The traditional organization chart is a vertical tree. Saaty points out in *Decision Making for Leaders,* that hierarchies or trees are the mechanism the brain uses to structure and store complex information.

FIGURE 5   *Selection Window Using Card Sort Headers*

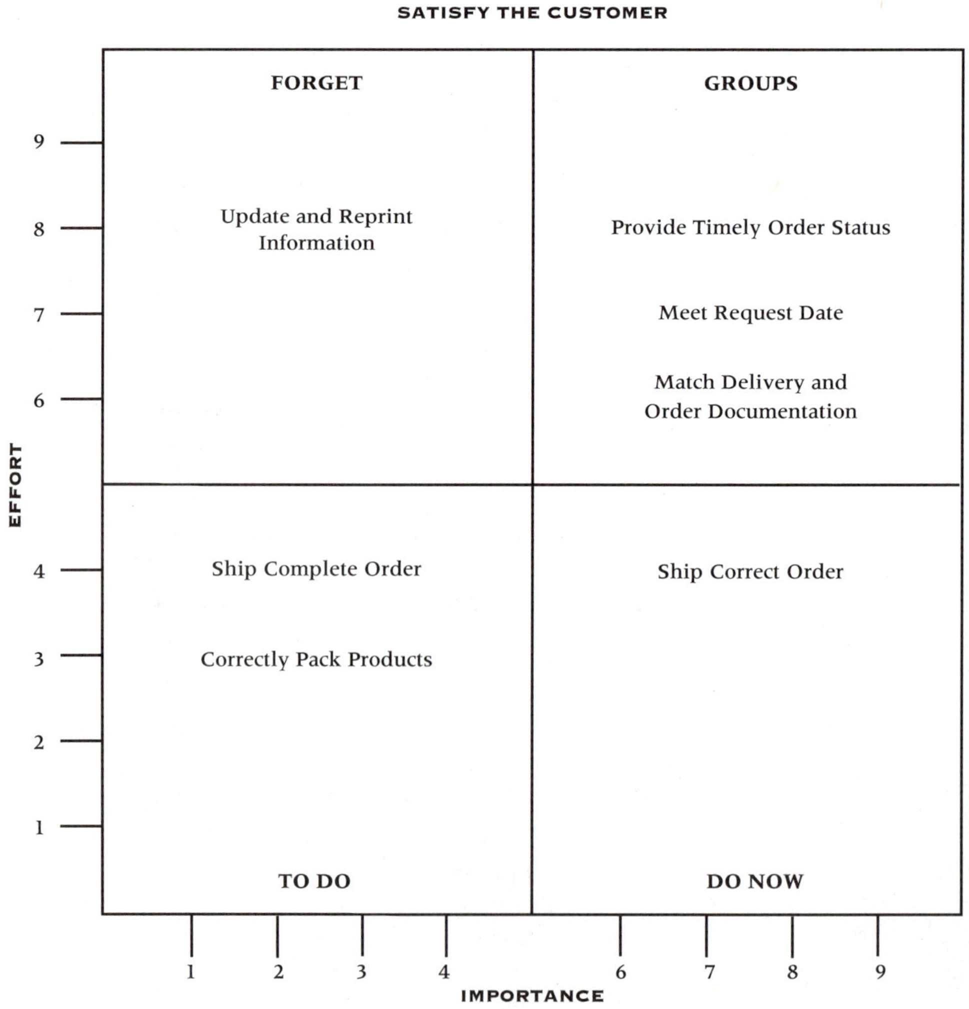

SATISFY THE CUSTOMER

	FORGET	GROUPS
9		
8	Update and Reprint Information	Provide Timely Order Status
7		Meet Request Date
6		Match Delivery and Order Documentation
EFFORT		
4	Ship Complete Order	Ship Correct Order
3	Correctly Pack Products	
2		
1		
	TO DO	DO NOW

IMPORTANCE   1   2   3   4   6   7   8   9

In *The 7 New QC Tools,* Mizuno introduces the systematic diagram with the alternate name of *dendrogram* from the Greek word for tree. The dendrogram is used "to find the most appropriate option." Mizuno then goes on to describe the wide variety of uses for the tree diagram, including:

- Functional analysis (from value engineering)
- Correlation tree
- Reverse PERT chart
- Decision tree
- Fault tree analysis
- YS technique (Yabiki Seiichiro)

The tree diagram is designed to expand a purpose into the tasks required to accomplish it. In this form it is also called an *outline diagram.* The tree diagram starts with a stated purpose and enables you to view the full range of details required to accomplish your purpose. It is also a method to expand your purpose into tasks to be performed. It can be used by individuals or a group of people focused on the purpose. The tree diagram is one method for viewing a complete hierarchy of tasks and their linkages. It provides the structure to ensure a complete plan.

Begin the tree diagram by reviewing your purpose to be accomplished. Be sure everyone in the group clearly understands the purpose. A review of your criteria for success at this point can further clarify planning. Write the purpose at the top or the left of your work area. The tree diagram can be expanded in any direction, but the left-to-right format lends itself to using other tools after completing the tree diagram.

The diagram will be easy to read if you enclose the purpose and the other elements of the tree diagram in boxes. Using cards or Post-it® notes can make it easier to reorganize the tree if it grows in an unexpected direction. You cannot predict the number of branches that will be formed, or the number of divisions for each branch.

Generate all the high-level tasks, or "targets" that must be completed to accomplish the purpose. Targets are those things that combined together accomplish the purpose and can be developed by applying brainstorming to the purpose. Another method is to use the headers or idea cards developed in a card sort performed on the purpose. A tree diagram cannot be completed by simply turning a card sort on its side.

Place each of the targets in a box, lined up to the right of the purpose. Leave plenty of space between each target to allow for growth of the tree diagram. Connect the targets to the purpose to form the first branches of the tree diagram. Expand each target to define the subordinate tasks that are necessary to accomplish each target. Use group dialogue, or any creative process, to define tasks. When the subordinate tasks have been defined and recorded for each target, draw the lines that will connect them to the target.

Each subordinate task should then be subdivided into further levels of subtasks until the final level is achievable. Each subtask should be broken down until it can be given to a person or group to be completed. This expansion may add more levels to your tree. Levels of detail may be added unevenly, causing one branch to grow larger than others.

The final step in making a tree diagram is to test the validity of the work. This is done by reviewing each task and level on the tree diagram to see if it logically connects to the tasks above and below it. You might consider expanding to a larger group that includes the people who will actually perform the tasks. Their knowledge and experience may help you see gaps or unnecessary tasks. When this is complete, review each subtask to ensure its necessity to the completion of the task. Expect this questioning process to cause change in the tree diagram. A tree diagram is shown in Figure 6.

FORCE FIELD ANALYSIS

Stephen R. Covey mentions the force field analysis in his book *The Seven Habits of Highly Effective People,* Simon & Schuster, (1989). He credits sociologist Kurt Lewin as the developer of this model that shows the driving forces as rising and restraining forces as pushing down. Lewin's focus on the dynamics at work in any change process began over 40 years ago. During World War II, our government tried to

FIGURE 6   *Tree Diagram Using Card Sort Headers and Ideas*

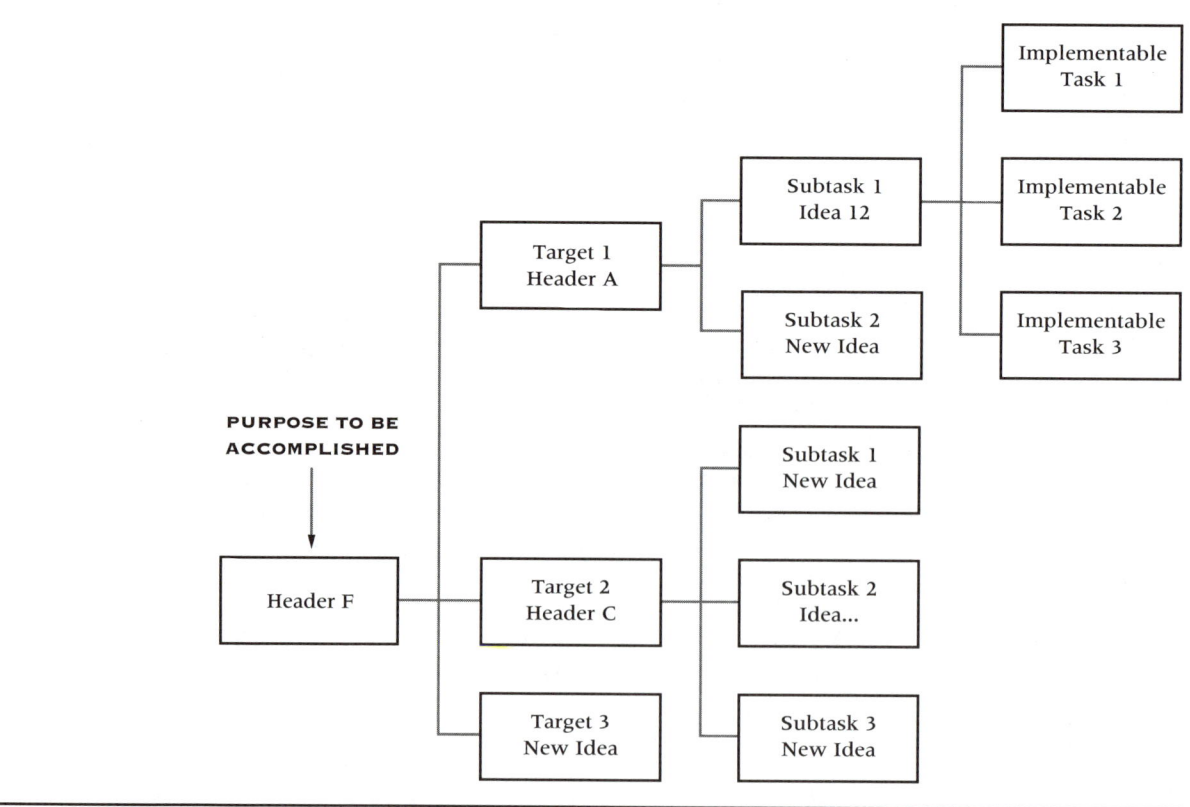

change the beef-buying habits of housewives to expand use of internal organs and to limit the use of muscle cuts to aid the war effort. Women were unwilling to change at first because they did not know enough about selecting and preparing the recommended meats. However, when the president's wife got involved in the problem and began to understand the benefits, change began to happen. Lewin learned:

> *When people become involved in a problem, they become significantly and sincerely committed to coming up with solutions to the problem.*
>
> LEWIN

Moran, Talbot, and Benson in *A Guide to Graphical Problem-Solving Processes* (1990) described the procedural steps for the force field analysis as it is more typically shown and used.

The force field analysis is a technique to visually identify the forces affecting accomplishment of your purpose. It is a way to show supporting and resisting forces. Force field analysis can help you analyze the depths of your resources to overcome the resistance by providing a clear picture of the situation to share with others. It can be completed by one person, but it is most effective when applied by a diverse group with a clearly defined purpose and a method to accomplish it.

Begin by drawing vertical and horizontal lines. Make the spaces large enough that there is plenty of room to write. At the extreme right, under the horizontal line, print your purpose. This is to provide focus for the generation of supporting and resisting forces. It may further help to add an arrow to the horizontal line to indicate the direction of positive accomplishment. Further clarity can be added by marking the left side as driving forces and those on the right as resisting.

List the forces driving toward your purpose on the left side of the vertical line and those resisting your efforts on the right. These lists could be created by using brainstorming or simply by carefully examining your initial plan. When each list is complete, go over the lists again and assign a strength to each force. A scale from high to low provides a good initial view of the situation. Now draw an arrow under each force pointing to the vertical line. The arrow's length indicates the strength of the force.

Evaluate the results. Force field analysis provides a clear visualization of the forces with which you are dealing. Examine both the driving and resisting forces for opportunities for improvement. Your goals are first to seek ways to reduce or eliminate resisting forces. This action serves to conserve resources and reduce the effort required to accomplish your goal. If necessary, you should seek additional resources to aid in overcoming the resisting forces.

A completed force field analysis is shown in Figure 7. As shown, there is not always a resisting force for every driving force. By adding the strength of the force, it is easier to see which driving forces can be added to and which resisting forces can be decreased.

MATRICES

The matrix format of rows and columns has long been used to guide the gathering and organization of large amounts of information. Matrices are created manually

FIGURE 7   *Force Field Analysis on Implementable Task from Tree Diagram*

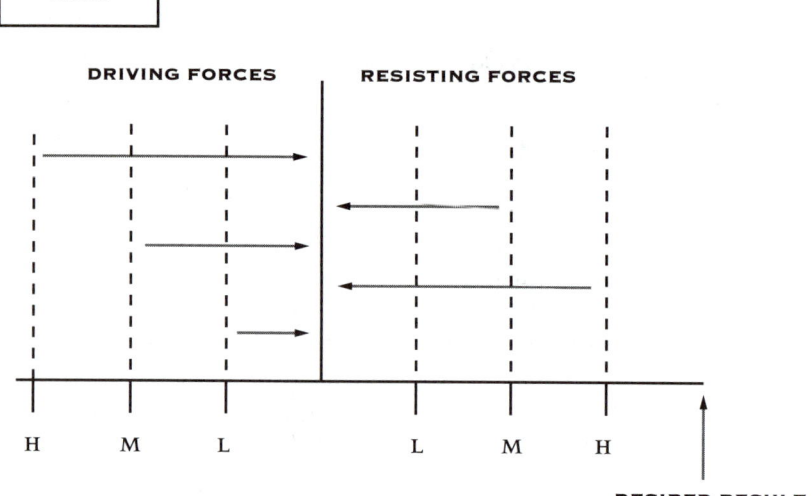

or through a variety of semi-automated and automated vehicles including the computer spreadsheet. The number of rows varies widely, based on the application. The number and width of the columns varies based on the size and type of the data contained. The value of a matrix is defined by its contents. Two major types of matrices are the most common. The first type contains information and the second contains correlations between two sets of variables. Examples of both types of matrices follow.

S.M.A.R.T. PLAN

The S.M.A.R.T. plan is defined by the information it contains. This matrix provides the key information that is necessary to build a successful plan. The S.M.A.R.T. plan requires a set of tasks to accomplish your purpose. It can be a vehicle for guiding a group in the development of a working plan that defines clear accountability and goals. It is a technique for structuring task details, which includes a measure of completion, assignment of responsibility, resources required, time to complete, and predecessor tasks. It is a way to plan the implementation of the tasks necessary to accomplish your purpose.

Like all decision making and planning tools, the S.M.A.R.T. plan begins with a clearly defined purpose. Write this purpose at the top of your work area. List the tasks or specifics necessary to accomplish your purpose. These can be created as part of the process of building the S.M.A.R.T. plan, or they may be transferred from a completed tree diagram. The process of selecting the implementation details of each specific provides an additional test of the work performed in a tree diagram. If you find a specific or task is not sufficiently detailed, do not hesitate to return to the tree and modify it before continuing.

Now that the S.M.A.R.T. plan is set up, the work of defining the implementation details begins by identifying the measure of completion for each specific. A measure is a clearly visible indicator that the specific is complete. Measures can include dates, quantities, or performance levels. There must be no doubt when the measure has been reached. A good measure can also show progress. Measures are agreed upon by consensus.

Each specific must be assigned to a person or a group to assure its completion. Assignment is one of the keys to success in any plan. Assignment provides accountability. It must be very specific. In addition, it must provide opportunity for participation. No assignment should ever be made without at least the agreement of the assignee. The ideal situation is one in that qualified groups or group members have sufficient motivation or interest to volunteer.

Completion of each specific requires the availability of resources. Resources include time sufficient to create quality results as well as capital, capital equipment, raw materials, and supplies. Personnel with appropriate skill, knowledge, experience, and commitment are also essential.

Any form of planning requires an understanding of a desired endpoint. In more advanced planning techniques, the duration of each task is also included. The S.M.A.R.T. plan assumes that the group has considered project time as one of the resources. Timing provides a target for task or specific completion, a guide for planning the details of task implementation and acquiring resources, and an early start date for any task dependent on, or succeeding, this task.

Putting the proper priority and sequence on specifics requires an understanding of the linkages between them. A predecessor defines what must be done before this task can be accomplished. Predecessors provide an outline of the order in which tasks must be done as a guide for planning the implementation details and utilization of resources. A specific may have one, many, or even no predecessors.

For short specific lists, write the specific in the predecessor column. For longer lists, number the list of specifics and use the number of the predecessor. Figure 8 shows a S.M.A.R.T. plan type of matrix.

FIGURE 8   *S.M.A.R.T. Plan Matrix on Implementable Task from Tree Diagram*

SPECIFIC	MEASURABLE	ASSIGNMENT	RESOURCES	TIME	PREDECESSORS
Implementable Task 3	Deliverable	GH	8 Person Hours	1 Week	Target 1 Subtask 2 Implementable 4

CORRELATION MATRIX

The second type of matrix is a correlation matrix. In this form of matrix, one list of variables is compared to a second list of variables. They are often compared with numbers or symbols. The most common symbols are ◎ for a strong relationship, ◯ for a medium relationship, and △ for a weak relationship. The number 9 is often substituted for the strong relationship symbol, the number 3 for the medium, and the number 1 for the weak. These numbers are based on experience and are not numerically valid. The reason for the multiple is that it surfaces the most important items. These symbols come from the Japanese symbols for win, place, and show at the horse racetrack. The first translations contained these symbols, and they have become common in U.S. quality documentation. An example of a correlation matrix is shown in Figure 9.

PROBLEM PREVENTION PLAN (CONTINGENCY PLAN, PDPC)

What could go wrong? This question is an essential part of planning. Unfortunately, we often do little other than worry. The problem prevention plan is a method for planning around contingencies and creating alternatives or solutions for every foreseeable contingency.

The earliest reference to a contingency planning method that formulates the same questions is the process decision program chart (PDPC) described in *The 7 New QC Tools* by Shigeru Mizuno. This tool structures the implementation steps of a plan, and then asks "what if?" and prompts for possible countermeasures.

FIGURE 9   *Correlation Matrix*

	Process 1	Process 2		Total
Customer Need 1		◎		9
Customer Need 2	△			1

The two common methods used to implement the PDPC often cause confusion. The first is a modified tree diagram where each level of questioning is exploded downward. The second is a "book" outline format where process steps, their contingencies, and possible countermeasures are related by outline numbers like the chapters in a book.

The problem prevention plan is a much easier, more thorough method of contingency planning. It is also easier to understand. It is an enhanced implementation more closely related to the potential problem analysis used by J.D. James in the quality leadership process. In addition to defining the "what ifs?," now called *potential problems*, the tool defines potential causes to allow a more specific focus on feasible countermeasures, or preventions. The last enhancement is the ranking of the levels of the plan based on achievement of the goal.

The problem prevention plan is a technique to determine what can go wrong with your plan before it does. It is a method for rating the seriousness and likelihood of potential problems, a vehicle for investigating the causes of potential problems, a way to identify actions that can prevent problems from occurring, and a tool to trigger implementation of preventive action. The power in this tool is the structured "worrying" process that yields precise actions to keep our plans on track and helps us accomplish our purposes.

The problem prevention plan requires a purpose to be accomplished and a plan to accomplish it. It can be especially valuable when uncertainty exists or risk is high because it provides a comprehensive strategy before a major plan is implemented. This type of planning can help you identify and remove roadblocks to your success.

Begin the problem prevention plan by defining a list of what could go wrong with your plan. Write the purpose to be accomplished at the top of the page, board, or chart pad. Consider using a creative tool, such as brainstorming, to develop the list. Look for potential problems that could get in the way (perhaps from a force field analysis). A potential problem is something that can prevent a plan or process step from occurring or producing the planned output. It can alter the quality of the resulting output or cause delays.

To construct the problem prevention plan, place the list to the left of a board or sheet of paper and create columns for probability and seriousness. For each of the potential problems, rank both the probability of its occurrence and the seriousness. Probability is the likelihood that the potential problem will happen. Seriousness is the impact on the accomplishment of the purpose if it does happen, ranked high to low.

Identify the potential problem with the highest probability of occurrence and of a most serious nature, marking them for further analysis. For each identified potential problem (high probability and seriousness), develop a list of potential causes. List the potential problem at the top of a page. Search for potential causes using dialogue, brainstorming, or some other creative process. Rate the probability of occurrence of each of the potential causes on a scale ranked high to low. Select the potential causes that are most likely to happen. Further analyze them to attempt to prevent them from happening.

For the highest probability, discuss and select actions that can prevent a future problem. List the potential cause at the top. Search for preventions using dialogue, brainstorming, or some other creative process. For each prevention, define a trigger that will signal the beginning of the prevention. A trigger can be an event, a time, or a measure.

In this planning stage, solutions are changes in our plans to prevent the possibility of a problem. Alternatives are actions that can be taken to minimize or eliminate the problem if it occurs. Figure 10 shows a problem prevention plan on matching delivery and order documentation.

PERT CHART (CPM, ARROW DIAGRAM)

Some useful project planning and tracking methods have come from the work of Henry Gantt. The best known of these is PERT, or **p**rogram **e**valuation and **r**eview **t**echnique, and the PERT planning method.

FIGURE 10 *Problem Prevention Plan*

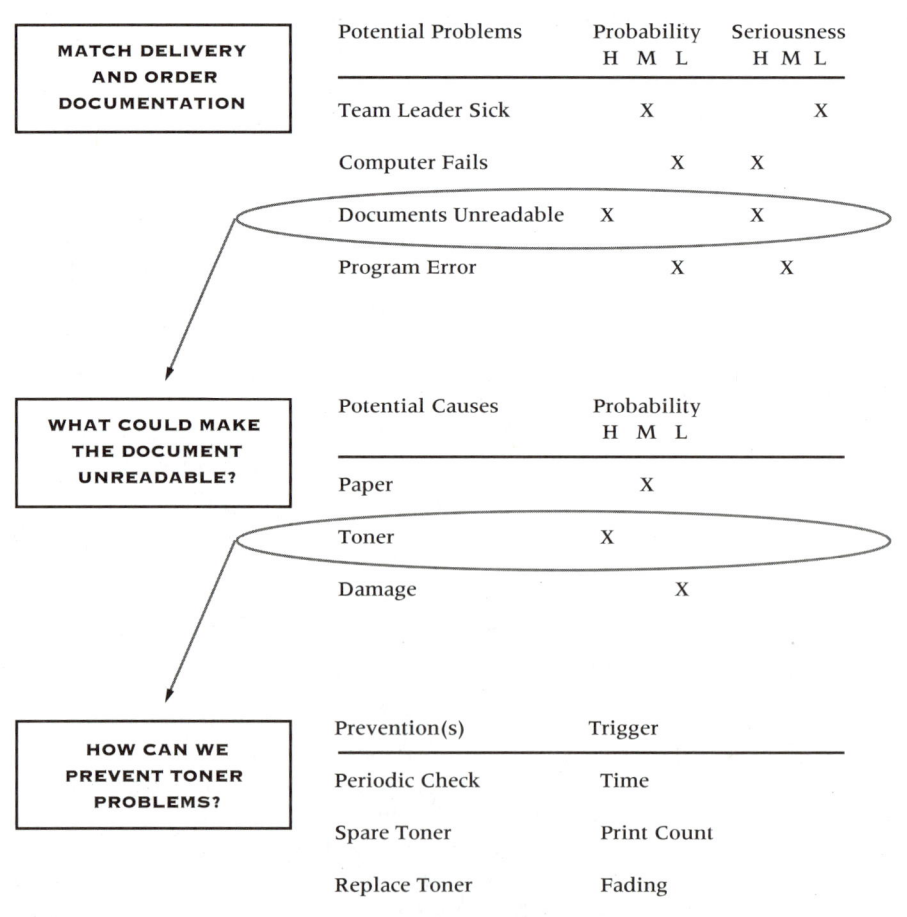

A PERT chart is also called an *activity network diagram. Project Management with CPM, PERT and Precedence Diagramming* by Moder, Phillips and Davis, Van Nostrand Reinhold (1983) places the origin of the PERT chart in the work of a Polish scientist, Karol Adamiecki, in the early 1930s. Adamiecki created the "Harmony Graph" matrix with a time scale on the vertical axis and activities on the horizontal axis. Movable strips under each activity indicated the duration of the activity, and the horizontal axis contained a reference to inter-task dependencies.

The PERT Planning Method as we know it today was formed in 1958 by a research team from Lockheed Aircraft Corporation, the Navy Special Projects Office, and Booz, Allen, and Hamilton in their plan to develop the Polaris Missile System. The critical path method (CPM) was created concurrently by a team from DuPont and Remington Rand Univac. Their method identified the shortest, or critical, path through a project.

Today's PERT planning method has three variations based on the display and duration of activities. These include activity on arrow, activity on node, and precedence diagram. The full PERT planning method is extremely complex and can be confusing. The PERT chart contained in this article is a simplified activity on node diagram that includes the identification of a critical path. It is our goal to provide the benefits of PERT planning through a simplified charting technique designed to be used following the tree diagram and S.M.A.R.T. plan.

The PERT chart is a technique to organize tasks or activities into a schedule, a visual method for identifying predecessor activities, and a means of identifying the minimum time required to complete the project. It can identify gaps or missing tasks in your project plan, show the critical path through your project plan, and track your project to completion. The PERT chart requires a clear understanding of your purpose to be accomplished and a knowledge of the tasks or activities necessary to accomplish the purpose. Most often, computer planning programs are used to facilitate completing and updating PERT charts.

As with any decision-making or planning tool, the most important place to start is with a clear understanding of the purpose to be accomplished. A concise purpose statement can improve substantially your ability to plan. Once you have defined your purpose, establish a list of the tasks that must be performed. The PERT chart depends on other tools, such as the card sort, a tree diagram, or a S.M.A.R.T. plan, to define the tasks necessary to accomplish your purpose.

Record the predecessors for each task. These are the tasks that must be completed before the current task can be started. This information from the S.M.A.R.T. plan is recorded in the first blank column. For each task, define the task duration. This is the total time required to perform the task with the assigned resources. Use the same unit of time for each task, that is, hours or days. Assigning duration requires knowledge of the manner in which the work will be performed. The assistance of those who will perform the work can be invaluable. If the task is not sufficiently detailed, you will have difficulty. This can be an indication that the task needs to be subdivided.

The second key to defining duration is a knowledge of the resources available. Often an unacceptable duration can be shortened through the application of more resources. Warning: There are some operations that by their nature are sequential and cannot be done in parallel. Ensure that the availability of additional resources will help and not hinder or waste.

The PERT planning method works backward from the purpose to be accomplished to build a linked, time-driven plan that identifies each task and its starting point in order to meet a desired completion date. The reality of PERT is that it is often worked both ways several times to gain understanding and to help all the tasks fit together in the best possible manner.

The original PERT did not have the array of judgmental tools that we have today, nor was it assisted by today's computer technology. With the use of other judgmental tools, such as the S.M.A.R.T. plan and the tree diagram, it becomes possible to work forward from the earliest possible start to determine the actual completion of the purpose.

To use a PERT chart, create a temporary calendar scale that covers the time from a starting time to the date when it should be complete. Working forward or backward requires an initial calendar scale to facilitate the location of tasks on the chart. The final calendar scale is defined by the creation of the PERT diagram on the chart and can be placed only after the diagram is completed.

Working from the first task to be accomplished, place the tasks to be completed on the chart. Each task should be enclosed in a circle or ellipse with its required completion date written clearly above or below it. Remember this comes from the S.M.A.R.T. plan. Add the task number to the task. On large or complex charts, the task number will be vital to maintaining order and conserving space. Draw an arrow from the task to the next task to be accomplished. For the last task to be done, the arrow is drawn to the purpose. Place the task duration, or time required to complete the task, on the arrow as shown in Figure 11.

FIGURE 11   *PERT Chart on Implementable Tasks from S.M.A.R.T. Plan*

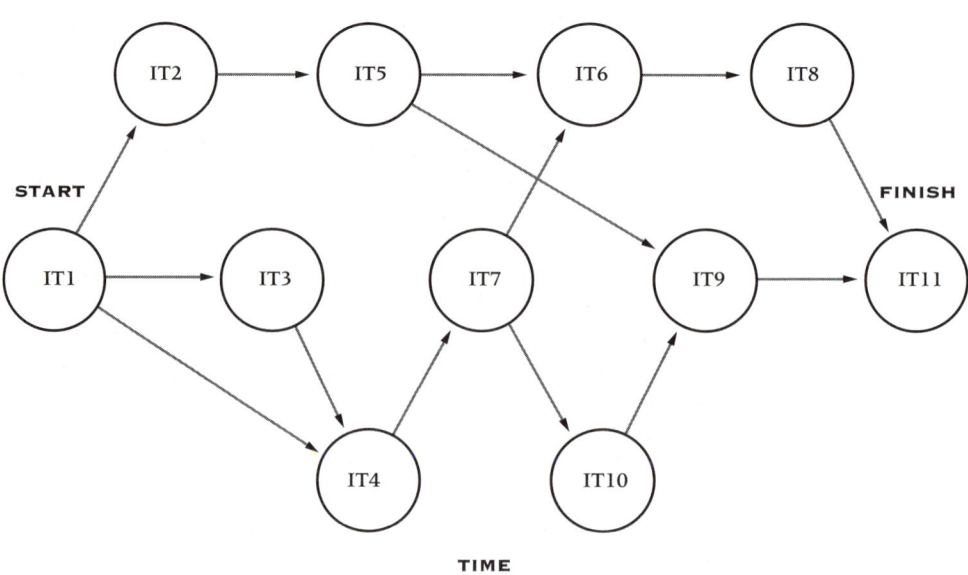

The completed PERT chart will provide a network of tasks that must be completed to accomplish your purpose. The total time to get from the start to a completed purpose will depend on how many tasks can be accomplished in parallel. The more things you can do at the same time, the sooner you will be done, but there is a limit. That limit is the critical path through your network of tasks. The critical path is the longest path of predecessor/successor tasks in the network. It is discovered by adding the duration of tasks together for each of the possible paths through the network. The path with the longest duration defines the minimum time required to accomplish your purpose. Clearly mark the critical path with double lines or color for all to see. The critical path will also determine the time or length of your calendar scale. At this point, redraw the calendar scale and PERT network to assure harmony between the network and scale and to ensure coherency of task placement.

Considerable development work has been performed on the PERT chart since it was created. Entire courses exist to teach the PERT/CPM (critical path method) planning method. There are also a number of computer programs on the market that implement this process. In a more intensive study, you will encounter some of the following terms:

Activity	The task to be done (or specific).
Node	The circle or ellipse in which the task to be done is written (or event).
Predecessor	A task that must be completed before the current task can be started.
Successor	A task that cannot be started until the current task is completed.
Duration	The time required to complete a task.
Early start	The soonest a task can be started.
Late start	The latest a task can be started and still stay on schedule.
Early finish	The soonest or most optimistic time a task can be finished.
Late finish	The latest a task can be finished and still not delay the following tasks.
Slack	The difference between the time a task should start and when it must start.

When used on a PERT, these terms are often abbreviated, such as EF for early finish and LS for late start. Figure 11 shows a completed PERT chart.

Reengineering: Process Redesign

By Terence T. Burton

Process redesign is the first element of a reengineering framework. The objective of process redesign is to reinvent, reposition, restructure, and de-departmentalize critical business processes in a manner that creates a renewed focus on customer need, not business as usual with a few added enhancements. Process redesign demands that we abandon the parochial rules about business and adopt a start-over mind-set.

Ultimately, our goal is to reengineer what is typically a homogeneous business into several stand-alone focused value centers. This is typically accomplished by a complete overhaul of the company's infrastructure, including such processes as:

- Physical
- Business
- Technical
- Information
- People

Some of the activities characteristic of process redesign include:

- Linking business processes together to decrease product and informational movement, defective business process queues, work-in-process, material or information handling, time, complexity, and associated costs.
- Reducing cycle times by overlapping business process activities, such as processing a customer order, developing a new product, purchasing raw materials, or preparing compliance documentation.
- Creating the conditions for an immediate exposure and solution to business process problems and opportunities achieved by the entire workforce.
- Providing real-time feedback mechanisms to business process and subprocess owners. This supports the creation of self-management, self-measurement, and self-adjustment.
- Process redesign has focused traditionally on making the "as-is" incrementally better. Reengineering causes individuals to work from a much broader definition

Selected text and illustrations from *The Reengineering Toolbox* by The Center for Excellence in Operations, Inc. (CEO), Nashua, New Hampshire, Terence T. Burton, President. Reprinted by permission.

of process redesign than occurs with traditional continuous improvement methods. Process redesign in a reengineering sense depends largely upon an organization's distance from its desired, or "ultimate," state.

In our implementation experiences, we have found that process redesign evolves to a new level of breakthrough improvement. Every organization performs at different levels, from excellent to poor, depending on the process and goal. Therefore, it is logical that the next generation of process redesign include concurrent activities focused on the following analyses:

1. Some business processes currently meet or exceed customer needs, and the proper activity to support process redesign is reinforcement of current practices. This usually includes the soft aspects of traditional continuous improvement, such as team building and improving facilitation and leadership skills.
2. Other business processes fall short of meeting customer needs and require small, incremental improvements. The proper activity to support process redesign is continuous improvement of the "as-is." This usually includes the soft aspects of continuous improvement as previously described, plus the traditional TQM problem solving tools (for example, The 7 Old Tools, The 7 New Tools, SPC, charting and measurement techniques, and so on).
3. Every organization has business processes that, no matter how much reinforment or incremental improvement is pursued, will never meet the customer's need within the customer's time window. These are the candidates to be reinvented or rediscovered. One of the largest causes of reengineering failures has been the lack of tools to deal with reinvention needs.

Unfortunately, many reengineering initiatives are nothing more than slash and burn downsizing efforts, recycled TQM or continuous improvement activities, in vogue movements, or a new list of MIS projects. The major causes of reengineering failure include overreliance on technology as a solution and application of old tools that focus on continuous improvements of the "as-is." *Old* tools focus on competencies (for example, how to make current conditions better). *Reengineering* tools focus on antecedents (for example, what needs to be done) and encourage entrepreneurial thinking and invention of new business processes. Anything else results in what actually is downsizing, TQM, continuous improvement, created activities, or a new list of MIS projects.

CEO's Breakthrough! Reengineering™ framework addresses the full spectrum of inventing, managing, and implementing breakthrough improvement. The purpose of *The Reengineering Toolbox* is to share our implementation methodology and "out-of-box" tools because we feel these are critical to achieving real breakthrough results. Successful implementation makes the difference with reengineering separate organizations that "wish" or "think" things will automatically change simply because they have launched a reengineering initiative.

The Breakthrough! Reengineering™ BPR tools presented in this article are from CEO's book, *The Reengineering Toolbox.* These tools are much more difficult to apply in real life than, for example, the seven standard TQM tools because they must be applied by entrepreneurial process redesigners. We have learned from our implementation experiences that there are many reasons for this fact. The most pronounced difference in reengineering is that in many situations, the process forces you to start in the abstract to create a new reality. There may not be a process because it may not yet exist. Additionally, many of these tools are applied to knowledge-based activities, in which definitions of customers, products, processes, quality, performance, and success are often unclear.

Applying Pareto charts, run diagrams, and check sheets to real-life situations on the shop floor is a structured, linear problem-solving process. The operator typically is provided with quality and workmanship standards, process/routing, work instructions, set-up sheets, quality measurement criteria, and tooling/gauges. The operator has the benefit of a defined product and process and can measure physical results against a predetermined standard. Imagine how much success this operator would have if he or she were sent to an empty space to apply these tools! This is the challenge of reengineering. Application of these new reengineering tools for process redesign requires a totally new thinking process characterized by out-of-box thinking and business as unusual.

PROCESS REDESIGN

TEN P BUSINESS REENGINEERING CHECKLIST

The 10 P Business Reengineering Checklist (Figure 1) is used in conjunction with business process mapping. The 10 P checklist adds dimensional value for each activity that is a business, technical, or administrative process. It also helps in rationalizing the real needs of a business process and to remove any unnecessary activities.

Business processes in most organizations have evolved over decades. As a consequence, many of the activities that are routinely performed in organizations do not stand up to the test of the 10 P checklist. Often, activities are identified that produce an unnecessary or incorrect product or have no customer. In practice, it is not unusual to find that some of the 10 P checklist items have no answer.

BPR Methodology:

1. Decide and describe the business segment or process to be analyzed.
2. For each of the checklist categories, fill in the answer to the category in as much detail as possible.
3. For each answer provided, check off whether it is a complete, partial, or missing answer.
4. Total the number of check marks in each of the rating columns.
5. If you have 80 percent or more of the check marks in the "complete" rating column, you understand your business segment or process very well. Experience has shown that most organizations usually have most of the check marks in the partial or missing columns, indicating that much work is required.
6. Identify the data required to complete the answers to the categories, determine the data sources, and decide who will obtain the data and when.
7. Collect the data.

FIGURE 1   *Ten P Business Reengineering Checklist*

Process Description: Date:

Category	Answer	Answer Rating			Data Collection				
		Complete	Partial	Missing	Source	Data	Required	Who	When
Purpose									
Procedure									
Practice									
Participants									
Pace									
Place									
Period Frequency									
Product									
Purchaser									
Performance									
	Total Check Marks								

BPR Results:

- Clear understanding of a business segment or reason for a process's existence.
- Compelling reason to eliminate the business segment or process where no clear answer can be found.

BUSINESS PROCESS MAPPING

Business process mapping (Figure 2) is a scoping tool used to document and diagnose the standard internal business processes that deliver products and/or services to the customer. This tool helps the enterprise understand the sequence of activities, relationships, process element cycle times, resources consumed, process cost, information and physical activity flows, and process participants.

Business process mapping is a flexible process that can be adapted to the preferences of the organization. Business process mapping can be accomplished through post-it notes, brown paper analysis, computer-generated flowcharts, freehand drawings, flip charts, and the like. The approach we choose is not as important as the purpose and results achieved.

FIGURE 2   *Business Process Mapping*

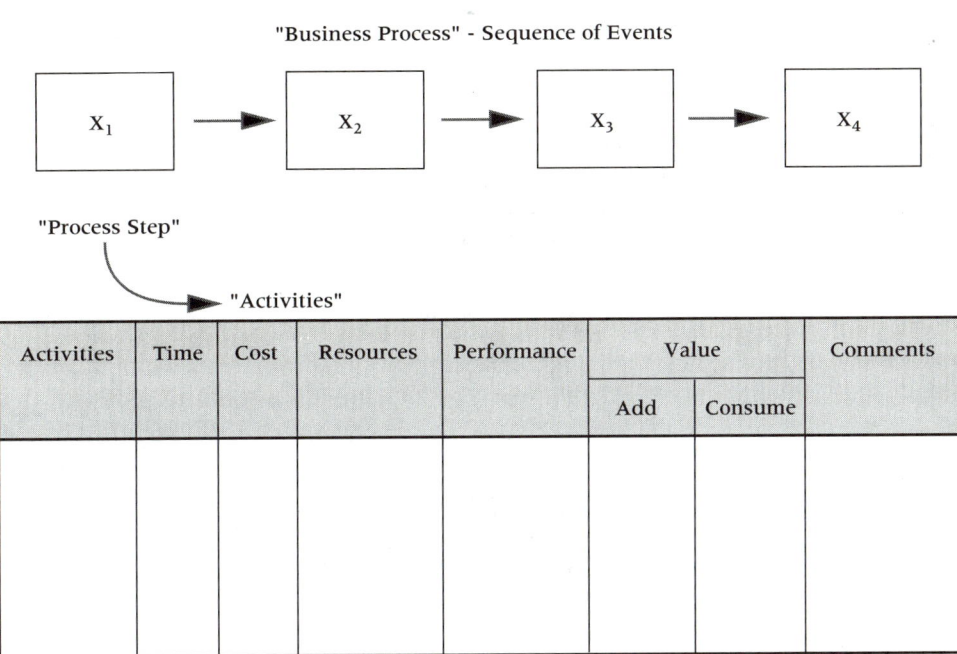

BPR Methodology:

1. Chart the major cross-functional process steps and the sequence of events in a business process.
2. Document the specific activities and elements of each process step.
3. Determine critical descriptive data to analyze and assess the activities that are required to complete each process step.
4. Apply the 10 P Business Reengineering Checklist to each activity in the process.
5. Segment value-adding and value-consuming efforts in the process and begin identifying opportunities to eliminate, combine, or streamline process activities.

BPR Results:

- Cross-functional business process maps.
- Process dynamics, redundancies, disconnects, waste.
- A solid foundation for breakthrough change.

THROW IT AWAY (TIA) ANALYSIS

Throw It Away Analysis (Figure 3) is a tool designed to stimulate innovation and reinvention. Throw It Away Analysis is conducted as a structured small group

FIGURE 3   *Throw It Away Analysis*

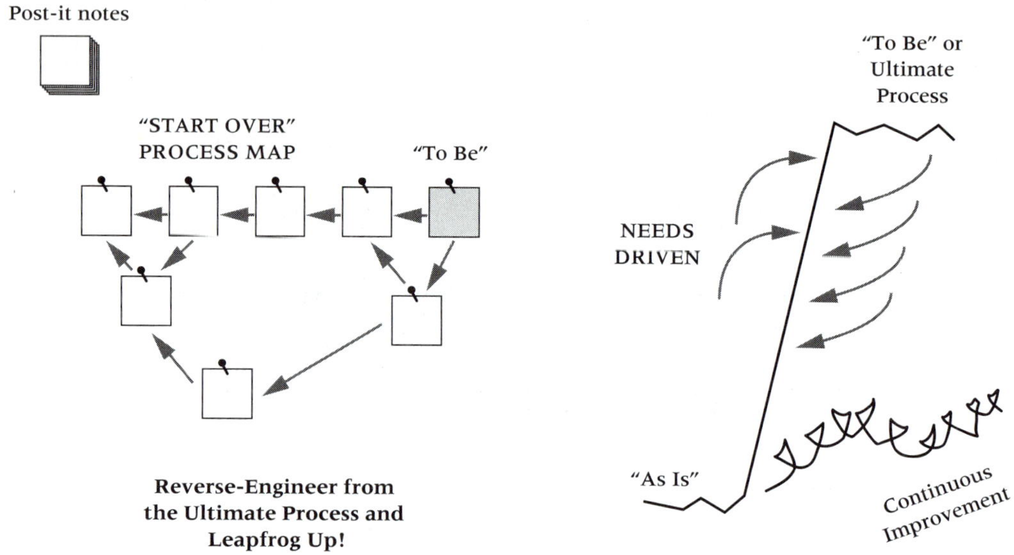

Post-it notes

"START OVER"
PROCESS MAP   "To Be"

"To Be" or
Ultimate
Process

NEEDS
DRIVEN

"As Is"

Continuous
Improvement

**Reverse-Engineer from
the Ultimate Process and
Leapfrog Up!**

Business Segment of Process:_____   Date:_____

Sequential Process Steps	Throw It Away or Rearrange it	What Could Happen	Potential Impact	Potential New Process Flow

exercise made up of process participants and those who might be helpful who come from outside the business process. These forward-thinking individuals usually ask tough questions, such as "Why is this done and is it necessary?" The objective of this exercise is to get the process owners to think out-of-box and raise possibilities that may seem crazy, unthinkable, impossible, and ridiculous. Be aware that some of the results of Throw It Away Analysis may well be impossible or ridiculous but often one leads to the creation of a process breakthrough.

BPR Methodology:

1. Assemble a small team of six to eight process and non-process owners.
2. List out the sequential steps on a flip chart using post-it notes.
3. Have the participants explore what would happen if one of the process steps were removed. The facilitator removes the process step post-it note from the flip chart so it is viewed as being thrown away. The facilitator should remove one post-it note at a time and encourage the team to rearrange the process flow without that step.
4. Record the results of the exploration on the Throw It Away Matrix.
5. Stop the exercise after each of the process steps has been subjected to the Throw It Away Analysis.

BPR Results:

- A detailed analysis of each process step's worth and contribution.
- A potentially new flow or simplified one.
- Development of an attitude favorable to change.

TOUCH VERSUS ELAPSED ANALYSIS

Touch Versus Elapsed Analysis (Figure 4) is an opportunity identification tool designed to define the ultimate potential improvement in an "As-is" business process. This tool compares the elapsed time documented from the business process mapping with the cumulative actual work time. This comparison is made through a pilot exercise where a subassembly, product, or document is walked through each of the process elements without any delays. Process participants are made aware that this exercise will happen and must give their immediate attention to it. They are instructed to drop whatever they are doing and complete their aspect of the business process as fast as possible. Once the exercise is completed, each participant is asked to analyze what is preventing him/her from continuous processing all of the time.

BPR Methodoloy:

1. Record the sequential process steps from the business process mapping tool and the documented elapsed time.
2. Inform all those involved in the pilot exercise of their roles and responsibilities.
3. Run the pilot exercise and record the actual work time.
4. Calculate the Reengineering Improvement Ratio.
5. Identify the process steps for reengineering or elimination.

FIGURE 4   *Touch versus Elapsed Analysis*

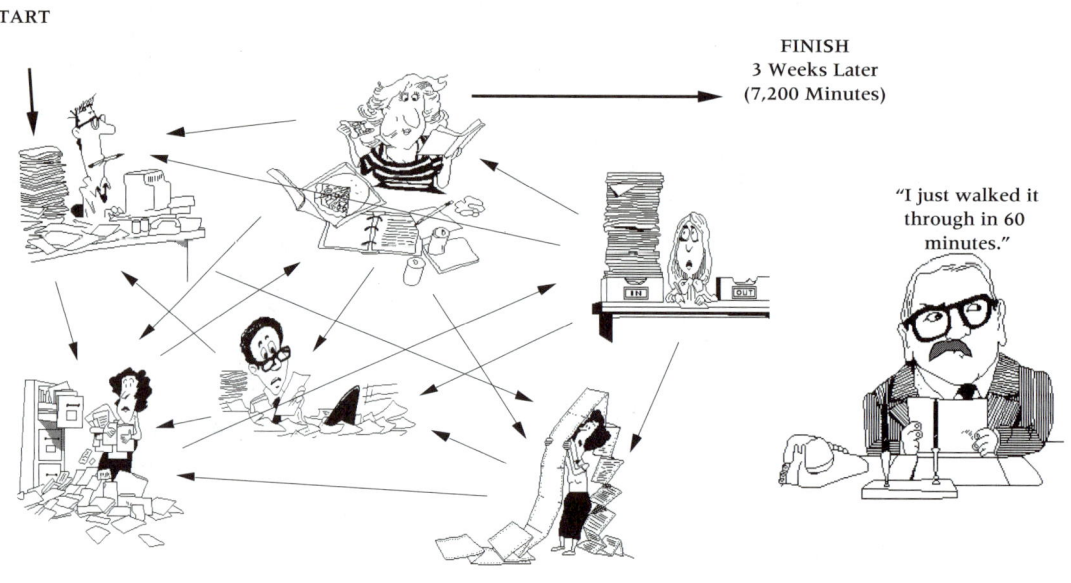

START

FINISH
3 Weeks Later
(7,200 Minutes)

"I just walked it
through in 60
minutes."

EE:AA = 7200:60
= 120:1

Business Segment of Process: _____   Date: _____

Sequential Process Steps	Documented Elapsed Time	Actual Work Time	Reengineering Improvement Ratio	Focus of the Reengineering Effort
Total			Elapsed / Actual, Expressed as an EE:AA Ratio (for example, 100:1)	

BPR Results:

- A calculated ratio of actual work to total elapsed time.
- Targets of process reinvention to greatly reduce cycle time.

TOTAL ENTERPRISE QUALITY MANAGEMENT

ADAPT PROBLEM-SOLVING NETWORK

ADAPT (Figure 5) is an analytical network to support reengineering that is similar to the PDCA cycle for TQM. Solving business problems via the reengineering ideology requires out-of-box thinking. This type of problem solving is unstructured, nonlinear, and random in nature. The ADAPT network is used to encourage entrepreneurial behavior and risk.

FIGURE 5 *ADAPT™ (Out-of-Box PDCA)*

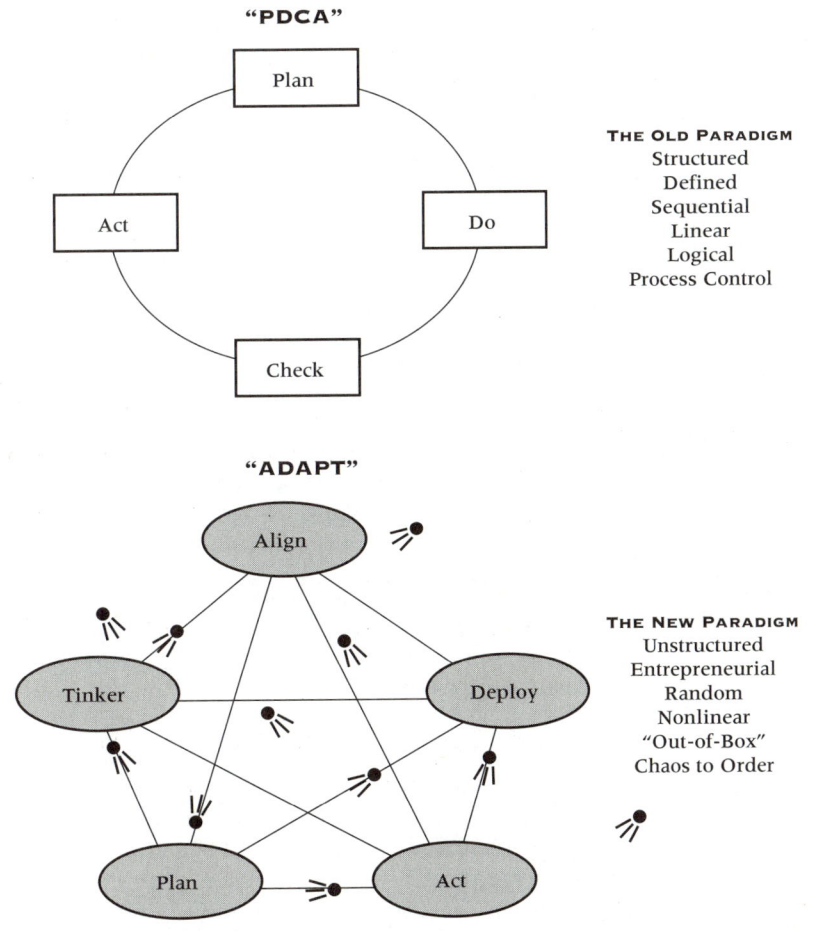

PDCA is a repetitive sequential process, and ADAPT is a network of conceptual activities connected by tightropes. Imagine the spatial masses moving on and off the page on a Z-axis. You might be in the Deploy space and determine that the next step is Plan. However, because of real circumstances (for example, the tightropes intersect and lead you on a new course of action), there is not enough time for planning. The importance of ADAPT is to help us to recognize which space we are in, to determine the next space of the reengineering process, and to adjust if you land in a different destination. Reengineering is forced (but well managed) chaos and disequilibrium followed by order at a higher performance level.

BPR Methodology:

1. *Align* resources toward a common set of reengineering goals and objectives that will generate new organizational orders, such as agility, seamlessness, self-management, and the best possible performance.
2. *Deploy* resources to work toward the achievement of reengineering goals.
3. *Act* or try something new. Keep in mind that with reengineering it is difficult to plan until you take action first (that is, unplug the existing PC-based 3 week quotation system and start from scratch).
4. *Plan* the next set of actions and the definitions of success.
5. *Tinker,* or check and adjust your progress based on the latest information.

BPR Results:

- A new awareness of managed chaos and development of individual thinking capabilities.

SUPPLY CHAIN MANAGEMENT

SUPPLY CHAIN ACTIVITY NETWORK (SCAN)

SCAN (Figure 6) is a method for diagramming the elements of a company's supply chain. This tool provides a generic framework for baselining the "as-is" supply chain, its execution steps and cycle times, and its performance criteria. SCAN also provides the foundation for out-of-box process redesign to eliminate or simplify the supply chain.

BPR Methodology:

1. Expand the framework of SCAN to reflect the specific operational elements of the company's supply chain (that is, create the detailed supply chain map of your company).
2. Detail other descriptive elements of the supply chain, such as process elements, cycle times, methods deployed, and so on. Note: Detailing can be accomplished through the use of other tools such as Purpose and Process Mapping, Touch versus Walk-through, 10P, Journeys between Charting, Bill of Resources, and the like.
3. Analyze the completed SCAN of your company for redundancies, duplicate efforts, waste, or non-value-added activities.

FIGURE 6   *Supply Chain Activity Network*

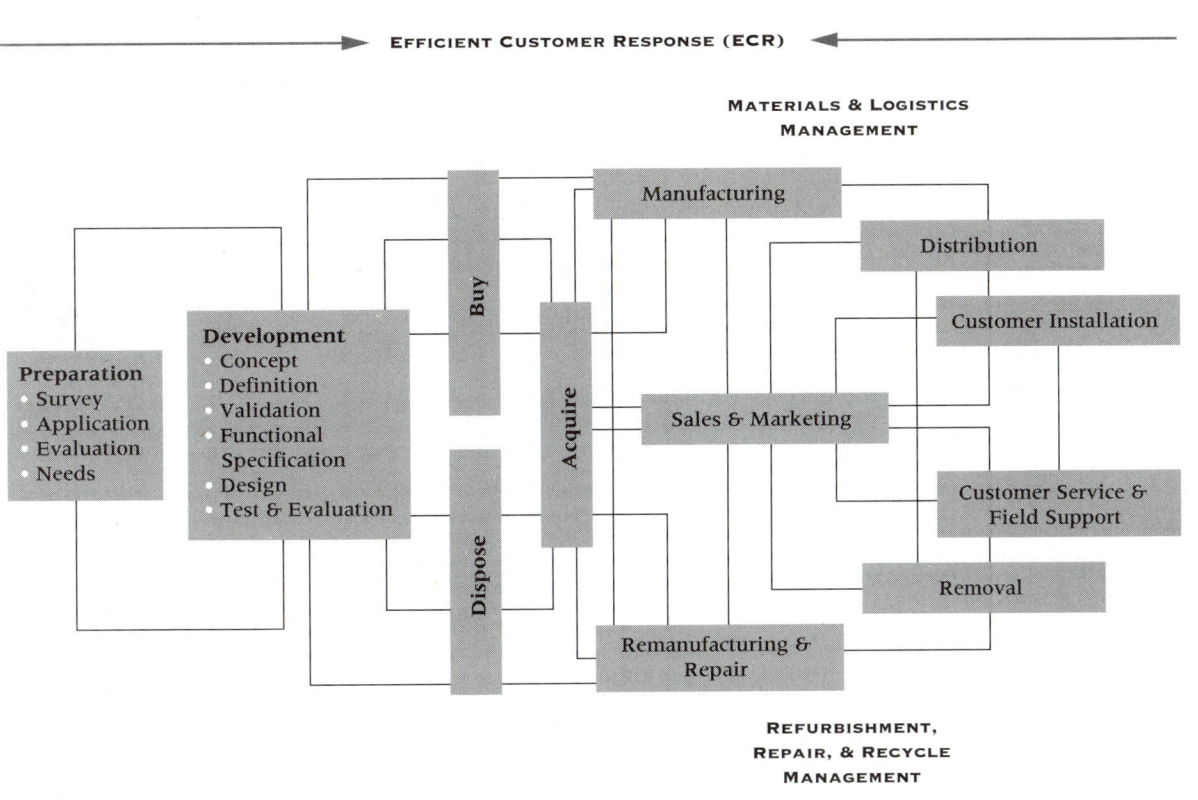

4. Brainstorm, discussing how to break the homogeneous SCAN into multiple purpose value centers with fault tolerant logistics characteristics.
5. Reengineer and simplify the SCAN. Define the implementation steps, resources, and organizational implications of the SCAN after reengineering.

BPR Results:

• An "as-is " SCAN.
• A "to-be" SCAN.

SERVICE COST VALUE MATRIX

The Service Cost Value Matrix (Figure 7) is based on activity-based costing and management approaches. Its objective is to analyze a business process in terms of values added versus values consumed.

BPR Methodology:

1. Define the services provided to the organization and the level of resources consumed to provide these services.

FIGURE 7   *Service Cost Value Matrix*

Product/Service	% of Resource Consumption	Cost of Product/Service	Value of Product/Service

2. Identify an individual chart of account costs directly related to the business process and accumulate costs into a business process cost bucket.
3. Calculate ratios of total resource consumption based on services provided by the business process (this is used as the statistical base for allocating costs).
4. Allocate total costs to services provided based on the level of resource consumption.
5. Compare the value added with the value consumed and determine activities any future reengineering or continuous improvement efforts will focus on.

BPR Results:

• An analysis of value of service versus cost of service for major elements of a business process.
• Definition of cost drivers.

ORGANIZATIONAL ROBUSTNESS

ORGANIZATIONAL INVOLVEMENT MAPPING

The Organizational Involvement Mapping tool (Figure 8) is a process to understand better the core business or technical processes that deliver a valued product or service to your customer. Most organizations have between five to eight core business or technical processes that should not be confused with business functions. A few parts of many business functions are included in a business process. Organizations are arranged in a vertical hierarchy, but business processes flow in horizontal and diagonal directions and do not necessarily follow the formal structure. Organizational Involvement Mapping depicts visually the business and technical process flows, and who is involved in their execution.

FIGURE 8   *Organizational Involvement Mapping*

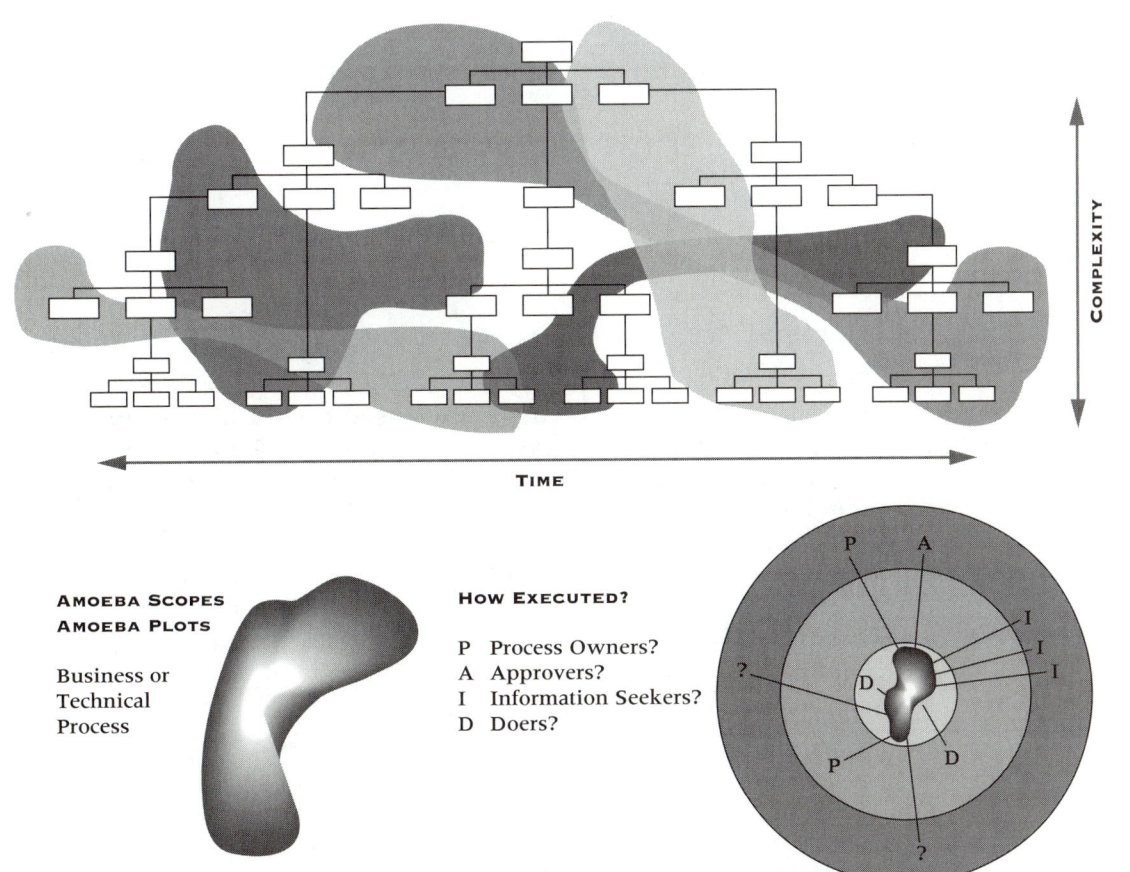

AMOEBA SCOPES
AMOEBA PLOTS

Business or
Technical
Process

HOW EXECUTED?

P   Process Owners?
A   Approvers?
I   Information Seekers?
D   Doers?

BPR Methodology:

1. Construct a detailed organization chart of the company or division under study.
2. Develop a listing of the core business or technical processes that deliver a valued product or service to the customer. Most organizations have between five to eight core business or technical processes.
3. Plot on the organization chart how each of the business or technical processes is accomplished. Connect the plotted points with a freehand amoeba figure that embodies all functions that make this process a reality.
4. Develop an execution plot that shows the level of involvement of each person who is identified in a function that contributes to this process. Identify each person as either a doer, a process owner, an approver, or an information seeker.
5. Determine if any of the work being performed in the rings can be eliminated or transferred to the doer ring. Most of the outer rings cause the majority of delays that the doer ring experiences.

BPR Results:

- Identified core business or technical processes.
- Visualization of how these business or technical processes interact and are accomplished.
- Classification of those involved in these processes.
- Identification of work that can be moved to doers or eliminated.

SPEED-TO-CUSTOMER

DEVELOPMENT PROCESS MAPPING

Development Process Mapping (Figure 9) is a reengineering tool used to define the structured, logical steps and the elapsed cycle times an organization deploys to develop new products. This tool can be used in conjunction with other reengineering tools (that is, touch development time versus elapsed development time, Development Process Capability, 10 P Checklist, Journeys between Charting, Organizational Involvement Mapping, and so on). This tool pinpoints areas and practices of the existing product development process that can be examined to reduce cycle times and improve development product and process quality. It can also be used as a basis for developing "fast lane" development rules that bypass normal development practices for certain exceptional situations.

BPR Methodolgy:

1. Define the current product development phases, guidelines, check sheet items, and formal approval requirements.
2. Determine organizations, functions, departments, and specific activity skills involved in the current development process.

FIGURE 9 *Development Process Mapping*

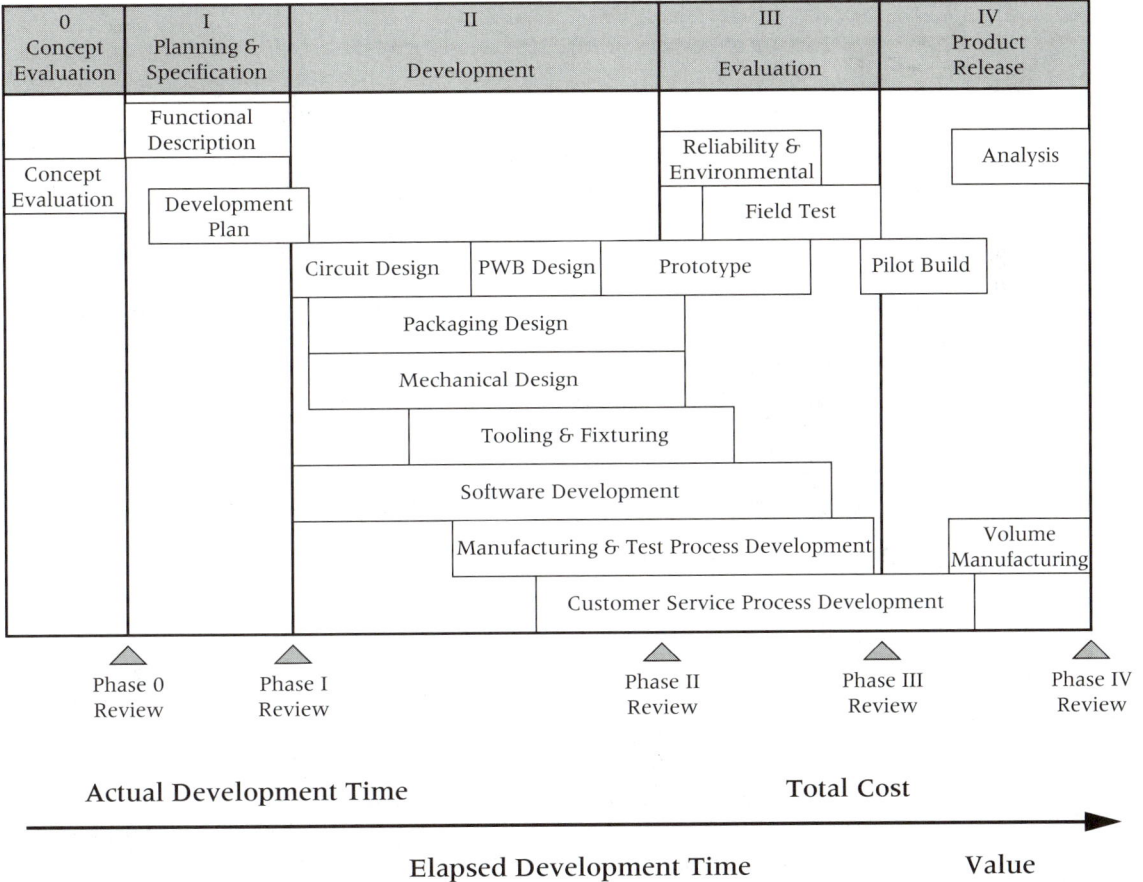

Sample Product Development Structure

Actual Development Time   Total Cost

Elapsed Development Time   Value

3. Develop "as-is" Development Process Maps for those new product development efforts that are known (for products currently being developed, or for products already released for commercialization).

4. Supplement Development Process Maps with descriptive or performance information, such as cycle times, development costs, time-to-market performance, organizational involvement, budgets, and so on.

5. Develop "to-be" Development Process Maps based on questions, such as, "How would you develop this new product all over again knowing what we know today?, What would you have done differently?, How could we have saved 50 percent of the time?, How could we have reduced product cost by 20 percent?, What changes will produce breakthroughs in product development?" Note: These maps can be developed in focus groups or brainstorming sessions.

6. Reengineer the Product Development Process, including Phase Definitions, Roles and Responsibilities, Phase Review and Gatekeeping, Design Review Procedures, Project/Resource Management Methodologies, and Success Measurement.

BPR Results:

- Directions and requirements for developing a flexible, agile, rapid-response development process.

DEVELOPMENT PROJECT MAPPING

Development Project Mapping (Figure 10) is a reengineering tool used to take an inventory of development projects-in-process. This tool can be used in conjunction with MVP Filtering to reconcile product/technology strategy and product development. In the majority of cases, organizations can "purge" their open development projects and thus regain focus and resource capacity for programs that are strategically important.

Development Project Mapping is typically an emotional and political exercise similar to reducing work-in-process on the plant floor. The philosophy is to avoid being caught up in developing faster processes to execute what you should not be doing in the first place.

BPR Methodology:

1. Create an inventory of Product Development Efforts based on the following classifications:
   - *Derivatives:* Projects that are cost-reduced versions or enhancements of existing products.
   - *Platforms:* Fundamental improvements in cost, quality, functionality, or performance over previous generations.
   - *Breakthroughs:* Significant developments to existing products and processes.
   - *Research & Development:* Creation of new technologies that eventually translate into commercial development.
   - *Strategic Alliances:* Activities outside the boundaries of the map that fit one of the categories previously mentioned.
2. Develop a descriptive profile for each project (for example, resources, costs, priorities, market potential, risk, and so on).
3. Determine Phase-To-Date and Phase-To-Finish facts, such as cost, cycle time, financial impact, resource constraints, trade-offs, and so on.
4. Purge the development workload based on short-term criteria and particular time-to-market needs.
5. Repeat the process monthly to manage development resources, program work flows, resource gaps, budget overruns, and development velocity.

BPR Results:

- An effective Product Development Management tool to prevent overload conditions.

FIGURE 10 *Development Project Mapping*

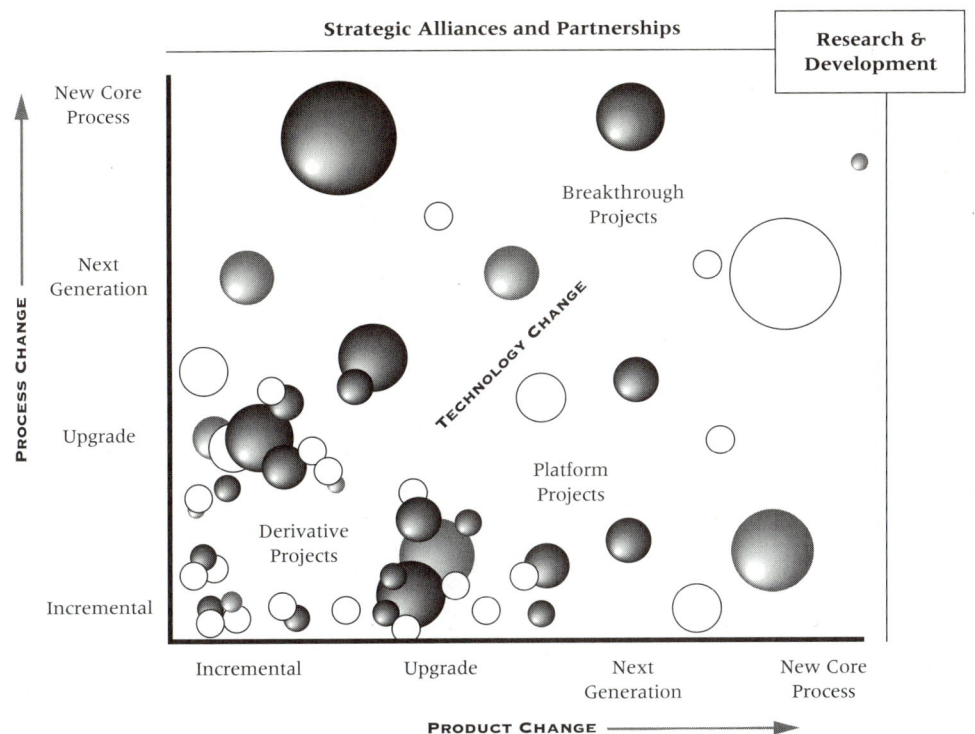

Strategic Alliances and Partnerships

Research & Development

New Core Process

Breakthrough Projects

Next Generation

TECHNOLOGY CHANGE

PROCESS CHANGE

Upgrade

Platform Projects

Derivative Projects

Incremental

Incremental Upgrade Next Generation New Core Process

PRODUCT CHANGE

PROBLEMS
Too Many Projects (50%–75%)
Wrong Mix of Projects
Incorrect Execution Sequence
Misuse of Resources
Loss of Focus
Missed Market Windows
Products without Customers
Technologies without Markets

Development Project Map

	A	B	C	D	E	F

Business Plan?
Market Definition?
Projects by Category?
Resources by Category?
Project/Resources Gaps?
Phase-to-Date Status?
Phase-to-Date Cost?
Phase-to-Finish Resources?
Phase-to-Finish Cost?
Program Value-Added?

PART 3

TRAINING AND MANAGEMENT DEVELOPMENT

Executive Education for Total Quality Management

BY ELLEN DOMB

"Train, train, train" is a prerequisite for success in all the works on quality transformation, from the classics (Deming, Juran, Crosby, Feigenbaum) to the popular (Peters, Byham, Blanchard, and others). Training is needed because the concepts of customer-focused quality, structured problem solving, continuous improvement, open communication, and fact-based decision making are not natural behaviors in many organizations. Many years of product (or finance, or technology) oriented decision making, of "firefighting" problem solving, of distrust between employees and managers must be overcome to begin to find the advantages of TQM. Training *alone* will not change people's behaviors, but training in the new skills is the first step toward the change.

The key to sustained change in behaviors is constant reinforcement on the job. The reinforcement is both internal—when the person sees that the new way *is* better than the old, and external—when the new behavior or its benefits are noticed by others. All agree that training must be "tailored" to the audience and the application environment, so that people can learn in terms that are meaningful in that environment.

Well-meaning TQM change agents take this advice and create a plethora of training classes specific to their industry or their organization (TQM for Health Care, TQM for Education, Problem Solving the XYZ Way, Teamwork at the RST Company, Facilitator Training for Process Improvement Teams, Team Leader Training, SPC is for Everyone!, Quality Function Deployment, Tools and Techniques, Listening skills, Teamwork, Robust Design, Developing Surveys, and so on.) Each of these courses has a place in the transformation of organizations. So why do so many attempted transformations fail?

They fail because training for the employees of an organization is only the first step. The constant reinforcement of the new behaviors is missing, because the leadership of the organization may have received the same (or abbreviated) *skill* training as the others, but did not learn their special responsibilities as leaders of the change process. Organizational leaders will recognize this scenario: you reached your present position by being excellent practitioners of the *old* way of doing things. As a leader, you have recognized the need for change, decided that TQM is the right choice for the future of the organization, and now you just want to get on with it. It seems cruel to expect *you* to lead people in changing to a new way, when your personal strength is your knowledge of the best of the old way.

You tell your organizational development staff, your training department, or your consultant to start getting the TQM change going. They organize classes and start coaching you and your senior executives on change, change management, how to be leaders, and the impact of the changes that you can anticipate. But organizing classes is the easiest and most visible thing that they can do, so it is a natural tendency to do a lot of it.

The executive leadership of the organization is most frequently neglected in this outpouring of educational opportunities. Occasionally, a special class will be formed for them (usually short, since the training department is told "they don't need the details, only the overview so they'll know what everyone is supposed to be doing") or specific to a task (how to be a good team sponsor for a problem-solving team, how to conduct a QFD design review).

The executive has special educational needs. Early in the organization's transformation you will need to make decisions on the process of change; on education and training; on customer, supplier and labor relations; on traditional and nontraditional organizational structures; and on how you will change your leadership styles to promote the new philosophy. And in many organizations, you have to make these decisions during a 3 day "management retreat" designed to kick off the total quality management "program." If you are a senior manager, but not the chief executive, you may be even more frustrated if you are being asked to make extensive changes that take you away from the patterns that have been your basis for success, without the chief executive's view of the need for change.

To avoid these problems, the Xerox Corporation pioneered the "cascade" approach to quality improvement education. The executive group learns from inside or outside experts and then each member of the group teaches her/his work group, coaching them through an application of the new principles, so that they can do the same with their groups. The change is seen as a waterfall, flowing down the organization chart.

There are many benefits to this approach:

- Executives and managers must address the implementation issues at each level of the organization, since they will be explaining it to everyone else.
- Cultural compatibility of the teaching, since people who have been successful in the operations of the organization are the people who create the classes and teach them.
- Implicit importance (if my boss spent weeks learning this and is now teaching it, it must be important).
- Direct application to the concerns of the work group.

Other large companies have been slow to adopt the cascade approach. The most common objections are

- It takes too long.
- Executives may not be good teachers.
- The message may be diluted by the time it filters through five, six, or seven levels down the organization.
- Workers may be inhibited about questioning their supervisors about the changes, or about the details of the classes. Also, the fear that workers *will* question their supervisors can create awkwardness and cause the most sensitive issues—job security, pay, responsibilities, personal change—to be brushed off, increasing the participants' insecurity.
- It requires substantial support by professionals to develop training materials and to assist the trainers.
- The emphasis on applications *within* work groups may cause substantive issues *between* work groups to be neglected.

Style may be as important as content in creating effective executive education. Whether the executive has formal management and technical education or has on-the-job education; whether the organization is a city government, a corporation, or a hospital; the leadership is most familiar with learning by doing. Lecture-style classroom education is remote from their successful experiences, yet it is the most easily packaged form of training and therefore the most common. You need to assess your personal learning style and select the mix of options that will help you understand what you need to start and sustain the changes in your organization.

Executive education style options include

- Structured classroom
     Internal (executive group of the one organization)
     External (classes [industry-specific or general] given by consultants or universities to mixed groups from multiple organizations)
- Interactive workshop, with the same options as the structured classroom, usually with several sessions devoted to simulations of application of the concepts in your work environment
- On-the-job coaching
     External consultant
     Internal consultant
- Benchmarking (formal, structured) or visiting (less structured) similar organizations that have more TQM experience
- Self-study (reading; video/audio tapes; attending conferences; computer-assisted training for technical subjects, tools, and techniques)

The chief executive has unique problems because of the traditional view of his/her position. If educational opportunities (classes, workshops, or any other options) are designed to explore the problems of the organization, and to help people learn the skills and behaviors needed to overcome those problems and to move into a proactive customer-focused future, those people may be reluctant to discuss with you what they see as past failures—either their failures or yours! If this is the case in your organization, it may be helpful if you start TQM executive education and training with private sessions for each executive, or for small groups without the chief executive, until enough of the new values are in place that they can share past "failures" as learning opportunities, and not hide them due to fear of reprisals based on past patterns.

The process of executive education for TQM is iterative—the executive needs to know *something* about TQM to understand the scope of change required, in order to participate in the decisions about the style and content of subsequent education. Leaders should see this iteration as a benefit, since it involves the leadership in developing the TQM model that will be effective for their organization.

The Plan-Do-Check-Act cycle (Deming cycle or Shewhart cycle) shown in Figure 1 describes a basic learning process of data gathering, situational analysis, hypothesis (PLAN), experiment (DO), evaluation (CHECK), and adoption or modification of the hypothesis (ACT). The Plan-Do-Check-Act (PDCA) cycle is taught as a beginning element of TQM (using a variety of acronyms to allow the various consultants to attempt to distinguish their own approaches).

The executive group will learn to apply PDCA to all aspects of managing the enterprise. They can learn the PDCA cycle by applying it to their own education, creating something new, rather than echoing the experiences of others.

In a typical scenario, the Plan phase includes assessment of your own learning styles (usually based on past failures and successes), survey of available resources (consultants, seminars, industry resources), and a decision on how and when to initiate your educational activities. The Plan phase may contain one or more PDCA loops within it, as options are tested by individuals or groups within the leadership. If the introduction of TQM is the personal transformational concept of a powerful chief executive, these steps will be stylistically different from an introduction that comes from a group decision by an executive team, but will have the same elements of assessment, evaluation, and decision.

FIGURE 1   *Plan-Do-Check-Act Cycle*

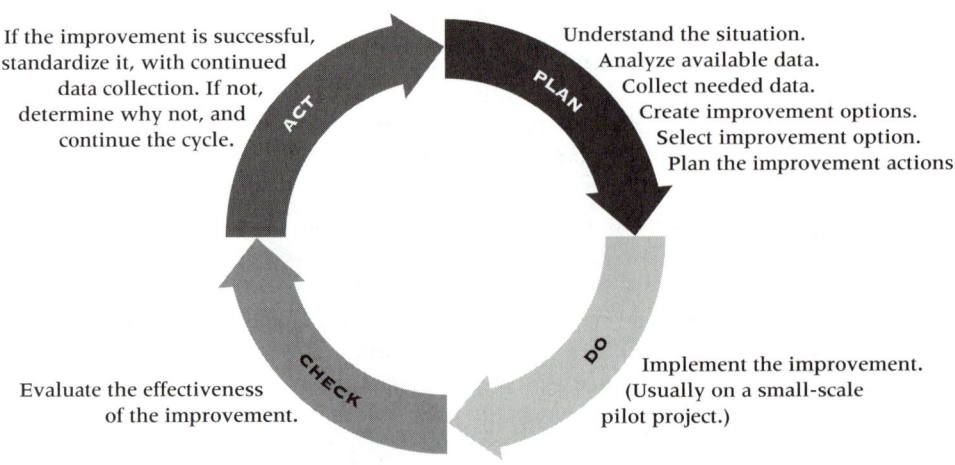

The Do phase is initial education, in any of the styles, or any mix of the styles noted previously. This ranges from one action, such as the chief executive reading a book, to lengthy meetings of the leadership with visiting experts to whole-company meetings. The simple acquisition of knowledge of the business occurs in many ways. Examples abound:

- Discovery that the Customer Service Department at a medical laboratory does *no* customer service—it only fixes mistakes made in doctors' offices or at the lab.
- Learning that no one in an aerospace engineering department had ever viewed the manufacturing group as a customer, to whom they had obligations.
- Learning that the employees of a high-technology firm that superficially prizes technical achievement overall distrust management, think problems are solved based on hierarchy (not on data), and know that incomplete products are frequently shipped to customers in order to book sales by the end of the month. Repair visits that cost more than the product (not just more than the profit!) are then scheduled in later months.
- Discovery that a city government was planning a new airport based on interviews with airline passengers (the ultimate customers) but had no data at all from the airlines, car rental companies, food vendors, and other businesses that would work in the airport.

The Check phase is often skipped when people are new to TQM and new to the structured PDCA thinking in particular. In Check, the leadership needs to ask if the education was effective. (You "planned" it and "did" it; was it any use?) The most stressing part of Check is establishing criteria for evaluating your own learning—at what stage will you review mastery of content (simple testing) and at what stage will you look at the effect on the way you run the business (return on your investment in total quality management)?

Act flows relatively easily from Check; if the education and training helps, do more of it. If it does not, find out why and change the style or method so that it will help.

The executive team's learning *about* learning at this stage can be its own best lesson. If you have been a Do-Do-Do organization, or a Plan-Plan-Plan how to write a plan-organization, then Plan-Do-Check-Act will be a major cultural change. If you have been an actively learning organization, Plan-Do-Check-Act will be natural. This will be part of your learning about how to change yourselves and your organization.

You may have difficulty generating these insights within your executive group. Many organizations use external consultants throughout their TQM transformation for guidance in managing change, in creating and delivering training, and in maintaining the flow of learning. The consultant conducts or assists the executives with the "check-act" phases, as they learn to do it themselves, and as they learn the complete Plan-Do-Check-Act cycle as a natural part of their working style.

The benefits of working with consultants are in gaining outside perspective on your organization. Consultants bring cumulative lessons learned from other organizations, both in your industry and outside, depending on the range of the consultant's practice. The consultant brings an immunity to company politics, which can lead to objective advice and training in sensitive areas.

A recent experience of the author's can illustrate this:

EXAMPLE:

I had my first 4-day experience with the company, conducting an assessment of what they had already done to initiate TQM, and working with the executive group to create an implementation plan. At the end of the last day, I reemphasized PDCA and asked for C and A (actions we would each do before the next meeting so we could Plan an effective session).

The CEO started the Check by saying that he had gotten great value by how *uncomfortable* my questions made him, since most insiders are reluctant to ask those questions. Then he turned to the other executives and asked if they were *comfortable* working with me, and wanted to continue. They realized within a few moments that he valued both their sense of comfort and his own, that his discomfort was stimulus to learning, and that this was valuable insight into their own culture.

Drawbacks exist as well as benefits. If you have engaged a consultant to implement a "TQM package" and do not do the work to discover how to make total quality function in *your* culture, for the benefit of *your* customers, then you may have short-term benefits (lots of problem-solving teams are typical, and they will solve some important problems), but you will not create a sustained change in your organization's way of working.

When PDCA is applied by the leadership to their own education, the subject matter of executive education in TQM blends smoothly into the decisions that must be made to implement TQM throughout the organization. Whenever "Check" shows that you need to know more to make TQM effective, you will "Act" to get what you need.

Executive groups in North America are impatient with theoretical discussions that do not have practical examples that they can immediately apply to their own situation. The typical format for executive education that is acceptable in this impatient environment is workshop-style consulting sessions. A concept is taught when (*only* when) the leadership group needs to apply it to their organization. The drawback of this approach is that the leadership is dependent on the consultant to judge what they need, and when they need it. The Japanese saying "when the student is ready, the teacher will arise" suggests that this is true in other cultures as well.

It may be necessary to distinguish between training and action—during a meeting you will hear the question, "Is this practice or are we really committed to the decision that we make?", particularly if the participants do not have all the data needed to *make* a decision in the meeting, and they are learning a decision-making technique.

Regardless of whether the organization is using Crosby's 16 step implementation, or Creech's 5, or GOAL/QPC's 10 elements of TQM implementation (or any of the others proposed as frameworks for planning by Juran, Berry, Harrington, or Hinton, among others), the CEO must make certain decisions, and the executive leadership will have to make decisions about how, when, by whom, and with what resources TQM will be introduced into the organization.

You will further decide how the introduction will be evaluated and modified, and how, when, and with what resources to move from introductory to organization-wide TQM. In other words, you apply Plan-Do-Check-Act to the process of introducing TQM.

This implementation plan is the basic process of leadership education. The leaders need to know the technical side of TQM to be able to understand how it will be used and how it will change your way of doing business. You need to understand the human side of TQM to understand the change process, the time it takes, and the dynamics of change in the organization, so that you can anticipate and manage the structural, logistical, and social changes that will be needed to support the change to TQM.

For example, if your reward system is now based on individual supervisors assessing the work of individuals as observed by the supervisor, how will you have to change when you move to a team environment where the value of work is measured by its usefulness to customers? If you now work in functional departments (Finance, Administration, Purchasing, Accounting, Engineering, Sales, Marketing, Manufacturing, Distribution, and so on or Nursing, Rehabilitation, Laboratory, Surgery, Emergency, and so on), what changes will be needed when you move to management of customer-focused processes? If information access is now limited, what will change (philosophy but also hardware and software) to get information to whoever needs it whenever they need it because employees need information to help customers *now?*

The quality initiative can stall if the leadership tries to understand the whole scope of TQM, to anticipate all the changes, and to put all the new structures in place at the start. This is so much simultaneous effort that no actual change in *how* people work takes place—they are so busy preparing for TQM that they do not start practicing TQM! Generally, it is best to start with basic principles and enable the leadership to apply those principles to their own work (especially the work of implementation), actively practicing PDCA so that what they learn by doing is applied to the next stage of planning.

An illustration is provided by the president of a technology company. In the opening stages of TQM education, he and his executive team learned about identification of customers and processes. They then visited their customers for several months. Instead of attending routine executive conferences, they asked to see their product in use in the customers' environment and to see all of their products in use (not just the technical product, but their invoices, packaging, instruction manuals).

"The customers told us time and again that we were lucky that our technical product was so good, because they hated doing business with us, and only bought from us because our competition was behind us technically. The customers had great difficulty installing and maintaining the product in their systems. Our paperwork was always wrong. They had a long list of complaints.

Because we had always judged success by sales, we had never known that customers hated dealing with us. Our rewards had always favored adding technical sophistication to our products. We had never paid attention to the impact using our product and dealing with our business systems have on customers."

When the executives shared their findings, they had no trouble with motivation for change. They did not embrace TQM because a consultant told them it was right, or because it was the latest management buzzword, but because it helped them to help their customers and achieve competitive advantage in the entire relationship with their customers, rather than the narrow technical advantage they had before.

The next phase for the executive team was to start a series of pilot projects, the Do phase of PDCA, to improve some of the processes that were causing the worst impact on customers. The executives learned the process analysis and problem-solving methods that the project teams used, so that they could participate where appropriate, review the work of the teams, and remove any institutional barriers to the success of the teams.

With this approach the *work* of the company becomes the education of the leadership in TQM. The amount of classroom time was small, a few days initially on the general concepts of TQM, another few days on process analysis and problem solving, but these executives immediately started changing their own work as leaders.

This same technology company tells their stories to others frequently in an effort to bring their whole industry into a TQM mode. Other companies react with shock that the senior executives spent so much personal time in the start-up of TQM. That shock is a measure of a general failure to understand that the way of managing the organization is being changed, so the work of management will change. That change encompasses all work, not just some special TQM meetings.

An outline of the issues that the executive leadership will deal with in TQM implementation is shown in Figure 2. Education and training can be used to start each of these; seminars, books, videos, consultants, and trainers can show the leaders how other companies have struggled with the same problems.

If executive education has similar style and content to that offered all employees in the organization, there will be *some* benefit. The executives will typically learn methods of process analysis, problem solving, understanding variation, techniques for teamwork, and later policy deployment (hoshin management), as well as other special topics that apply in their area of responsibility (quality function deployment, voice of the customer, statistical process control, business system reengineering, just-in-time, and so on). But if you do not learn within the context of your responsibility for creating and managing the transition to Total Quality Management, you will see TQM only as a collection of tools, try to delegate responsibility to middle managers, and join the ranks of company leaders that are disappointed that they have not realized the promise of TQM.

What can be done if an organization has fallen into the trap of training everybody in the tools of TQM, but has not practiced the disciplines and philosophies of TQM at the leadership level? *Start!* If thorough, complete, data-driven, process-oriented Plan-Do-Check-Act is applied to the entire body of work of the leadership, the organization *will* move from management to Total Quality Management, for the benefit of its customers, employees, and the entire society.

FIGURE 2   *Content of Executive Education*

Topics will be covered over 1–2 years, as needed to create and manage the transformation.

1. **Technical knowledge of TQM**
    1.1. Process analysis
    1.2. Problem solving/process improvement (sometimes called *The Quality Improvement Story*; PDCA)
    1.3. Understanding variation, basic statistics
    1.4. Teams and teamwork, how to be a team participant, role of senior management in support of teams
    1.5. The elements of TQM: combining 1.1 through 1.4 for daily management, policy deployment, and cross-functional management
    1.6. Creating and managing the implementation plan; selecting, modifying, and using a model (Applying PDCA to their own work)

2. **Specific issues for their business** (Depending on the level of sophistication of the executive team, this may or may not be necessary. Any absent elements need to be in place before attempting company-wide deployment of TQM. They are frequently developed concurrently with the pilot project introductory phase of learning about TQM.)

    2.1. Elements of strategic planning—Mission, vision, values, long- and short-term business plans and implementation plans
    2.2. Customer knowledge
    2.3. Supplier relationships
    2.4. Competitor situation
    2.5. Employee relationships, labor relations
    2.6. Financial and operational measures

3. **Organizational culture**
    3.1. Trust
    3.2. Problem-solving style
    3.3. Past change efforts
    3.4. Leadership and management

4. **Why change? Why TQM?**
    4.1. Benefits of TQM
    4.2. Costs and risks of TQM
    4.3. Formulation of policy
    4.4. Creation of Steering Committee
    4.4.1. Role of Steering Committee
    4.4.2. Relationship with existing management structures

5. **Developing an implementation plan**
    5.1. Options, risks, benefits, cultural fit

FIGURE 2	*Content of Executive Education (Continued)*

5.1.1.   Pilot projects, learn by doing

5.1.2.   Simultaneous change

5.2.   Self-assessment as part of the implementation plan

5.2.1.   Malcolm Baldrige National Quality Award Criteria (or state awards, or similar awards in other countries)

5.2.2.   Organization-specific review criteria

5.2.3.   Using the review as an element of management TQM education

5.3.   Staffing and other resources (for any of the options)

5.3.1.   Training: Cultural and technical issues

5.3.1.1.   By trainers (internal or external)

5.3.1.2.   Cascade, by managers and colleagues

5.3.2   Applying training

5.3.2.1.   Special projects

5.3.2.2.   Daily management

5.4.   Planning for continuing education

5.4.1.   Overview of advanced topics (designed experiments, robust design, JIT, 5S, benchmarking, compensation system change, quality function deployment, policy deployment, and so on)

5.4.2.   Recognizing when advanced topics are needed

REFERENCES

Survey of TQM Concepts and Extensive References

Costin, Harry. *Readings in Total Quality Management.* Fort Worth: Harcourt Brace College Publishers, 1994.

Implementation

Berry, Thomas H. *Managing the Total Quality Transformation.* New York: McGraw Hill, 1991.

Byham, William C. *Zapp! The Lightning of Empowerment: How to Improve Quality, Productivity, and Employee Satisfaction.* New York, Harmony Books, 1988.

Creech, Bill. *The Five Pillars of TQM.* New York: Penguin Books, 1994.

Harrington, H. James. *The Improvement Process: How America's Leading Companies Improve Quality.* New York: McGraw Hill, 1987.

Hinton, Tom, and Winny Schaeffer. *Customer-Focused Quality: What to Do on Monday Morning.* New York: Prentice Hall, 1994.

Juran, J.M. *Juran on Quality by Design.* New York: The Free Press, 1992.

Peters, Tom. *Liberation Management.* New York: Knopf, 1992; *Thriving on Chaos.* New York: Harper & Row, 1987; and *The Tom Peters Seminar: Crazy Times Call for Crazy Organizations.* New York: Random House, 1994.

Scherkenbach, William W. *Deming's Road to Continual Improvement.* Knoxville, TN: SPC Press, 1991.

Xerox Quality Solutions. *A World of Quality: The Timeless Passport.* Milwaukee: ASQC Quality Press, 1993.

Special Topics

Camp, Robert C. *Benchmarking.* Milwaukee: ASQC Quality Press, 1989.

Katzenbach, Jon R. and Douglas K. Smith. *The Wisdom of Teams.* Boston: Harvard Business School Press, 1993.

Managing across the Organization: Lateral Management

By John W. Moran

Organizations today are exploring many options to make themselves agile and "boarderless,"[1] in order to take advantage of opportunities for increasing customer satisfaction, growth, and profitability. Many good opportunities are abandoned each year because of the difficulty in managing complex organizational relationships.

In the near future, organizational structure will be very lean and agile. It will be composed of three types of management:

• Strategic Management
• Lateral Management
• Daily Management

This structure will allow the organization to act on each good opportunity to improve internal and external relationships and to please its customers. This structure reduces unnecessary complexity and promotes cooperation and collaboration.

The relative degree of agility in American industry can be termed organizational robustness—the gradual change toward a flat and seamless organization. Many executives agree with the need to streamline and simplify their organizations, but relatively few companies are making the dramatic structural changes required to make organizational robustness a reality.

Companies are continuing to give priority to employee involvement and empowerment as the number of job classifications and organizational levels shrinks dramatically. Eventually, the steady and predictable path of promotion up a hierarchical organization will become obsolete, replaced by a horizontal, fast-track structure that provides valued employees an array of work experiences and more free time to acquire new skills. As companies eliminate their unnecessary activities, they will be able to restructure their organizations into boundary-less customer pools that resemble those of professional services firms. They will also continue to make investments in their own people to increase the organization's competency. One might think, "This all sounds great, but what does it look like and how does it work?"

In the agile organization, there is one single box on the organization chart called the *customer success function*. This function is comprised of critical customer processes (amoebae plots), or fractals of resources assembled on demand to increase customer value. Critical customer processes are comprised of physical and business processes that generate activity in the organization. We often describe these structures as dynamic antibodies (a great noun for organizations) that are redeployed to capitalize on market opportunities or to destroy waste. In practice, this redeployment process might resemble a 1960s lava light moving 100 miles per hour! This kind of structure may seem fragmented and unstructured. However, it is extremely agile, structured, and very disciplined at creating customer success.

THE STRUCTURE

Strategic management is one of the permanent structures in the organization that works to develop the strategic goals of the organization, deploying them to all the daily management work units and reviewing the progress on meeting these goals. Strategic management develops three types of goals:

• Efficiency goals—related to resource utilization
• Effectiveness goals—related to customer commitment
• Agility goals—related to responsiveness to change

Strategic management deploys efficiency and effectiveness goals to the daily management structure that has control over the means to accomplish changes in these goals. Flexibility goals are deployed to the lateral management structure that has the ability and resources to work across the organization, initiating changes to accomplish "agility" goals. Lateral managers help to define the common areas between functional daily managers, in order to improve the flexibility and responsiveness of the organization.

Strategic management focuses on keeping the agile organization on the right course. It plans major shifts in emphasis, tracks the marketplace's and customer's shifting needs and expectations, and plans major interventions to remain a viable entity in the global marketplace. Strategic managers must work on common problems that cause obstacles in the rest of the organization. Strategic managers must help align routine work with the efficiency and effectiveness goals. Strategic managers must also develop and put in place the appropriate organizational structure that will help to accomplish the strategic goals. If not, stress will occur within the organization, causing wasted hours and unsatisfactory goods and services.

The strategic management structure must help the organization to understand that financial organizational goals are not mutually exclusive. The reward system can align financial goals with organizational goals. For example, one organization operates a gain-sharing program that rewards an employee $1,200 for achieving financial goals, but only $100 for achieving customer satisfaction goals. Employees in this organization do not see the connection between customer satisfaction, increased sales and loyalty, and the achievement of very short-term financial goals. Customers are second-class citizens in this organization.

In an agile organization, strategic management is the external focus. The members of the strategic management team spend their time and energy on planning the future and monitoring the external environment. Strategic managers do not become involved with the day-to-day or micromanagement issues. However, they do insure that the daily management of the organization is aligned to both present and future needs of the organization.

Lateral management is a temporary structure in the organization that focuses on the achievement of corporate-wide agility goals and objectives. This form of management is virtual. It is formed as needed to accomplish important boundary-breaking and breakthrough solutions to organization-wide needs. This type of management structure is in the total reengineering business. It works on the system to change the culture, in order to accomplish the "whats" that help achieve ongoing operational goals. Lateral good management focuses on the "hows" that make the "whats" happen.

Lateral management assignments will become more attractive to those in the organization, since they will be the new route to promotions. Today middle management jobs are disappearing at an exponential rate as organizations attempt to become lean and profitable. Lateral management assignments will provide the fast trackers in the organization an opportunity to learn about the complexity of their organization, as well as the sense of feeling promoted and valued. This is an important way to build a person's self-esteem and loyalty to the organization. Lateral management assignments, even though temporary, will broaden daily managers into strategic managers over time.

Daily management is a permanent structure in the organization that focuses on the routine work that accomplishes the functions that transform inputs into needed and value-added customer products and services. Daily managers focus the ongoing work units on continuous improvement of the routine work processes. Continuous improvement is incremental improvement and is part of the fabric of the way daily work is performed in an agile organization.

Daily management is composed of functional management and the majority of the organization's associates. Daily management, concerned with the effectiveness and efficiency goals, is internally focused but ready to change as the organization moves forward.

Lateral management, on the other hand, can be described as follows:

• An activity based on interdivisional cooperation
• A horizontal integration process that helps an organization achieve efficient, organization-wide flexibility goals
• An organizational barrier-breaking approach that reduces organizational layering

Lateral management affects the organization in the following ways:

• Expands the scope of strategic activities and actions
• Deploys some of top management's functions
• Changes the culture of the organization
• Expands empowerment
• Defines the common ground between functional units to facilitate smoothly the flow of horizontal work

Lateral relationships are complex because the exercise of power and the authority to maintain and protect the vertical boundaries of turf are constantly working against it. Reward structures also complicate smooth lateral relationships since individual performance is more prized than cooperation and teamwork.

Today we force these lateral or cross-functional relationships by using executive power and authority. These forced lateral relationships are often based on urgency or survival and produce short-term results with disastrous long-term consequences.

An agile organization has learned through experience that the old approach of looking for culprits and punishing them for problems is not effective. Major problems are better approached in a lateral manner since the organization's memory tells those in authority that a lateral alliance is an effective way to solve major problems since innovation happens quicker, change is accomplished faster, implementation is smoother, and ownership is widespread.

In an agile organization, decision makers charged with managing change that is complex do not go it alone. They become effective influencers. They seek out those with the useful ideas and knowledge in the organization. They seek colleagues' ideas and involvement and reach a consensus with different points of view.

Lateral management decision makers have four major responsibilities in any lateral management alliance they lead:

- Define purpose and goals
- Create an atmosphere for new behavior
- Develop knowledge and learning
- Establish accountability and control
- Document and review progress on a regular basis

Figure 1 shows the complexity of a lateral manager's job.

Lateral managers are alliance builders who influence others in the organization to work together as a team to accomplish organizational-wide goals and objectives. Lateral managers have to create the right atmosphere in order to accomplish their purpose. Lateral managers have to balance the needs of the lateral team with the needs of the organization. Lateral managers work with team members who come from different sections of the organization with different cultures: they take the best of similarities and differences. Figure 2 shows the four major purposes they must balance to accomplish the team's purpose.

In order to develop a successful lateral team, managers need to use the plan described in the following outline.

I. Define
   A. Purpose
      1. Define the reason for the existence of the lateral team
      2. State the benefit ratio for this project
   B. Goals
      1. State what is expected of this lateral management team
      2. Define the boundaries of the project
      3. Detail the expectations of management
   C. Roles

FIGURE 1 *Complexity of a Lateral Manager's Job*

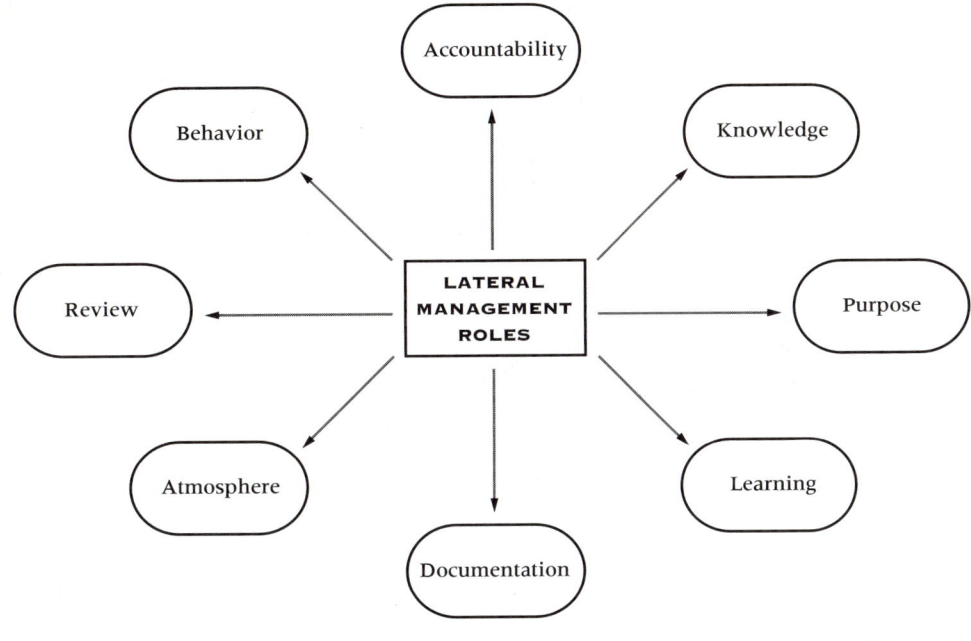

1. Management must define the structure of lateral teams
2. Management must define the general roles of each position on a lateral management team
3. Management must define its role
D. Commitment—management questions
   1. How will management show commitment?
   2. How will we reward lateral teams?

FIGURE 2 *Purposes of Lateral Management*

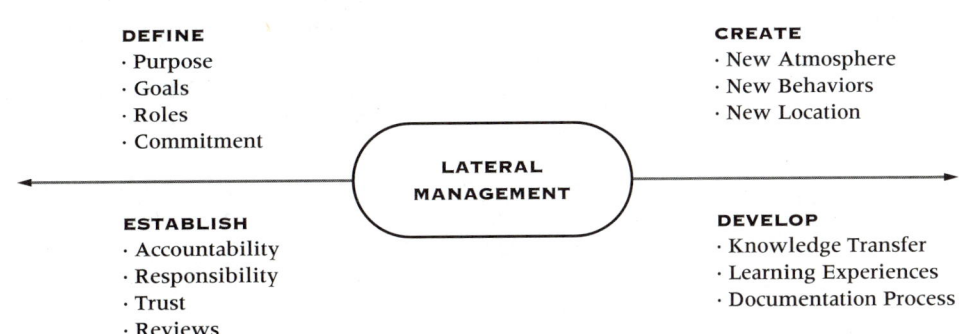

3. How will we support lateral teams?
4. How much empowerment will we sanction?

II. Create

A. New atmosphere
1. Trust
2. Truthful
3. Cooperative
4. Competence
5. Reduce confusion
6. Create enthusiasm
7. Humility
8. Ownership
9. Stress-free
10. Open and collaborative
11. Noncompetitive
12. Clear focus—purpose
13. Nonnegotiating—no trading favors
14. Win/win situations
15. Sense of urgency—importance of the project or program—high organization priority
16. Widespread involvement of the organization—honestly seeks inputs from a wide section of the organization

B. New behaviors
1. Sense of purpose
2. Surface hidden conflicts
3. Focus on process (root cause) not people
4. Supportive of peers
5. Jointly define roles, processes, relationships, and expected results
6. Cooperation rather than competition
7. Keep promises
8. Follow through on commitments
9. Admit errors
10. Use influence rather than power and authority
11. Free to express ideas

C. New location
1. Establish a co-location for the lateral management team
2. Eliminate functional barriers by moving team members to a common location
3. Co-location allows for a free-flowing interaction that builds trust
4. Co-location helps to create interdependencies—we need each other to survive
5. Co-location increases productivity—no need for meetings to pull the team together—we are together all the time
6. Co-location contributes to the trust-building process
7. Co-location contributes to a smooth information flow

III. Establish

A. Accountability

      1. Set group goals (not individual)
      2. Communicate needs clearly
      3. Set group structure
      4. Shared responsibility for achievement
      5. Develop time lines
      6. Subgoals achievement
   B. Responsibility
      1. Define who is the lateral team leader
      2. Define the lateral team leader's roles and responsibilities
      3. Define the later team members' roles and responsibilities
   C. Trust
      1. Trust is the key ingredient to a smoothly functioning lateral team
      2. Trust cannot be decreed—it must develop
      3. Management must supply the necessary environment and support for the development of trust
      4. Trust is a fragile commodity—easily broken and difficult to rebuild
      5. Trust development is a key responsibility of the lateral team leader
   D. Reviews for objective self-evaluation
      1. How are we doing as a lateral team?
      2. How are we doing on our task?
      3. How do others perceive us as a team?
      4. How are we exercising our empowerment?
      5. What has worked well? Why?
      6. What have been our failures? Why?
      7. How can we transfer our reflections to other lateral teams?
IV. Develop
   A. Knowledge to transfer
      1. Integrate alliance members with different perspectives
      2. Integrate alliance members with different demonstrated competencies
      3. Common consensus decision-making process to integrate alliance members with different decision-making skills
      4. Alliance members educate one another
      5. Why we use lateral teams—innovation happens faster—training on innovation
      6. How to make collaboration work
      7. Creative ways to innovate—new tools
   B. Learning experiences
      1. Always interested in learning
      2. Always open to learning
      3. Learn from our own and other teams' mistakes
      4. Learn from one another
      5. Learn from others outside our group
      6. Learn a common problem-solving methodology
      7. Learn consensus decision making
      8. Learn communication skills
   C. Documentation process
      1. Understand processes we are working on

2. Understand our cross-functional management process
3. Understand our successes and failures
4. Understand our progress to our goal
5. Understand the customer needs and wants
6. Understand our needs and wants

Lateral management is the change process. Lateral managers are rotated through this management structure to receive a broadening view of the organization and to gain the skills of influencing without authority.

Lateral managers focus on issues of flexibility that create a competitive organization. Typical issues for analysis are listed in Figure 3.

A recent survey[2] reported that the top issue that could improve competitiveness is customer service, while the main barrier to growth is regulatory requirements. Both of these issues can be handled efficiently in a lateral management structure, since they are company-wide in scope.

The first of these lateral management structures has shown up in the automotive industry as platform teams. Chrysler used the platform team approach to develop the Viper sports car in just 3 years.

A recent analysis of Deming Prize winners in Japan[3] showed that the main results after the introduction of cross-functional, or lateral, management were as follows:

- Strengthened cooperation between divisions
- Reduction of process defects and defect losses
- Expansion and improved sales of new products
- Increases in net sales, numbers of products, and number of customers
- Reduction of claims and customer inconveniences

FIGURE 3 *Typical Issues for Lateral Management*

COMPETITIVENESS	GROWTH
• Customer Service	• Regulatory Compliance
• Organization Excellence	• International Competitiveness
• Technological Innovation	• Marketing Capability
• New Product Development	• Organizational Barriers
• Time to Manufacture	• Overhead
• Time to Market	• Health Care Cost
• Strategic Partnerships	

The lateral management structure is a temporary alliance that is built and nurtured to achieve its stated purpose and then is disbanded. Lateral managers then return to a position in either of the two permanent paths of the organization: strategic management or daily management. The permanency of the strategic management and daily management structures is usually measured in terms of years. Strategic management and daily management are semipermanent in that they can be changed or modified as an organization's needs and objectives change.

In order to accomplish this integrated alliance building, a lateral manager may employ a lateral flow chart to show the interrelationships of the various functions being represented on the lateral team.

An agile organization must not become an extended bureaucracy but instead should be flexible, responding quickly to a changing market environment and/or customer. A key to accomplishing this flexible but fluid organization is lateral management.

LATERAL MANAGEMENT SUMMARY

1. Lateral management teams are formed for the purpose of managing an issue critical to the success of the organization across the various functions and business units of the company. Secondarily, lateral management helps to create broader perspectives for future general managers.

2. Lateral management teams are led by a member of senior management and comprised of management committee members. Each lateral management team reports to the management committee. Each lateral team has a facilitator and requires staff support from related functions. For example, to prepare for its monthly meeting, a lateral team on customer satisfaction may require some information from customer relations or marketing.

3. Lateral management teams can have permanent full-time members or can be composed of members who are part-time and meet 3 to 4 hours weekly. It is best if the members are full-time and permanent, since they will devote their full time and energy to important company-wide goals. If the goal is really important to the future of the organization, permanent full-time members are necessary.

4. Lateral management teams can form process improvement teams from time to time as needed. These are not permanent teams, and in general will be led by a member of the lateral management team. When issues are very technical or beyond the expertise of the team, a leader who is not on the lateral management team may be chosen. Members of the process improvement team will come from the functions most affected by the targeted process.

5. Lateral management teams realize that primary responsibility for implementation of the cross-functional goals lies with the daily management structure. Their job is therefore to recommend and monitor progress through the management committee and departmental objectives.

6. Lateral management teams recommend that certain activities be filtered down through the organization and will monitor progress and report to the management committee from a company-wide point of view. Lateral management teams recommend overall policy changes and ways to remove obstacles to the process.

7. Lateral management teams may also involve themselves in the management review process so that company-wide issues are adequately broached and discussed.

8. The key focus of a lateral team leader is the building of trust in the alliance he or she is leading. Trust building is a task that requires an enormous amount of time and energy of a lateral team leader. Trust is not the same as trading favors, utilizing past relationships, or calling in a debt that is due. Trust is more than just being honest.

   Trust is a process of being able to depend on other team members for help, support, knowledge, companionship, and friendship. It is a bond that develops around mutual supportiveness. This bond is very fragile and, if broken, is difficult to repair. A lateral team leader must focus on six key areas in building trust in a collaborative atmosphere. He or she must spend time and energy to build the team's commitment to the six key areas. These six key areas are defined as follows:

   Attitude—Lateral team members exhibit an internal and external noncompetitive attitude toward one another in all interactions. This noncompetitive attitude helps to improve the free flow of information vital to learning about the project assigned and in making lasting changes.

   Collaboration—Lateral team members freely and willingly share their skills and expertise with one another and with those outside the team.

   Joint Accountability—Lateral team members understand that this is a joint venture and not a solo flight. There is no individual glory or blame in this process. We need one another to complete our assignment and survive.

   Acknowledgment—Lateral team members must acknowledge errors or mistakes freely, as well as admit uncertainties. There can be no bluffing in a lateral team environment.

   Commitment—Lateral team members must be personally committed to this process and believe in teamwork. There is no place for hidden agendas. Egos cannot be indulged.

   Cooperation—Lateral team members must follow through on their promises, assignments, or duties. Team members were selected because they are the best.

   Lateral team leaders have to nurture quickly this trust-building process since lateral projects are virtual and finite. To expedite this process, the lateral team leader should start by creating a set of shared values with the team members based on the six key areas defined previously. It is essential for the lateral team leader to seek an agreement from the team on how they will work consciously to honor the agreements on the shared values. These agreements become the "Hows" of accomplishing the "Whats" that have been assigned.

   The lateral team leader must audit how the team is doing on the agreements and understand how well the lateral team is working together. At regular intervals, the team leader and the team should discuss honestly their progress toward their goals and commitments. The lateral team leader can rate each one of the six categories individually. Each score should include a rationale to be discussed with the team. For each low score, a plan of action should be drafted to deal with the issues raised and improve the score quickly.

Individual as well as group responsibilities may be assigned to make the changes required. This process of checking on agreements gives the lateral team leader the pulse of the team and allows for timely intervention. As the team matures, this process can be more of an audit to insure the team is functioning appropriately.

9. Being part of lateral management is a risk for team members since there are many points of potential failure. Senior management must constantly be in touch with lateral management teams to ensure that they are functioning smoothly. Senior management must help lateral teams by removing obstacles and by providing needed resources. Lateral management teams will not survive unless they are nurtured.

10. Successful lateral management requires behavioral changes as well as organizational changes. Organizational changes can be done very quickly, but behavioral changes take time and nurturing. Lateral management helps to break down the traditional, functional "stovepipe" barriers that impede smooth-flowing, collaborative work in the organization. If the company does not change, the mentality and associated behaviors of those involved will result in the creation of horizontal dictators instead of vertical chimney dictators.

Organizations have experimented with the concept of lateral management at the daily work level by organizing around processes without any attention to the behavior changes that are needed by those involved. These organizations have been amazed at how fast vertical chimney dictators made the change to horizontal process "czars." These organizations still have the same problems as before but they are now organized differently.

Successful lateral management, at any level in the organization, requires attention to the six key behavioral changes detailed earlier:

- Attitude
- Collaboration
- Joint Accountability
- Acknowledgment
- Commitment
- Cooperation

Attention to these behavioral change areas plus the reward and recognition structure that supports lateral management helps to insure successful change. The process of changing how an organization is run, from authority and control to consensus and collaboration, requires more than just tipping the organization on its side and calling it "lateral management."

NOTES

1. "Boarderless Management," *Business Week,* May 23, 1994, 24–26.
2. "From Debate to Dialogue," Special Advertising Supplement, *Research and Development Magazine,* July 1993.
3. "An Analysis of the Deming Prize Winners: The Importance of Cross-Functional Management in Improving Corporate Health and Character," Kozo Koura, Abstracts of the EOQ '93 World Quality Congress, Helsinki, Finland, June 1993.

Pathway to Leadership: Training Issues for First-Line Supervisors

By Joann DeMott and Paul H. Wang

INTRODUCTION

With the words, "You got the job!", the work life of the new supervisor is changed. With the change of title to "supervisor" or "Coach" or "Team Leader" comes a new peer structure with new relationships to build. There is different work to be done and more responsibilities to assume with increased authority.

Indeed, congratulations are in order, for the path toward formal leadership has begun. Yet the exhilaration of being chosen is often coupled with concerns and questions about the new job ahead. What will the new job be like? Can I do the work? Do I know enough? Can I handle what's expected of me? Will I be good at it? Will my work friends still like me? What am I supposed to do . . . really? With this new authority, will people willingly and actively follow me or simply obey or even subvert me because of my new position?

As the news of the selection spreads, the attitudes of the work team vary. With alarming speed, a promoted worker can be moved by his peers from being "one of us" to being "one of them" where suspicion reigns. Some workers, however, look forward to having someone they know and trust as the new supervisor, hoping to have access to someone working as a catalyst for improvement and innovation. Yet, whether they feel cautious or hopeful, all workers wonder what changes are in store.

CHANGES FOR THE NEW SUPERVISOR

Although shifts in the attitude of peers are rapid, sometimes surprising and often painful, changes in the work itself and the responsibility to be carried cause the greatest anxiety.

Since much of a supervisor's work is accomplished behind the scenes, a new supervisor might not know exactly what to do. In the eyes of many workers, the supervisor's job is too little "doing" and too much "talking about doing." In their opinion, the *real* work is done by those who make the products or provide direct services. The new supervisor must learn what his new work will be and how to effectively set priorities with a new set of variables. He is also expected to do more—that is, he either voluntarily takes on more work because he believes he should or he is given more work because he is paid to do so. Unfortunately, no more hours in the day are issued with the new job, and the supervisor must learn new methods of allocating his time to complete the work.

The new supervisor also has greater responsibility with more authority. She is now responsible for the work of the team as well as orchestrating the effectiveness and productivity of the work processes in her area. She becomes the safety net for the team and is accountable for the work area's contribution to the system. When staff workloads are full, there simply is not anyone left to do extra work. It is the supervisor who must quietly and confidently fill in the gaps as needed.

From the moment the new position is accepted, the new supervisor must begin balancing the propelling forces of her vision as well as the opposing forces of her changing relationships and responsibilities. With acceptance of the supervisor's position must come a commitment to a new learning journey, to obtaining and applying new knowledge, skills, and behaviors that will allow the supervisor to support the operation of the business, as well as her desire to become an organizational leader of people.

TRAINING SUPERVISORS TO BECOME LEADERS

In order to answer the questions, "What knowledge and skills do I need and how am I to behave in order to effectively lead?" the new supervisor will expect and require formal training.

Too often training designed for supervisors, if given at all, is limited to providing information about how supervisory tasks should be done. We may attend a 3-day seminar to learn how to properly authorize time cards and will listen to a trainer talk about problems and issues around Equal Employment Opportunity. We may also find out ways of handling difficult employees since employees who experience new supervisors are expected to be resistant. We are taught to expect staff to test the new supervisor with unproductive behaviors and possibly even subvert the organization during the initial break-in period. What is needed by organizations and is desired by supervisors, however, is a more comprehensive, long-term training series where the knowledge, skills, and behaviors needed to become an organizational team leader are developed.

It is important at this point to define "leader." A portion of the authors' definition is taken from the root word *lead* which is defined as "position at the front: vanguard." Being in front usually means the individual has a high-level position of authority. Regardless of an individual's original source of power—power over resources, expertise, punitive power, official appointment, or charisma—leadership is viewed by the authors of this article as **"a person that others will willingly and actively follow, regardless of his or her relative position of authority."**

A supervisor needs to know how leadership comes about as well as what needs to be learned in the process. Therefore, this article will introduce the reader to a process for the effective development of supervisors as leaders as well as provide suggested content for formal and informal supervisory training and developing a mentoring relationship.

HOW DO LEADERS EMERGE?

What is the process that effectively develops an individual into a leader? What process can we use to earn the respect and, ultimately, the right to be called a leader in the hearts and minds of people?

Figure 1 is a visual map of how leaders emerge over time. The learning process links together formal and informal training and mentoring with the deliberate and conscious application of our accumulated knowledge, skills, and high-performance behaviors.

DIAGRAM COMPONENTS

The personal learning diagram is divided into upper and lower sections.

ABOVE THE DOTTED LINE

The upper section is the continuous process of learning. An individual first identifies the areas in which she needs to learn. If she wants to learn to become a leader, she may be influenced by the direction in which her organization is moving, she may get an idea from something she has read or heard about in a conversation, or she may get advice from someone she admires and trusts.

Next, she seeks out opportunities to learn through formal or informal training or by building a learning relationship with a respected mentor. In her new area of learning, she actively seeks out the knowledge, skills, and behaviors that need to be displayed.

She then deliberately and consciously applies the knowledge, skills, and behaviors in the workplace. By planning an application, consciously doing it, checking to see what happened, and then making adjustments based on the results, learning has begun.

A formal application strategy may be unnecessary for some individuals. Some of us are filled with an internal force—we are intrinsically motivated—that drives our improvement efforts. We seem relentless, trying out new methods, monitoring the results of our actions, and making adjustments for the next application.

Other individuals are not as easily motivated from within. There is a greater desire for external motivators, and a process is needed that can help consciously apply new knowledge, skills, and behaviors to make changes in the workplace. A simple system to deliberately and consciously apply any new learning is described later in the reading.

FIGURE 1 *Pathway to Leadership*

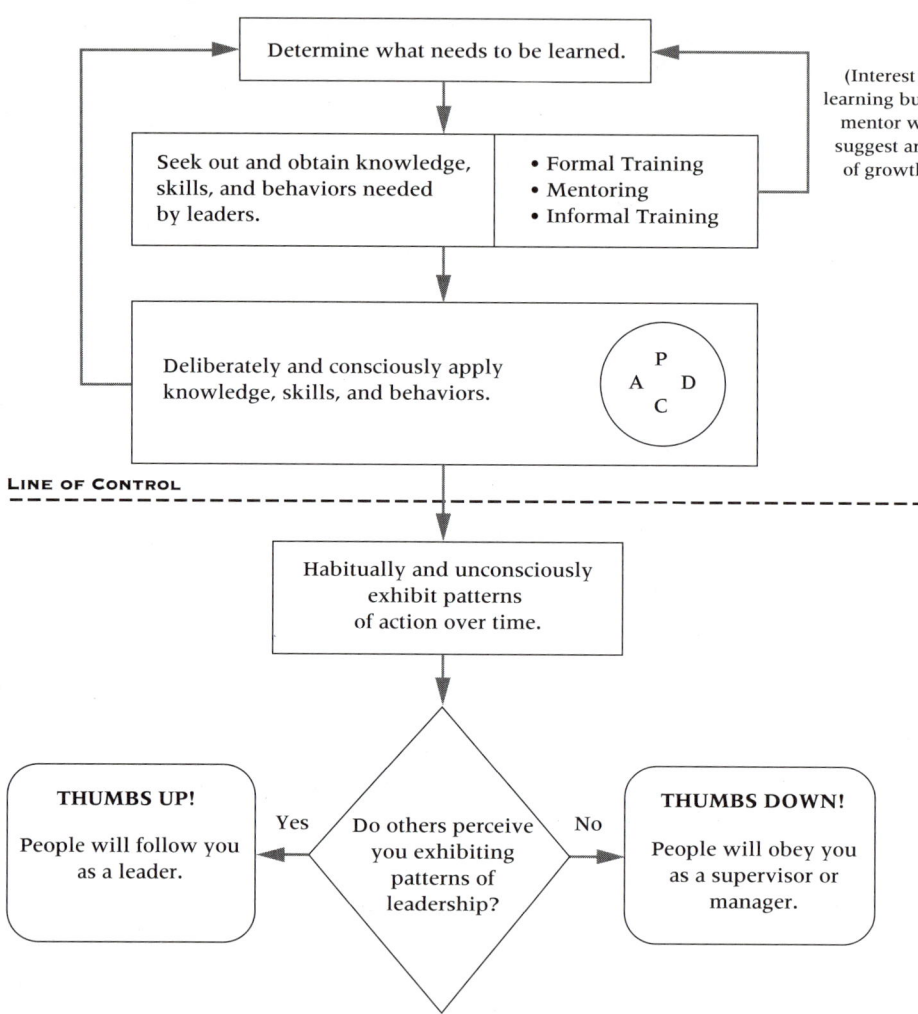

Possible Results:
- increased morale
- interest in the future
- high performance
  as a work unit
- people willing to take risks
- trust of others
- loyalty to leader and work unit
- work unit energized
- open communication
- refreshing work atmosphere
- high levels of learning
- self-directed initiatives
- empowerment

Possible Results:
- authority's efforts are
  subverted
- fear used as a motivator
- dysfunctional unit
- guarded communication
- disregard for others
- apathy
- unit performs at minimum
  levels
- absence of loyalty
- limited growth of staff

Continuous movement through the developmental loop of the upper section is the responsibility of the learner. It is the learner who has control over what is learned and how—or if—it is applied in the workplace. The most satisfied learner self-directs her new areas of development.

Unfortunately, a surprising number of individuals believe that attending a training session, reading a book, or watching a training video qualifies as learning. We hear the words, "I've heard all this stuff before," or "I already know this," or "I took that class 3 years ago." Deliberate and conscious application of the knowledge, skills, and behaviors is not seen as a required part of the learning process for these individuals. Yet the absence of direct, visible application has its consequences in the lower section of the diagram.

BELOW THE DOTTED LINE

A dotted line divides the diagram into upper and lower sections and indicates the separation of ownership between the learner and the rest of the world. It is the lower section of the diagram that is intriguing.

Whether others will treat a supervisor as a leader and choose to willingly follow her is not in the supervisor's direct control, for it is others who watch the supervisor over time and determine whether the person exhibits the desired set of knowledge, skills, and leadership behaviors. Like anything we judge in life, we look for a pattern of behaviors that exhibits those characteristics we desire in someone we choose to follow. Therefore, no person can be a leader by his or her own choice; one is only identified as a leader by others.

We often believe that we can consciously control what people believe about us. We believe that by saying the right words—"I believe in Quality!" or "I believe people are our greatest asset!"—others around us will give us credit for our intentions. We believe that "saying it makes it so," and then are shocked to learn that others perceive us as unapproachable, shallow, or frightening or accuse us of not "walking the talk." In truth, we are not conscious of the patterns we exhibit; they are habitual and unconscious. The consistent application or lack of application of our knowledge, skills, and behaviors creates patterns of character that are clearly seen by others.

Since others identify leadership characteristics and judge how we live those characteristics, each supervisor must understand the definitions used by his work team members, his new peers, and his leaders. These characteristics are most often listed:

"Someone I choose to follow ..."

- is a listener
- is trustworthy
- displays compassion when another stumbles
- can make decisions and follows through
- keeps commitments
- continuously learns
- has vision
- can be trusted

- is knowledgeable
- is skillful
- is honest
- is sincere
- is supportive
- is friendly
- is courteous
- is kind
- is caring
- is a risk taker
- uses common sense
- is fair
- is genuine

As an example, we will choose the accepted leadership trait: trust. Except in extreme cases, trust is not made or broken on single events. One trusting act could be viewed as circumstantial; a nontrusting act could be a simple mistake. In most cases, trust is developed by watching the behaviors of a person over time, through thick and thin, in good times and bad. Judgments are based upon evidence informally collected by both parties; they are based on the aftereffects of personal risks taken between individuals. Time, too, becomes an essential ingredient to leadership, for it is over time that people make judgments about us.

Being perceived as a leader is not necessarily connected to the position one holds within the organization. Even though a person may not literally be in a position of authority, he may be looked to for guidance, strength, and wisdom and be seen as "in front" even though he is not, literally, in front. This seems particularly true in an authoritarian management system. Administrators and managers hold positions of authority and position power, and may, indeed, be obeyed. Invariably, however, individuals without formal authority are seen as the "real" leaders. They have both a great following and substantial positive power within the organization.

We look into areas where these leaders have emerged and listen to staff. "We work hard, and we are happy," they say, which seems too good to be true. We consider these "good areas" to work. Looking deeper, we see that leaders' patterns are perceived to reflect trust, integrity, and honor, and staff are choosing to move with the leaders, not after or in spite of them; staff are happy, performance is good, production is high—indeed, perceptions have created reality.

The pathway to leadership diagram helps to make the learning path clear, and its implications for the supervisor—for all of us—are profound: in every moment, we must choose and display behaviors that, when linked with our growing knowledge and skills, will emerge as consistent patterns of characteristics exhibited by a leader. And it is only over time that a person's interactions with others become a visible and personal tapestry that will inspire others to follow . . . or not.

TRAINING STRATEGIES

Now that we know how our learning is judged by others, let us start the learning journey by explaining three strategies for training: *formal training,* which is most often conducted in a classroom with other learners; *informal training,* which usually occurs on ones own; and *mentoring* as a professional relationship with an experienced, respected, and trusted leader.

STRATEGY #1: FORMAL TRAINING

The purpose of formal training is to accelerate the learning process. Rather than stumble across what needs to be learned, supervisor trainees attend a series of training seminars over time that will prepare the supervisor to perform the responsibilities of his position and work to become an organizational leader. During the series, supervisors obtain knowledge of various theories, tools, and methods; practice new skills and high-performance leadership behaviors; and apply all components through activities in their day-to-day work.

There are many types of formal training, and it is, therefore, important to consciously select the right type with the highest impact for delivery. This is especially true for the adult learner, for we carry our prejudices and old learning habits with us into every formal learning situation.

Those supervisors who have had poor training experiences in the past might have more difficulty learning from the formal training pathway. All instructional strategies, therefore, would be orchestrated to reach the adult learner.

Learning to combine the knowledge, skills, and behaviors of a leader and consistently exhibit patterns of leadership characteristics is a long-term process. The recommended training series would be spread over a 18-month period to allow for learning new materials, developing new skills, and applying them in the work setting.

Instructional staff must be experienced supervisors, serve as leadership mentors, and be seen as consistently exhibiting patterns of leadership. They should be proactive learners who are deliberately and consciously applying their own knowledge, skills, and behaviors in the workplace. They should also be skilled in the use and application of quality and systems thinking tools.

In addition to a formal training manual, a training binder would be kept. All trainee information would be contained in the binder, along with notes, journal entries, handouts, articles, activity records, and other materials collected throughout the training series.

Here are some of the concepts that would drive the designs of formal training seminars:

* Adults come with their own expectations about what should be covered in the training. It is essential, therefore, to generate a list of questions participants expect to be answered. The initial content of the training is then aligned with what the customers expect and want. As the content is expanded to include the knowledge and skills new supervisors will need, a finalized agenda is formed and distributed to participants in advance of the training. Training manuals and background articles should be distributed prior to the training so they can be perused.
* Adults expect to be able to quickly and easily use their new knowledge and skills in their work environment. Therefore, each portion of the training relates

directly to the purpose of the training and can immediately be applied in the workplace. There are no "filler" activities.

- Self-esteem and pleasure are motivators of adults, and active participation in learning is essential to "making it stick." Therefore, learning activities (especially during tools training) are experienced in short segments to bring about fairly quick results. Then, as one tool builds on another, a feeling of completion and achievement increases longer-term satisfaction.
- Adults are not willing to sit for long periods. Therefore, short but frequent breaks are taken throughout the morning and afternoon sessions, and an hour is set aside for lunch.
- Adults bring with them an extensive background of knowledge, experience, training, and work wisdom. Learning is faster when new knowledge is integrated with what is already known. Therefore, participants learn primarily in teams to share and incorporate what they already know with the new material.
- Adults prefer a variety of activities. Therefore, the following is incorporated: verbal presentation, reading, use of visuals, activities in small groups, kinesthetic manipulation of training materials, on-site customer interviews, process demonstrations, and dialogue in large and small groups.

CONTENT OF FORMAL TRAINING: THE NEW ROLES OF THE SUPERVISOR

Formal training is recommended in the following areas:

- Developing effective *facilitating* skills by learning to help groups experience collective thought and coordinating group efforts.
- Learning and implementing proactive *planning* using quality tools and a planning methodology.
- Practicing efficient and innovative methods for *improving* work processes using quality and systems thinking tools.
- Adopting a knowledgeable and supportive partnership within the work team while *sponsoring* functional and cross-functional process redesign teams.
- Learning the art and science of *training* adults in a variety of workplace settings.
- Establishing a rational and compassionate approach to *evaluating* staff's personal and professional performance and helping to orchestrate their growth.

Let us take each of the components and detail the knowledge, skills, and behaviors required to perform as a supervisor who is evolving into a leader.

FORMAL TRAINING IN FACILITATING

Facilitation skills are fast becoming the common denominator among leaders. Organizations now expect those they hire or promote to exhibit a basic level of facilitation skills much as we expect a keyboard operator to perform at a minimum keyboard entry speed. Supervisors in the facilitator role need to learn and practice the techniques used as groups of staff meet together to make decisions, improve processes, solve problems, and plan.

What does a supervisor do as a facilitator in the workplace?

- Listens with interest
- Speaks simply
- Speaks about the system and work processes
- Engages with staff frequently
- Tells the truth
- Asks for the truth
- Designs meeting processes to reach the meeting purpose
- Meets with customers and suppliers in person
- Asks customers what they need, expect, and want from the work unit
- Asks about staff's processes. What's working? What's not?
- Responds to requests, ideas, worries, complaints . . . now
- Visits with staff
- Recognizes the efforts of staff
- Brings out the best in staff
- Operates as the servant of the group without being servile
- Makes the work environment comfortable, if possible

Supervisors must take every opportunity to facilitate meetings and activities to gain experience with individuals and groups. Effective facilitating within the workplace is hard work, and to emerge as a facilitative leader, the knowledge, skills, and behaviors that must be patterned cluster in two major areas: listening and facilitating group process.

LISTENING

The supervisor as facilitator must learn to listen intently. Staff will invariably have concerns, ideas, thoughts, and worries that need to be addressed in the workplace. Without the ability to listen—listen to the words, to the body language, to the intent of an individual—the supervisor will miss important information about the day-to-day work, the thinking of staff, and the work environment.

To establish an effective listening pattern, supervisors must experience listening without visual filters; they must listen to the inflections and the delivery. Yet listening is not done just with the ears. Listening also includes being able to observe the body language and behaviors of another, perceive what the person's behavior might mean, verify with the individual that the supervisor's perception is accurate, and then act. Finally, as a facilitator of groups, the supervisor must listen to the contributions of all participants, remember the major themes, and summarize the statements to help the group reach consensus.

FACILITATING THE GROUP PROCESS

Helping a group to make a decision, develop an implementation plan, or resolve a conflict requires the facilitator to plan a process to be followed during meetings.

Each process will be unique to the group and to the purpose of the meeting, and supervisors must learn to set effective strategies.

Supervisors must continue to learn the essentials of facilitation within the workplace, and suggested training activities are provided in the appendix to this reading to develop and practice some of the needed listening and group process skills needed by the supervisor. Additional topics for conversation and facilitator skill-building, however, include:

- Talking with staff about personal problems
- Moving from "resolving conflict" to "reaching agreement"
- Intervening to improve individual behaviors in meetings
- Using the flipchart and other visual aids to make meetings effective
- Being the servant of the work team without being servile
- Deciding when and how to hold conversations for group problem solving
- Knowing how to create effective interactions with team members
- Understanding how to orchestrate the decision-making process as a group

FORMAL TRAINING IN PLANNING

As the supervisor begins to hone his facilitation skills, learning to plan becomes increasingly important. Actively engaging all levels of workers in the development of plans that will result in a desired future is essential to creating a cooperative, invested work team.

Collective planning occurs within a range of areas, from long-range scheduling of work to creating a unit vision that is aligned with the larger department vision. In collective planning, the supervisor works with others to think, plan, and operate with a more system-wide perspective. The team follows a series of structured steps called a "thinking progression" using various quality and systems thinking tools to set the ultimate objective and then create, coordinate, and implement plans to reach the intended goal. Planning begins with the outcome in mind and then rigorously sets the strategies to get there.

If the working environment has supported collective planning by teams and the new supervisor has come from a pool of trained in-house workers, many tools will already be known and practiced. If, however, engaging the workforce in planning efforts is new, more thorough training in both tools and methodology will be needed.

Formal training for the least experienced supervisor should include the following:

- Systems thinking basics
- Systems archetypes
- The quality management and planning tools
- The step-by-step thinking progression or methodology for planning
- A process for conducting periodic reviews

SYSTEMS THINKING BASICS

Understanding the basics of systems thinking allows the supervisor to see multiple interrelationships within his system and the larger, organizational system. It is essential that the supervisor understand that a system is not simply a set of parts, each acting alone to do their part of the work. Rather, a system is a set of inter-dependent and interrelated parts that work together to create a whole.

This understanding has become increasingly important as we try, at all levels of the organization, to understand how our organizations work and how we fit within them. Supervisors are asked to continuously improve, which cannot be done by focusing their efforts simply on their own areas of responsibility. Supervisors must be trained to think systemically, concentrating on the whole and understanding how each part can best affect the whole.

A "must read" basic text on systems thinking has been written by Draper Kauffman, titled, *Systems 1,* available from Pegasus Communications, Inc., in Cambridge, MA. It is an inexpensive and easy to understand primer in soft cover that should be in every organization's library.

SYSTEMS ARCHETYPES

Systems archetypes are patterns or maps of recurring problems that show the interrelationships of the various parts of the system and how they influence the outcome of the whole. Peter Senge and others from the Massachusetts Institute of Technology, and Innovation Associates (Framingham, MA) have identified ten basic patterns or recurring stories that supervisors may find within their work environment. The ability to draw pictures of recurring problems and identify the points of leverage can be especially helpful to supervisors and their work teams.

The following scenarios, described by Pegasus Communications, Inc., in various issues of their newsletter "The Systems Thinker," (edited by Colleen Lannon-Kim) tend to recur in the workplace. Supervisors will find it helpful to learn to map these situations within the workplace as they develop.

Drifting Goals—In the "Drifting Goals" archetype, a gap between the goal and current reality can be resolved by taking corrective action or lowering the goal. The critical difference is that lowering the goal immediately closes the gap, whereas corrective actions usually take time.

Escalation—In the "Escalation" archetype, one party takes actions that are perceived by the other as a threat. The other party responds in a similar manner, increasing the threat and resulting in even more threatening actions by the first.

Fixes that Fail—In a "fixes that fail" situation, a problem symptom cries out for resolution. A solution is quickly implemented that alleviates the symptom, but the unintended consequences of the "fix" exacerbate the problem. Over time, the problem symptom returns to its previous level or becomes worse.

Growth and Underinvestment—In a "growth and underinvestment" archetype, growth approaches a limit that can be eliminated or pushed into the future if capacity investments are made. Instead, performance standards are lowered to justify underinvestment, leading to lower performance, which further justifies underinvestment.

Limits to Growth—In a "limits to growth" scenario, continued efforts initially lead to improved performance. Over time, however, the system encounters a limit that causes the performance to slow down or even decline, even as efforts continue to rise.

Shifting the Burden—In a "shifting the burden" archetype, a problem is "solved" by applying a symptomatic solution, which diverts attention away from more fundamental solutions.

Success to the Successful—In a "success to the successful" archetype, if Person A is given more resources, he has a higher likelihood of succeeding than Person B (assuming they are equally capable). The initial success justifies devoting more resources to A than B. As B gets fewer resources, her success diminishes, further justifying more resource allocations to A.

Tragedy of the Commons—In a "tragedy of the commons" structure, each person pursues actions that are individually beneficial. If the amount of activity grows too large for the system to support, however, the "commons" becomes overloaded and everyone experiences diminishing benefits.

QUALITY MANAGEMENT AND PLANNING TOOLS

If not already known, it is essential for the new supervisor to become very familiar with several thinking tools and be able to train other team members in their use. These six tools seem to be the most useful:

Affinity Diagram—used when multiple ideas need to be organized. The affinity diagram gathers large amounts of language data and groups them. It also brings unity to the group by accepting and honoring everyone's ideas.

Interrelationship Digraph—used when areas of focus need to be chosen. Is especially helpful to groups who enjoy dialogue and are able to consistently reach consensus through dialogue. It seems particularly useful to nonlinear thinkers. The tool examines cause and effect relationships—that is, "If I do this . . . what else will be affected?"

Spider Diagram—used when multiple variables are to be evaluated on a single page. The spider allows a display of process data for large areas of the organization. The group needs to collect data on current reality and display it for each variable.

Tree Diagram—used when the team needs to think through and develop strategies for accomplishing a goal or objective.

Reponsibility Matrix—used when the team has data about ideas and wants to show the relative strength of relationships between the ideas or variables. This is a tool for displaying the details of the plan such as who will do what, when, where, and at what cost. The responsibility matrix is an application of the matrix diagram.

Process Decision Program Chart—used to anticipate what could go wrong and prepare for it before it happens. This is an exceptionally valuable tool for everyone!

STEP-BY-STEP THINKING PROGRESSION FOR PLANNING

A consistent method for thinking through all aspects of a plan can be very helpful to a supervisor. The thought progression found in Figure 2 can be used.

FIGURE 2 *Planning Teams/Planning Process*

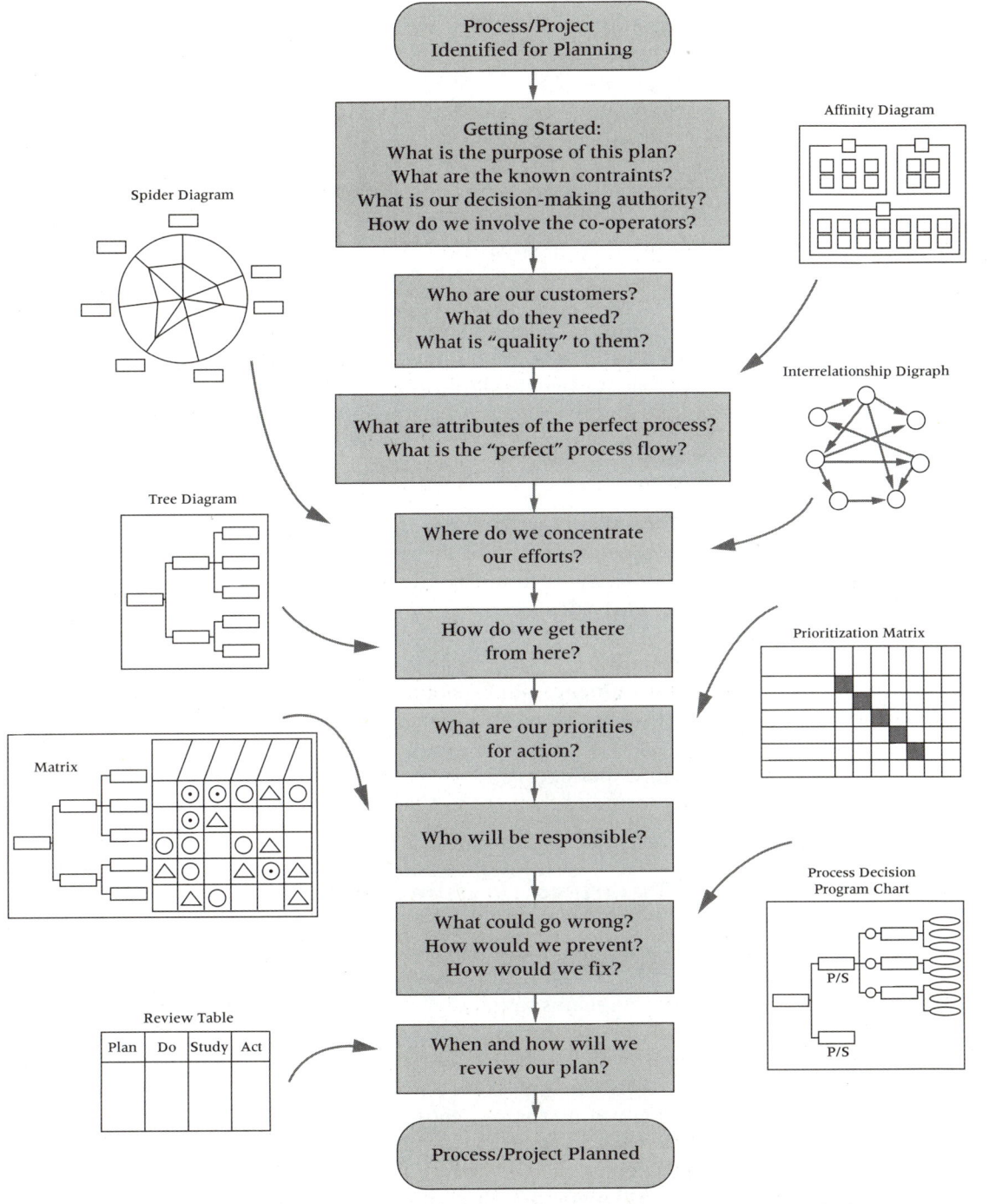

CONDUCTING PERIODIC REVIEWS

The best way to improve one's ability to predict is to compare consistently what was planned with what was accomplished during a given period. The periodic review allows staff to link their actual performance to their plan and make thoughtful adjustments.

As an example, process capability is often overlooked in planning. With the best of intentions, we commit to a completion schedule that our normal system is incapable of meeting; that is, our process actually takes 13 months to complete, yet we routinely commit to 9 months. We then force staff to show their commitment to us by working nights, weekends, and holidays to meet the deadlines. In truth, we create "heroes" and simultaneously drain our resources when we overestimate our process capability. As proactive planners, supervisors should know all process capabilities and select processes for redesign where customers or the market require shorter delivery times.

During periodic reviews, a supportive environment needs to be created. Supervisors and staff are encouraged to discuss what did not work as well as what did. A proactive review allows errors and problems to be brought to the table to be examined and fixed.

CONCLUSION

Good planning—planning that moves the unit or organization to the projected outcome—requires the ability of the supervisor and the work team to accurately predict their capacity to complete the activities and obtain results. Supervisors must ask questions, such as:

- Have we committed to more than we are capable?
- What factors influence our capability?
- How can those factors be anticipated in the future?

The wisdom, experience, and problem-solving abilities of the developing supervisors are reinforced as they are applied in the workplace.

FORMAL TRAINING IN IMPROVING

Continuously improving the organization's system and its various subprocesses are expected activities of a supervisor. Responsibilities include both improving the system by sponsoring teams to redesign work processes, and incrementally improving one's own work processes.

The supervisor must understand the system in which her work team operates as well as the critical processes that make up the system. These processes must be measured to determine their effectiveness; that is, performance measures indicate the efficiency and capability of the processes, while personal customer interviews help to determine the degree to which customers are satisfied with the outcomes. By reviewing the measures, critical processes in need of improvement can be identified. Process redesign teams are then formed to make process break-throughs that will, ultimately, improve the system as a whole.

Developing the skills needed for improvement requires formal training in the following areas:

- Identifying critical processes
- Measuring processes to obtain quantitative and qualitative data
- Selecting processes for improvement
- Applying the process redesign methodology and tools

IDENTIFY CRITICAL PROCESSES

To set priorities for action, the supervisor must identify the critical processes of the system. The supervisor begins by identifying all customers who directly receive the products and/or services of his or her unit. Next, she identifies her high-valued products and services and the indicators of quality for each from the customers' perspective. This requires the supervisor to conduct multiple interviews to deter-mine customer needs in her areas of responsibility. The supervisor then writes cus-tomers' answers to the questions on post-its (one answer per post-it) and clusters them using the affinity diagram process. Finally, critical processes are identified that must operate successfully to optimally satisfy customer indicators of quality for the high-valued products and services.

Customer information can be gathered by various methods. For a more detailed explanation of one method, the reader is referred to "Reading 24: Becoming Customer Oriented," by Mary Lou Roberts, *Readings in Total Quality Management*, Harcourt, Brace & Company, 1994.

MEASURE CRITICAL PROCESSES

Performance measures are set for each critical process and a system to gather data must be designed and set in place. Data may already be collected on the process, but it is usually inadequate. Data tied to indicators should be collected and tracked for a determined period of time. Supervisors can take the following steps to create their measurement system:

Part 1. Establish overall success criteria   Supervisors should refer to their cus-tomer interview data and review the question: "What would bring about your sat-isfaction in this process?" Customers will have identified their definitions of quality, which can be stated as quantifiable measures of their needs and can be charted.

Part 2. Establish process performance measures (PPM)   During the customer interviews, supervisors will have asked customers to use specific words to describe their satisfaction (indicators of quality), offer suggestions for improvement, or issue their complaints about problems in the process. To analyze the language data given by customers, each supervisor will first develop a Pareto chart and arrange the quality indicators by frequency. Using the information from this chart, the supervisor will develop process performance measures for the most frequently mentioned indicators.

For supervisors tempted to measure macro-processes, the task will be more difficult. During the initial design stage, the supervisor should not become paralyzed while trying to identify the "perfect" measure. The task is to look for a place (or places) in the process where patterns are visible and improvement over time can be judged.

Part 3. Develop a data collection system to obtain PPM data   Helpful questions concerning data collection might include:

- *What am I trying to find out?* In my customer interviews, how did customers define quality? What can I collect in my process that affects customers' satisfaction or other performance issues such as financial, employees' satisfaction, and so on?
- *Where in the process can customers' definitions of quality be measured?* Where will the data be collected?
- *What sampling scheme will be used?* Ask if there are important subgroups within the process that should be identified for data collection. Collecting data within separate subgroups will isolate the possible causes of variation, such as different times, different machines, different positions, different operators, or different shifts.
- *How much data should be collected?* Supervisors should be sure to consider resource constraints.
- *When and how long should the data be collected?* How often is the data available to be collected? How long can resources be allocated to collect the data?
- *How will the data be recorded?* When developing the data collection form, supervisors should involve those who will be collecting the data and design the form to make data analysis easy. Be certain to consider the display tool that will be used with the data. PPM data will likely be displayed using a run chart since it tracks data over time. However, data may also be displayed using the histogram, scatterplot, Pareto chart, or control chart, depending on what the trainee wants to know from the process.
- *Who will be responsible for collecting the data?* Supervisors are encouraged to collect the data themselves or request assistance from the work team members closest to the collection points.
- *For the data to be reliably collected, what training needs to occur, for whom, and by whom?*

Part 4. Refine the success criteria   Through the data collection system, the process will communicate its capability, controllability, and/or level of performance. Supervisors must let the process speak. However, it is important to consider what level of performance and customer satisfaction is desirable in order to consider the process successful. What level of performance is good enough to feel satisfied and let the process continue as it is? What level of performance will require a rework of the process design?

If specific process performance levels are identified by the supervisor, they are not to be seen as targets or numerical goals to throw at those who operate the process. They are simply levels of performance that indicate the next actions of the work team. A conversation, with the work team about the performance of the process in relation to the desired level is more important than the numbers.

SELECTING CRITICAL PROCESSES FOR IMPROVEMENT

Once data has been collected on the various critical processes, a single process is chosen to be redesigned. The selection is based on either poor performance or incapability. A Pareto chart can be used to display the levels of performance by process.

REDESIGNING PROCESSES

Unlike day-to-day process improvement, which makes constant incremental improvement, the purpose of process redesign is to make process breakthrough in key areas that need immediate attention and radical change. Processes are pulled apart and completely reconfigured. Process redesign is appropriate for its focus, its immediacy, its thoroughness and the expectation that it will produce radical change. The methodology is similar to organizational "reengineering," although it is confined to a specific process or system and takes into account the knowledge and expertise of the process "co-operators."

Supervisors must be knowledgeable and skilled in the thinking progression of process redesign. Therefore, supervisors must learn and practice the tools and methodology together during training and apply the same procedure with a team in their work area.

Figure 3 is a flow diagram of the process redesign methodology. In brief, the method follows this sequence:

- The supervisor, serving as sponsor, begins by forming a redesign team composed of those who operate the process on a regular basis, called "co-operators." To create a solid foundation for operating as a team, the Team Formation Plan is completed cooperatively by the sponsor and the team members. A copy of the Formation Plan is included as Appendix B.
- The team then develops a flow diagram of the current process, confining their process to ten steps or less. This provides a broad-brush look at the process as it stands and allows team members to see the process as a whole and what others do within it.
- Customer needs are determined through one-on-one interviews or focus groups. The language data is collated into a vision of the ideal process using the affinity diagram.
- The interrelationship digraph and spider diagram are used to focus the team's efforts on the areas of the vision with the greatest leverage.
- The team then redesigns the process using a process flow diagram or a tree diagram.
- The responsibility matrix is used to help the team think through the details of the new process such as who will do what, when, and where.
- The process decision program chart structures the team's thinking to anticipate what will probably go wrong in the new process and how the situations or factors can be prevented.

FIGURE 3   *Designing a New Process (Process Is New or Significantly Different)*

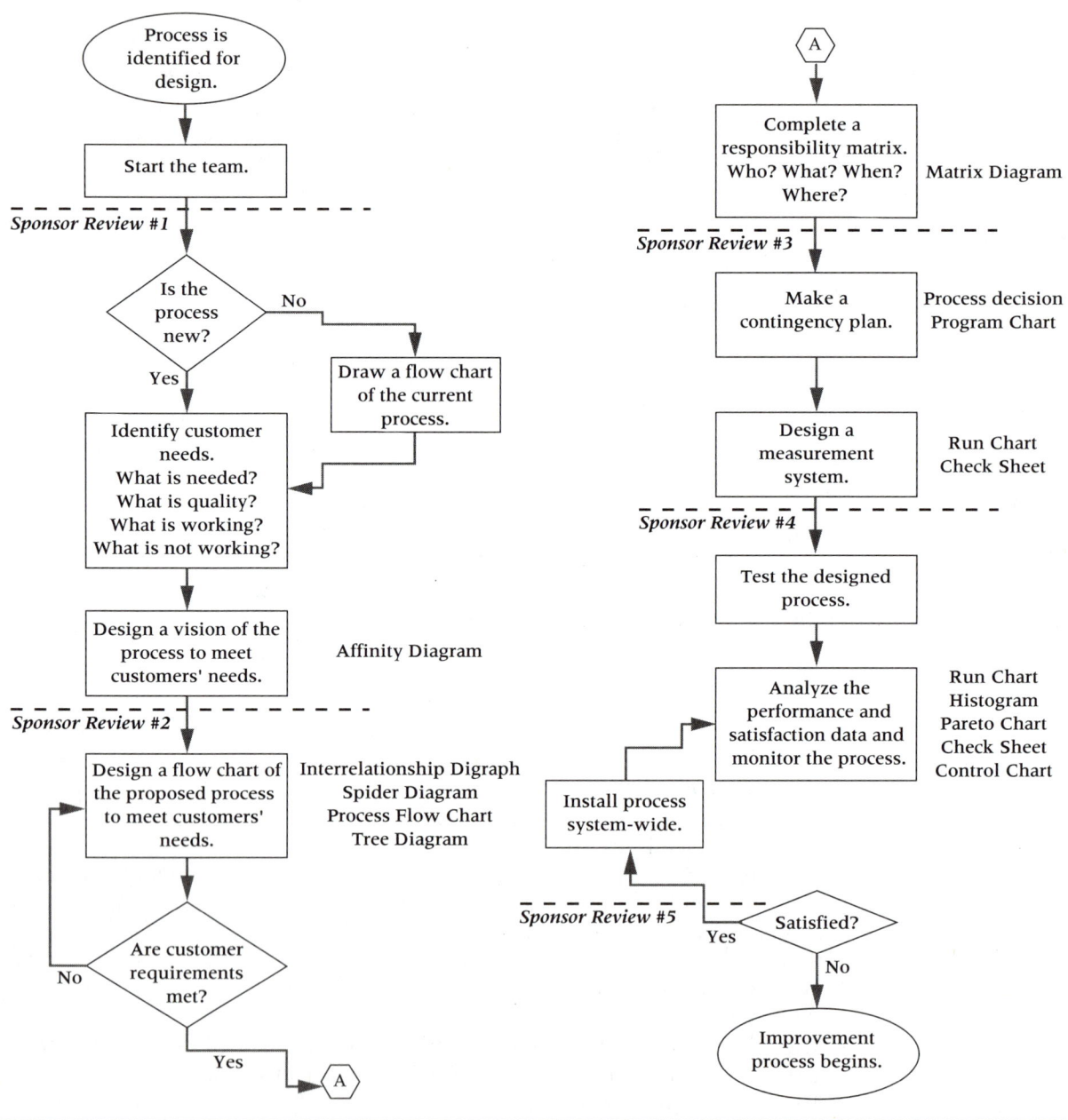

- A measurement system is then designed to ensure that the new process is, indeed, better than the old one.
- The process is then tested in one area of the workplace. Performance data is collected on the new design as well as the old one and then displayed using the

most appropriate tool. Examples of display tools are the Pareto chart, the run chart, the scatterplot, the histogram, and the control chart.
• When the process is shown to be a significant improvement over the old one, it is installed system-wide, and the team celebrates its success.

A detailed narrative of the process design methodology can be obtained from the authors.

FORMAL TRAINING IN SPONSORING

For many, working alone has been the norm. It is a familiar approach and is fairly simple. Working with others, however, is far more complicated. There are many opinions and ideas about what should be done; there is current experience with all aspects of a given process; more information is available to be understood and synthesized. Yet, because we now recognize our processes to be deeply interrelated and interdependent, there is an ever-increasing need to engage the thinking and creativity of all those who operate our processes day-to-day. The bringing together of process co-operators to make process improvements is the responsibility of the supervisor as sponsor.

During the training for the process redesign methodology, knowledge and skills needed to become a team sponsor should be incorporated, including creating and maintaining a partnership with the team and completing the Team Formation Plan. These practical activities of the sponsor allow the team to begin with a firm foundation of information and help the team continue to function effectively.

The role of sponsor, however, is more than simply a proactive champion for teams. Sponsors must exhibit characteristics that are found in the affective realm. The sponsor . . .

• is nurturing
• is supportive, with a vision
• is a cheerleader
• is compassionate
• is a defender
• helps others up from a stumble
• listens with empathy
• has a passion for the purpose
• is trustworthy

These characteristics require the supervisor to respond to others with feelings as well as action. Staff need to believe that the supervisor as sponsor will help them through their anxieties during stressful improvements or will eliminate barriers that might be in their way with other departments. The supervisor must provide vision and encouragement rather than tell the team how to redesign a process, how to improve the work environment, or how to reach agreement among team members.

Training activities in the affective realm that are designed to expose trainees to the qualities required of a sponsor can be found in the appendix to this reading.

The sponsor role of the supervisor is both practical and affective; yet both sides of the role deliver what the team needs during its redesign efforts . . . knowledge, support, and compassion while learning to improve within the system.

FORMAL TRAINING IN TRAINING

Training occurs in a variety of settings from an informal conversation in the workplace to formal training that requires advance planning and coordination.

In reality, the supervisor is "training" whenever he opens his mouth. People listen, and they take into consideration what he says. If little thought is given to what he says, staff may misunderstand and do things in ways he does not intend. In the extreme, staff may stop listening to him at all, believing that what he says has little value.

Training also occurs in an informal setting as plans are set, decisions are made, ideas are implemented, and problems are solved. A supervisor may teach the work team several structured tools, such as the quality management and planning tools. She may also teach the group how to plan or how to redesign a process. She may even teach the team how to listen and think collectively.

At the most formal level, some supervisors may conduct classroom instruction to teach specific technical skills or serve as instructional staff to new supervisors during their initial training series. Formal training of this kind will require planning and instructional delivery at the most detailed level.

The activities found in the appendix will provide valuable experience for a beginning trainer in the workplace.

FORMAL TRAINING IN EVALUATING

Performance appraisal systems have been highly criticized in much of the literature on quality. It is agreed that evaluation systems that reward or punish employees based on the performance of processes that they cannot control are damaging to staff and should be eliminated. However, in organizations that support innovation, continuous improvement, and customer satisfaction, most individuals want to hear how they are doing from their customers' points of view. They understand the personal and professional value of improvement and want to extend their own capabilities.

As evaluator, the supervisor supports staff as they listen with neither arrogance nor defensiveness to customers' assessments of their performance. Staff reactions to this evolving method of appraisal will vary since it is drastically different from the top-down approach of the past. In the newer evaluation systems, a performance rating is no longer given by the supervisor to the staff member. Effective evaluation occurs when personalized and accurate feedback from internal and external customers of the organization is assessed jointly by the employee and the supervisor. Their assessment goal is to create an action plan for personal and professional growth, designed to reinforce current knowledge, skills, and behaviors, or to adopt new skills and behaviors to the ultimate satisfaction of the customers.

Staff accustomed to serving the Supervisor instead of their customers may find this approach disconcerting. To find out from a variety of customers that their performance needs improvement is shocking to some staff who have not cared to know how satisfying their work is to others. "I can't satisfy *everybody*!" they will exclaim. As staff wrestle with ways to improve and develop, the supervisor must remain supportive, empathetic, and nurturing, yet remain clear about the messages received and the changes needed. The Supervisor must continue the support as improvement plans are implemented throughout the months ahead.

Other staff will welcome customer information and will begin making improvements immediately, whether the information is received at a regularly scheduled appraisal point or not. The supervisor may only need to offer training options or suggest activities. Support for these individuals may take less effort, but even self-directed staff need personalized attention and sincere recognition for their efforts.

Regardless of the abilities of staff to listen and respond to feedback, it is important that all evaluations be handled with extreme care, for it is through this process that we see ourselves, we see how others see us, and we learn to listen and react to both.

Training supervisors to follow a system of obtaining customer feedback and helping others develop a positive plan of action for personal and professional growth requires highly interactive and reality-based learning. By completing the planning, implementation, and evaluation stages of a personalized performance appraisal system focused on their own performance, supervisors are more prepared to replicate the system with staff in their area of responsibility.

A personal improvement plan, which can be found within the training activities in the appendix, should be the culminating learning activity of the 18-month formal training for supervisors. It should embody all the learning from the previous months of training and be used for continuous growth and development.

MOVING FROM FORMAL TO INFORMAL TRAINING

With the completion of an 18-month training series, the instructional staff and trainees may want to plan a customized celebration to mark the move from formal to informal training. It is essential to honor the relationships that have developed and encourage supervisors to meet informally long after the initial training has ended. Through in-depth conversations and activities, trainees and instructional staff will have formed valuable friendships—they know a great deal more about each other than they did at the start!—which they may want to continue over time.

STRATEGY #2: INFORMAL TRAINING

Informal training is usually the most frequently experienced training option. In the workplace, weekly meetings are often held with all supervisors of a given work area to learn to manage their budget or learn how to confront issues of safety, customer service, staff performance, or workplace maintenance. Effective managers will give supervisors the experience of conducting these regularly scheduled meetings in order to learn their own best style.

Continuous learning on one's own, another version of informal training, is attractive to many since it is held at one's own speed with one's own choice of materials, teachers, and tools. It requires no preset schedule. It has no ending. Informal training is easy and fairly inexpensive to obtain:

- read the latest books found in the business section of a favorite bookstore;
- check out articles, learning tapes, and books from the library;
- listen and talk with others at meetings and gatherings;
- attend social events;
- enter into conversations with leaders, supervisors, and workers from other organizations;
- watch the politics of the organization;
- listen for topics of interest;
- read industry literature;
- join associations in a field of expertise;
- listen to speakers on job-related topics; and
- participate in a speakers' forum.

The informal training strategy may seem especially attractive to those who value independence or prefer to move further and faster than their organization. The risks, however, are great: what we are learning may be disconnected from what the rest of the organization is learning; we will miss many valuable conversations; and new ideas do not always fully develop without the synergy of several minds working together. Orchestrating an informal learning group might fill the gaps caused by learning alone and create a place to learn from others.

STRATEGY #3: MENTORING

The final training strategy to be presented in this article is mentoring. This is not an easy learning strategy to orchestrate, yet it can be a most powerful one. The strategy requires the active cooperation of an individual who has more experience in the supervisor's desired area of learning and who is admired as a leader within the organization. Not all supervisors are fortunate enough to find a mentor. One has to be in the right place at the right time and must be able to establish a mutual connection with an organizational leader.

FINDING A MENTOR AND ESTABLISHING A RELATIONSHIP

The mentoring relationship often begins as an acquaintance between the supervisor and a well-respected and interested leader; it grows over time, with honesty and trust, into a professional friendship.

As a new supervisor looks for a mentor, she will want to seek out a leader who is personable and genuine. She should pay attention at staff meetings to see those leaders that come early or stay after the meeting to talk to attendees. As she watches for desirable characteristics, she should remember to look for patterns of leadership, not one-time occurrences. She will talk to senior managers at every opportunity. She will watch to whom other leaders talk for guidance. Since most of her learning will come from conversations, she will pay attention and listen intently. She will attend the organization's social events and talk with people informally over a hot dog and a soft drink. The informal atmosphere of a picnic often holds just the right opportunity to get acquainted.

Some supervisors do not enjoy or feel comfortable attending picnics and other social events. Other methods should be developed to establish connections and begin conversations with leaders. Volunteering for an organizational work group, perhaps, may be a more comfortable connection point for a less social supervisor.

Starting a learning relationship with a leader is part luck and part conscious strategy. Because sensitive organizational topics will eventually be discussed, honesty and candor are required. Each person must be willing to build an emotional connection just like any deep relationship between two people. It is because of the closeness that develops that it is often difficult to find a mentor.

Establishing the relationship can be risky for the mentor. During the course of mentoring conversations, he will be asked to talk through some of the informal activities going on in the organization, and he will expose his not-so-perfect qualities to teach the supervisor to cope with and compensate for human differences. It takes courage to trust that the supervisor will not take advantage of the relationship or talk behind his back.

Risk is present for the supervisor, too, who may worry that she has nothing to offer the leader or fears being turned down for lack of interest. The supervisor should remember that there are genuine advantages to the mentor. Those who have served as mentors report the following personal benefits. In their words . . .

- I like knowing my ideas and experiences are valued.
- I like to have someone to bounce my ideas off of.
- I like to be reassured. Believe it or not, I need reassurance like everyone else.
- It's nice to have someone I can talk with about the organization.
- I like to make people feel comfortable in their work.
- I like to watch persons grow over time.
- I like knowing that someone sees me as having desirable leadership characteristics…. I've worked a long time to be recognized as a leader.
- I like to tell what I know about how the organization really works.
- I like keeping up-to-date with the current thinking of new supervisors and managers.

HOLDING CONVERSATIONS WITH THE MENTOR

Once the leader and supervisor have agreed to form a mentoring relationship, orchestrating learning conversations can be a bit more complex. Up to this point, the meetings have occurred most often by chance. Conversations have been somewhat superficial, and there has not been a specific purpose to the topics. Now that will change deliberately. It is important for the new supervisor to be clear with her mentor and tell exactly what is on her mind.

At first, the topics will involve very little risk since trust has not been fully established. Topics might include training the mentor would recommend or where he sees the primary workload in the organization moving in the future. Keeping it informational and "light" will allow the relationship to unfold slowly, and keeping the exchanges conversational will create a more comfortable experience. The supervisor might also volunteer to work on projects or teams where the mentor is involved. Shorter conversations during breaks, before or after the meetings, can then occur around the meeting topics.

As the relationship evolves, the new supervisor might draw up a different list of topics, such as:

- *Organizational dynamics*—Why does the leadership react in a certain way to specific issues? What are their perspectives on the workings of the informal dynamics of the organization? How are the staff meetings operating?
- *Politics*—What are the sensitive areas? What are the current "political winds"?
- *Vision*—Where is the organization going? How do we interpret the strategic plan?
- *Focus and persuasions of current leaders*—Where do the various leaders stand on the current hot issues? How do they react to conflict or tough issues?
- *Self-exposure*—Am I seen from the center of the organization? How am I being perceived? Are my behaviors supportive? What are some suggestions for improvements, short- and long-term?
- *Leadership issues*—What are the dynamics of the senior team?

During the meetings with the mentor, the supervisor's responsibility is to listen. She should make mental notes of the information provided or take written notes if possible. She will want to store away the information for later use in her own workplace, not to use it against her mentor but to better understand how the organization operates. She will need to schedule time to be alone afterwards to write down her thoughts and ideas about what she heard.

- What difference did our conversation make to me?
- What did I learn that I can apply to my work situation?
- What would my mentor do in my work area that I'm not doing?

LISTENING DURING MENTORING CONVERSATIONS

The way to learn about an organization is to ask lots of questions and listen intently to the answers. Rather than trying to appear smart, the supervisor must stay with the conversation until he clearly understands the issues. He should not try to persuade or argue differing points of view. He will be wise to save his opinions until later when the mentoring relationship has grown and mutual trust has been established.

The supervisor should pay close attention to the conversations about politics. Ask for examples of the most current issues at hand and what senior leaders believe about them. The supervisor can log this information away in his memory to be retrieved when he is bringing controversial issues to a head. It is helpful to know about where the current leadership stands on an issue that affects the organization's future.

With the aid of the mentor's knowledge and experience, the supervisor learns to understand events and occurrences where she is either too close to see them (for example, how a seemingly small change in her department will affect the whole system), the events do not occur frequently enough to see them firsthand (for example, the effect on both the internal and external customers when the organization changed location), or she is too inexperienced to see them occur (for example, the effects of a departmental reorganization). Talking with a mentor and remembering what was said will be worthwhile if learning occurs, yet learning can only take place with direct application.

Although mentoring seems intangible, it can be very important to a supervisor's learning. It may be a difficult relationship to start, and it will take a significant period of time to grow. Yet once established, it can be a tremendously rewarding experience. Both mentor and supervisor can reap the benefits of invigorating conversation as they begin to see pathways unseen by others. But mentoring affords supervisors a special gift . . . the insight and confidence to carve out new pathways as they emerge as leaders in their own right.

DELIBERATE AND CONSCIOUS APPLICATION

As the Pathway to Leadership diagram depicts, the key to exhibiting patterns of character that identify one as a leader is deliberate and conscious application of the right skills and behaviors. The number of classes taken, the number of books read, or the number of mentoring conversations experienced makes no difference if the knowledge obtained is not applied. Skills learned initially must be honed in the workplace. Behaviors essential to leadership must be displayed over and over again to be judged as believable by others.

The following time-proven process follows the steps of the Shewhart/Deming cycle for continuous improvement, which incorporates one day's learnings into the work of the next.

- **Plan an application in the workplace (PLAN).** Start by choosing the concept, skill or behavior you want to make habitual or apply in the workplace. Next, visualize what it might be like if you tried the concept. What does it look like in the workplace? What might it look like if it worked? What would the consequences be if it worked? What if it didn't work? What could go wrong? How could you prevent things from going wrong? Finally, work out the idea, build a plan of action, and prepare for the event or action.
- **Carry out the plan (DO).** Just do it! Observe what happened from beginning to end. What are staff saying about what happened? What are staff doing as a result of the action? What difference is the action making?
- **Check the consequences (CHECK/STUDY).** What evidence did you collect that tells you it worked or it did not? What could you have done differently? What lessons did you learn?
- **Make adjustments for the next time, acting on what was learned (ACT).**
- **Begin again.**

At first the application process may seem formal and stilted, yet as we replicate this process over and over, continuous learning becomes habitual and unconscious.

CONCLUSION

In this article, we have explored six roles of the supervisor and three training methods to obtain the knowledge, skills, and behaviors needed in the roles. We have also presented a diagram that makes the day-to-day pathway to leadership visible. We have covered a lot of ground! Now it is time to decide what we are going to do.

One choice is fairly easy. We can accept the job of supervisor and learn to do the tasks we are asked to do. We can sign time cards and schedule work. We can discipline unproductive employees. We can fill out the employee ratings sheets and develop our plan for their improvement. We can attend training, read books, listen to others, and then walk away and do exactly what we did the day before. And people will probably do just what we ask—no more, no less—since we hold a position of authority.

The other choice is not easy and requires stamina. In this choice, we view supervision as a process that requires our continuous learning and development. We attend training, read books, and listen to others as we learn to facilitate, plan, improve, sponsor, train, and evaluate as a supervisor. With this choice, we must also deliberately and consciously apply our new knowledge and skills in the workplace while behaving in ways that characterize leaders. We must align our thoughts, speech, and actions to develop patterns of trust, honesty, integrity, and compassion, as well as other characteristics of leadership. Without our being aware of it, we will exhibit patterns of action that others will watch and judge. If others perceive our patterns to embody such characteristics as trust, honesty, integrity, and compassion, then people will look to us for leadership, regardless of our position, regardless of whether we have formal authority or not.

But what difference will it make? What about the changes we see in the future?

There is much agreement that our work world is rapidly changing. As we transform into a new kind of work structure, many supervisory and middle-management positions are being eliminated. Some organizations are reducing the numbers of supervisors they employ and asking each remaining supervisor to coordinate the efforts of several work units. In other organizations, traditional supervision is being eliminated altogether, and self-directed teams are being formed around multiple work processes. The latter structure is becoming an efficient and respected way to utilize the tremendous capacity of our workforce to meet customers' needs.

Changes in the workplace are closely related to the changes in organizational structure. Many entry level workers are being moved in and out of companies as workloads rise and fall with the pulse of the marketplace. Specialized workers are being hired on a temporary basis, coming and going as needed. More and more workers are finding themselves without the traditional company to call home. In fact, "home" is now a temporary services agency, complete with fringe benefits.

Where does this leave us as supervisors? Why should we make the effort to develop in a role where positions might be eliminated? Is it worth the personal and professional investment?

The answer is clear: those of us who have consistently demonstrated the knowledge, skills, and behaviors described here will have far more credibility with others and will be in demand. We will, at some time, be asked for leadership, and we must be sure the experience is positive. We may be chosen to be one of several remaining supervisors in our organization, for team leaders will always be in demand. We may take a management position in a different company. We may become a supervisor in a new start-up business down the street. We may even start a business of our own. The knowledge, skills, and behaviors of leaders are transferable to any setting and have cascading, positive organizational benefits.

Our choice has far greater impact, however. No matter where we are employed or what position we hold, with an honest pursuit of knowledge and skills centered on selfless values and personal principles, we can be more effective members while also more fulfilled and satisfied within. What better reason . . . this?

APPENDIX 9-A *Great Behaviors*

GREAT BEHAVIORS	UNPRODUCTIVE	INTERVENTIONS
Very interested; alert, energized, focused.	Interrupter	"One moment … I want to complete my thought."
	Side Conversations	"I'm distracted by more than one conversation. Let's stay together."
Can see many sides to an issue.	Crosstown Bus Driver	"I think we're off track. Let's move back to the agenda."
	Rambler	"So, to summarize your viewpoint …"
Participates; has lots to contribute.	Won't Talk	"What do *you* think?"
	Dominant	"I'd like to hear some other points of view."
	Side Conversations	"I'm distracted by more than one conversation. Let's stay together."
	Interrupter	"One moment … I want to complete my thought.
Very knowledgeable.	Dominant	"I'd like to hear some other points of view."
Presents sides to be sure everything gets covered.	Rambler	"So, to summarize your viewpoint …"
	Argumentative	"I see your perspective. What are others' ideas?"
Wants to see change because what currently "is" isn't working.	Griper/Whiner	"Those points need to be addressed, so let's put them on the parking lot."
	Argumentative	"I see your perspective. What are others' ideas?"
	Dominant	"I'd like to hear some other points of view."
Polite, respectful.	Won't Talk	"What do *you* think?"
Exhibits clear thought; succinct.	Won't Talk	"What do *you* think?"

APPENDIX 9-B *Team Formation Plan*

Name of Process: _____

Team Sponsor: _____ **Leader:** _____

Members: _____

The purpose of the process in the system is to:_____

_____

_____

The process was chosen because:_____

_____

_____

The team should not address the following: _____

_____

_____

The known constraints of the project are:_____

_____

_____

The team is charged with Level _____ of decision-making authority.

　　Level 1: "As sponsor, this is my decision to make."
　　Level 2: "As sponsor, this is my decision to make, but I want your input and
　　　　　　recommendations."
　　Level 3: "As a sponsor/team partnership, this is our decision to make."

The team's ground rules are:
• Ongoing Team: How will we know we are effective? _____

_____

_____

• Ad Hoc Team: How will we know when we are finished? _____

_____

_____

Start Date: _____

Target Completion Date: _____

APPENDIX 9-C   *Suggested Training Activities*

SUPERVISOR AS FACILITATOR

LISTENING

Activity #1: *Linking Observations with Perceptions*

To practice linking observations with perceptions, observe a group meeting, an event, or a gathering. Divide a sheet of paper in thirds, lengthwise. On the far left side, record the body positions of one to three participants. For example, at a department meeting, you might observe Bob sitting up at the table taking notes. Sally is slouching in her chair with arms folded across her waist. Mary is sitting back in her chair tapping her pencil on the table. In the middle section, list all the perceptions or conclusions one could draw from the observations. You might interpret Bob's behavior as alert, focused, and attentive (or, perhaps, he's working on something totally unrelated to the meeting!). Sally could be viewed as angry, uninterested, withdrawn, or freezing cold without a sweater. Mary could be viewed as cautious, contemplating the meeting content, or simply bored. Choose the perception you think most accurately fits the individuals' behaviors. At a break or after the meeting, ask each person to describe their experiences at the meeting and record the answers in the right-hand column. Compare your perceptions to what was reported. Was there a match? If not, what caused the confusion? What assumptions were made that proved inaccurate? How will you ensure your perceptions more closely match the actions of others in the future?

Activity #2: *Listening without Visual Filters*

To establish an effective listening pattern, you must experience listening without visual filters. To listen without the benefit of sight, sit in a circle with other trainees. Wear blindfolds. In a room with no background noise, hold a conversation around a given topic. After 30 minutes, remove the blindfolds and examine the process that took place. What differences did each person experience when the eyes were closed? How did the speed of the conversation change? How much did each trainee remember about the content of the conversation? When would wearing blindfolds at a meeting be helpful for a working team? What information was not available when blindfolded? Was it helpful not to see? How can the listening be replicated without using blindfolds? (Idea from The Dialogue Project, MIT, Boston, MA.)

Activity #3: *Listening to follow Directions*

To experience listening to follow directions, distribute several large sheets of unlined paper and a pen. One trainee will serve as "communicator" and will describe in words a prepared drawing of shapes and patterns. As a participant, listen to the communicator's verbal instructions and duplicate the drawing on the paper. At the end of the drawing session, compare all drawings to the communicator's. Are they identical? Are they even similar? If they are not the same, what did not work? What improvements could the communicator make to help the trainees hear better? What improvements in listening could you and others make to understand the communicator better? What implications does this activity have in the workplace?

As this activity is repeated over time, trainees will become progressively better at duplicating various drawings, and communicators will learn better techniques of giving easy to understand, verbal directions.

Activity #4: *Listening to Summarize*

As a facilitator of groups, the supervisor must listen to the contributions of all participants, remember the major themes, and summarize the statements to help the group reach consensus. To practice this skill, observe a canned conversation conducted by several instructors and volunteers. The conversation should include some deliberate twists and turns to teach trainees to log away important bits and pieces of the developing conversation and pull together summary statements. One trainee acts as group facilitator while the remaining trainees observe and record their own summaries. Repeat this activity at each seminar session, giving all trainees experience in the facilitation role. Sessions could be video-taped and played back for in-depth assessment.

GROUP PROCESS

Activity #5: *Facilitating Customer and Supplier Meetings*

To gain experience in facilitating meetings with customers and suppliers, complete at least one interview with your process customers and one with your suppliers. The following questions may be helpful while planning your interview:

- For which process will customers be chosen?
- Which customers will be interviewed?
- What questions will be asked?
- Are there any resource constraints (time, $, etc.)?
- Will I facilitate a focus group or conduct a personal interview?
- When will the interview take place? Where? What time?
- How will customer data be collected?
- What will be my opening statement?

Similar questions are used to plan supplier interviews, although emphasis is placed on giving information the supplier may not want to hear. Mock interviews could be conducted in the seminar setting to practice giving sensitive information about customer needs to a unreceptive ear.

Customer and supplier meetings could be video-taped with the permission of the participants and then viewed with the instructor to assess the trainee's facilitation skills. At a minimum, feedback should be given from other trained facilitators.

Activity #6: *Designing Meeting Strategies*

Develop a series of situations and design a meeting process for each situation. As a large group, examine each strategy for probable effectiveness. A finished example follows.

FACILITATING PROCESS EXAMPLE

Situation   One member of a six-person team consistently gripes and whines about the ineffectiveness of their team meetings. She is unhappy about the lack of an agenda, not starting on time, and members not listening to her ideas. Her complaints, though legitimate, are irritating the team members and causing them to withdraw. They want to improve their meetings, but they do not like her approach.

Meeting purpose(s)   The purposes of the meeting are to (1) make agreements on how future meetings will be organized and conducted, and (2) to reach agreement on how to work together peacefully.

A suggested process:
    I. Create the vision.
        A. Ask the question: "What are the attributes of the ideal meeting? What would it look like and sound like?"
        B. Use the affinity diagram to create the vision of the ideal team.
        C. Make agreements about who will do what at each meeting to help ensure that team members move their meetings toward the ideal.
    II. Make agreements about high-performance team behaviors.
        A. Introduce "Great Behaviors." (See Appendix A)
        B. Moving round-robin around the table, each member states the great behaviors they bring to the team meetings, the unproductive behaviors they revert to when their needs are not being met, and the interventions others can make to alert them to realign themselves to great behaviors for the benefit of the team.
        C. nformation is placed on individual table tents to be seen by other members at future meetings.
    III. Set the agenda for the next team meeting. Identify the purpose of the meeting and who will do what, and when.
    IV. Evaluate the meeting:
        A. What worked?
        B. What did not work?
        C. What did the members learn?
        D. What improvements could be made for the next meeting?

Projected Improvements   Creating a shared vision for the ideal meeting will surface the many attributes of an effective meeting. As the responsibilities are divided and commitments made to move to the idea, the complaints of the griper/whiner can be addressed productively.

The "Great Behaviors" activity will help the griper/whiner see the relationship between her positive intentions and her unproductive behaviors. It will also open the door for other team members to address the negative effects of the griper/whiner's behavior on their performance and attitudes. Actively meeting the needs of all team members should also be addressed.

The proactive approach of this activity cannot be overemphasized. We have been repeatedly taught *reactions* to members' poor behaviors. Instead, in this two-fold approach, we proactively create a process to meet all members' needs and then help persons realign their own behaviors if we miss the mark. Interventions, then, serve as a reminder to both the individual and the team to make changes.

SUPERVISOR AS PLANNER

Activity #1: *Systems Thinking*

As a large group, create a systemic picture of the organization showing the inter-relationship of its parts. Include all functions in a process flow diagram.

Next, create a systemic map on a smaller scale of your own area of responsibility, showing how the various subprocesses link together as a whole. The following steps can be followed:

1. Choose a cross-functional organizational process.
2. Map the process using the process flow diagram.
3. Place people's names within the process to show the interrelationships.
4. Exchange customer-supplier needs.
5. Hold a conversation about the interdependencies of the functions.

The example in Figure 4 shows the outlines of a chart that can hold the information you generate:

Activity #2: *Thinking Progression for Planning*

With other supervisor trainees, learn the quality tools and apply them in sequence using the methodology presented on page 149. As a group, identify an event or activity to be planned. Then use the thinking progression to develop and implement a plan of action.

Throughout the implementation of the plan, conduct planning reviews with the in-class plan you have created. Initially, instructional staff should role-play both positive and negative approaches to demonstrate the vastly different effects on team members.

SUPERVISOR AS IMPROVER

Activity #1: *Redesign a Process*

Use the thinking progression on page 149 and redesign a work process. Assemble the appropriate process "co-operators" and use the methodology and tools. For a detailed narrative on the methodology, contact the authors.

SUPERVISOR AS SPONSOR

Four-Part Activity: *Leadership Characteristics*

1. Select members of your work team to be interviewed. Questions to ask might be: What do the characteristic behaviors of exceptional sponsors look like in the workplace? What happens when these characteristics are not displayed? What are good examples you have experienced with past sponsors? Conduct the interviews and record the answers. Combine your list with those of other trainees and identify the most frequently mentioned characteristics of sponsors.

FIGURE 4   *Systems Process Flow Diagram*

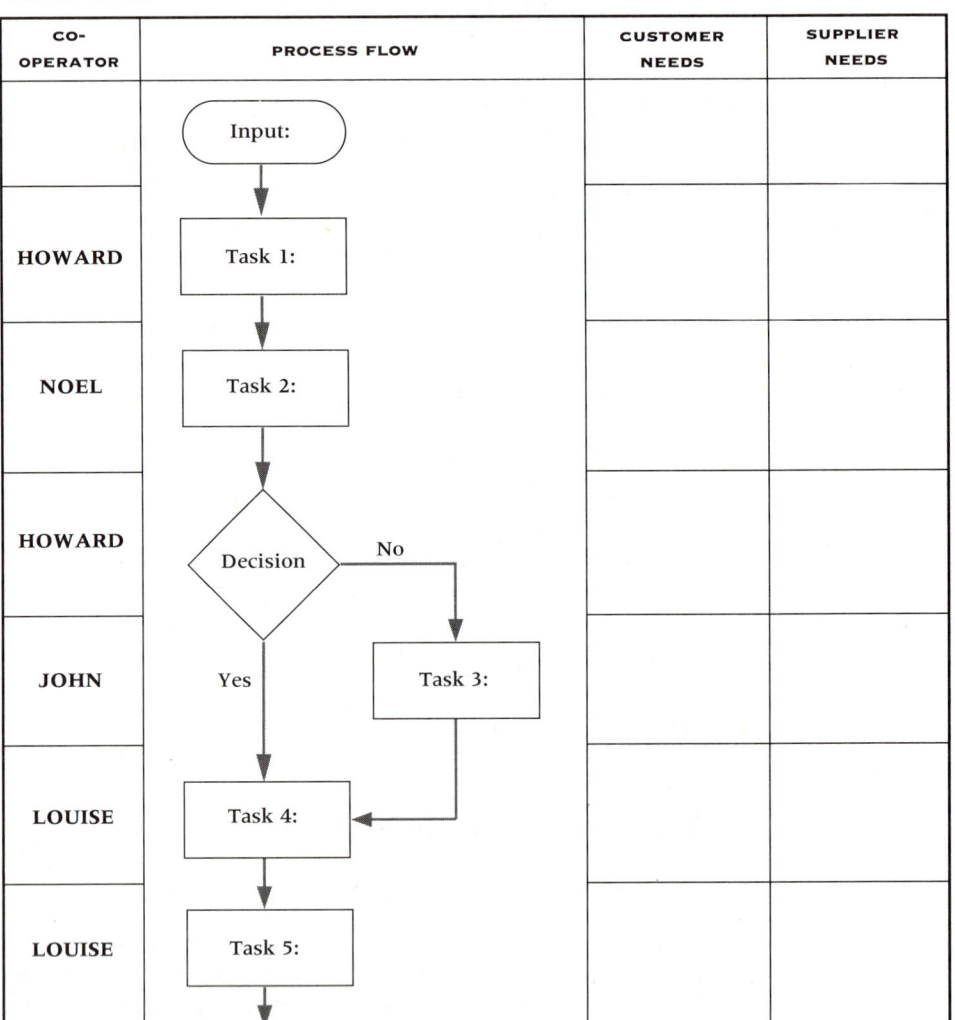

PROCESS NAME:

CO-OPERATOR	PROCESS FLOW	CUSTOMER NEEDS	SUPPLIER NEEDS
	Input:		
HOWARD	Task 1:		
NOEL	Task 2:		
HOWARD	Decision — No		
JOHN	Yes — Task 3:		
LOUISE	Task 4:		
LOUISE	Task 5:		

2. Once the characteristic behaviors of the sponsor have been identified, develop an operational definitions sheet. Definitions should be simple and clear, with examples given from the interviews.

3. Select one characteristic on which to improve and create a spider diagram of specific behaviors for that characteristic. Distribute the spider diagram (Figure 5) to your work team members for anonymous assessment.

4. Once the data has been collected, plot the scores on a single spider diagram. Determine what was learned from staff and what improvements, if any, need to be made. If you heard something from staff you did not expect, what will you do about it?

FIGURE 5   *Personalized Spider Diagram*

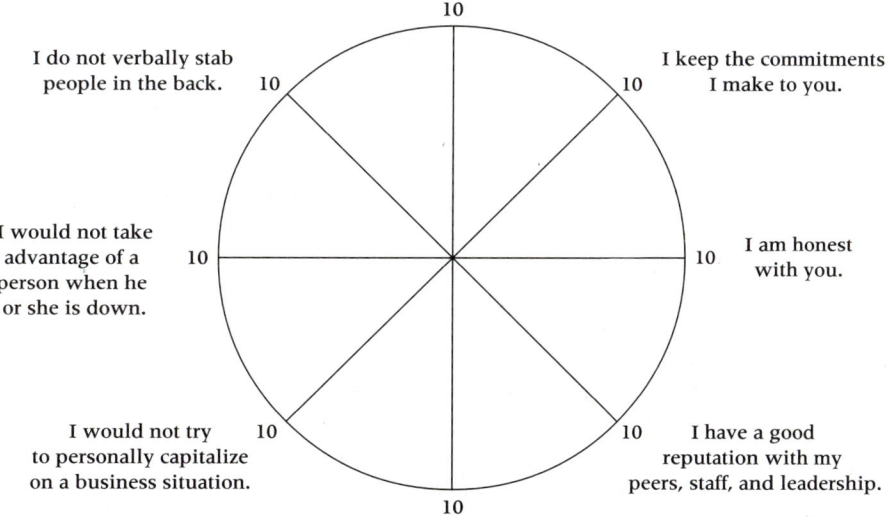

Date: _____

Rate the individual on a scale
from 1 to 10.

The outside of the circle is a "10,"
which means "This statement is true,
in my perception."

The center of the circle is a "1," which
means "This statement is not true, in
my perception."

LEADERSHIP CHARACTERISTIC

"TRUSTWORTHY"

If I cannot make an appointment or deadline,
I contact you in advance and let you know
so we can reschedule.

10

I do not verbally stab
people in the back.   10

I keep the commitments
I make to you.   10

I would not take
advantage of a
person when he
or she is down.   10

I am honest
with you.   10

I would not try
to personally capitalize
on a business situation.   10

I have a good
reputation with my
peers, staff, and leadership.   10

10

In private or public, I have not
made dishonest dealings or taken
unprincipled actions with you or others.

Skill Areas for Improvement	Specific Activities for Improvement
1.	a.
	b.
2.	a.
	b.
3.	a.
	b.

The risk for the supervisor is great when asking one's staff for an assessment of personal characteristics. If the work environment or the attitudes of the work team are not supportive or positive, supervisors may not want to ask staff at all. Fears and concerns should always be addressed and feelings respected.

SUPERVISOR AS TRAINER

Five-Part Activity #1: *Understanding Adult Learning Theory*

Trainees should know and understand adults as learners and be able to design a well-orchestrated training activity that meets adults' needs. To compare the benefits of incorporating the knowledge and skills, conduct a series of trainings in the following order:

1. As a large group, develop a set of success criteria for skills trainings, including characteristics such as clarity of presentation, use of props and tools, or the ability of trainees to demonstrate the skill after instruction.
2. Each trainee presents an impromptu training of 20 minutes, teaching any skill of interest to the trainees as a large group. No advance is done. Evaluate the success of each training using agreed-upon criteria.
3. Each trainee reads a summary of adult learning theory and prepares a 20-minute training on a topic of interest that incorporates visual, auditory, and kinesthetic learning modalities and considers the characteristics of adult learners. Conduct the mini-trainings and compare the first to the second. Did planning make a difference to the learning of the participants? Were more success criteria met than in Part 2?
4. Finally, trainees construct a learning system to train staff members in their area of responsibility in one new skill. An example might be training staff to use a systems thinking tool. Use the construction plan that follows.
5. After the third training has been conducted, compare all trainings. Was the third training most effective? How do you know? Did planning and new knowledge make a difference?

Activity #2: *Teaching the Management and Planning Tools*

Practice teaching the management and planning tools to your trainee group, incorporating what was learned during facilitation and training seminars. Supervisors acting as trainers report that teaching others the structure and use of the tools is not difficult. The tools are easy to understand, they follow a fairly fool-proof progression of thought and action, and they make good sense when completed. The most difficult part is holding the conversations—bringing out the thoughts of others, generating collective thoughts rather than discussions on disagreements, recognizing when the conversation has moved off track and bringing it back again, and making visible the personal agendas at the table.

CONSTRUCTION PLAN   Topic/Skills: _____

Date: _____

STUDENT LEARNING What should the trainees know, be able to do, and care about?	**PERFORMANCE ASSESSMENT** How will trainees demonstrate this learning? What evidence will be collected?	**LEARNING STRATEGIES** What strategies will bring about this learning?
RESOURCE INTEGRATION What tools, materials, technology, or other resources will support this learning?	**PERSONNEL** What will I need to do to prepare for this training? How will my preparation support student learning?	**SYSTEMS SERVICES** How does management of the timing, facilities, attendance, reporting, information collection and analysis, and refreshments support trainee learning?

SOURCE: Christine Tell, Lead Oregan, and Joann DeMott, The J. DeMott Company; 1993.

Activity #3: *Being a Trainer*

Complete the following activity as a large group.

The following statements have been made by professional trainers in their observations of supervisors as trainers. Hold conversations and demonstrations to answer the questions:

1. *"In order to treat everyone the same, you must treat everyone differently."* What is your view? How would a supervisor operate as a trainer within this paradox?

2. *"There is no room for arrogance or a patronizing attitude with learners!"* Demonstrate what it looks like and sounds like when a supervisor is arrogant and patronizing in the training role. What causes individuals to be arrogant? How would a supervisor let another person know that he is perceived by others as patronizing or arrogant? How might you expect the person to respond to your approach? Is it worth the risk?

3. *"Learning styles of learners are different and follow patterns."* What are the primary styles? How will you discern the differences in those you are training?

4. *"If you rushed through a tool and are not satisfied with your progress, it's OK to go back and make it right. A group does not lose face by going back. Shame comes from moving ahead just to be moving."* What are the risks and benefits of going back after rushing through a tool? What causes groups to rush? How can this be prevented?

5. *"Quality in the workplace is not about 'acting'. . . it's about 'being.'"* Demonstrate the difference between a supervisor who is "acting" like a trainer and one who is "being" a trainer. What are the differences between "acting" and "being" for the supervisor while operating in the various roles? How will you know what others think about how you are behaving?

SUPERVISOR AS EVALUATOR

1. Through interviews with staff, peers, and managers, list the knowledge, skills, and behaviors of an individual who would be "perfect" as a supervisor in your area of responsibility. Ask interviewees to specify what a supervisor in your area must know, what he must be able to do, and how he must behave to demonstrate mastery at a professional, personal, and interpersonal level. Record the exact words of the customers. Review your training binder and capture the information provided by customers from all activities throughout the year.

2. Write the language data on post-its (one attribute per post-it) and develop a personalized affinity diagram. This becomes your vision of the ideal supervisor in your area.

3. Using an interrelationship digraph, show the interrelationships of the vision elements and determine a hierarchy of influence. Indicate which of the vision elements is the primary driver and which is the primary effect.

4. Ask staff, peers, and managers in your area of responsibility as well as your supervisor to evaluate you on the various vision elements using a variable scale from 1 to 10. Include written comments on successes and possible areas for improvement. Conduct your own self-assessment as well. Collate the data and display it on a spider diagram.

5. Numerically link the data from the interrelationship digraph and the spider diagram and develop a combination factor for each vision element. Compare combination factors to determine the primary elements of focus for your improvement.

6. Using a tree diagram, develop strategies to reach your vision in the primary area of focus. Write a set of plans for achievement, identifying time lines for completion.

7. Develop a contingency plan using a process decision program chart. Identify actions or events that could go wrong and how you will prevent them.

8. Implement your personal improvement plan.

9. Review your plan monthly and quarterly with a designated manager or your mentor, using the plan review system learned during the planning seminar. Record what you intended to do during the quarter. Record what actually happened during the "do" stage and compare what was planned to what occurred. If there were differences, determine what you will do to move back on track.

10. At year's end, conduct an individualized, multiple-customer satisfaction survey to obtain data on your performance and how you satisfied customers.

11. Analyze the survey data jointly with your designated manager or mentor and update your spider diagram. Your interrelationship digraph should be reviewed to determine if any relationships have shifted.

12. Return to Step 5 to renew your plan for the following year.

Figure 6 illustrates the personal improvement process.

FIGURE 6   *Personal Improvement Process*

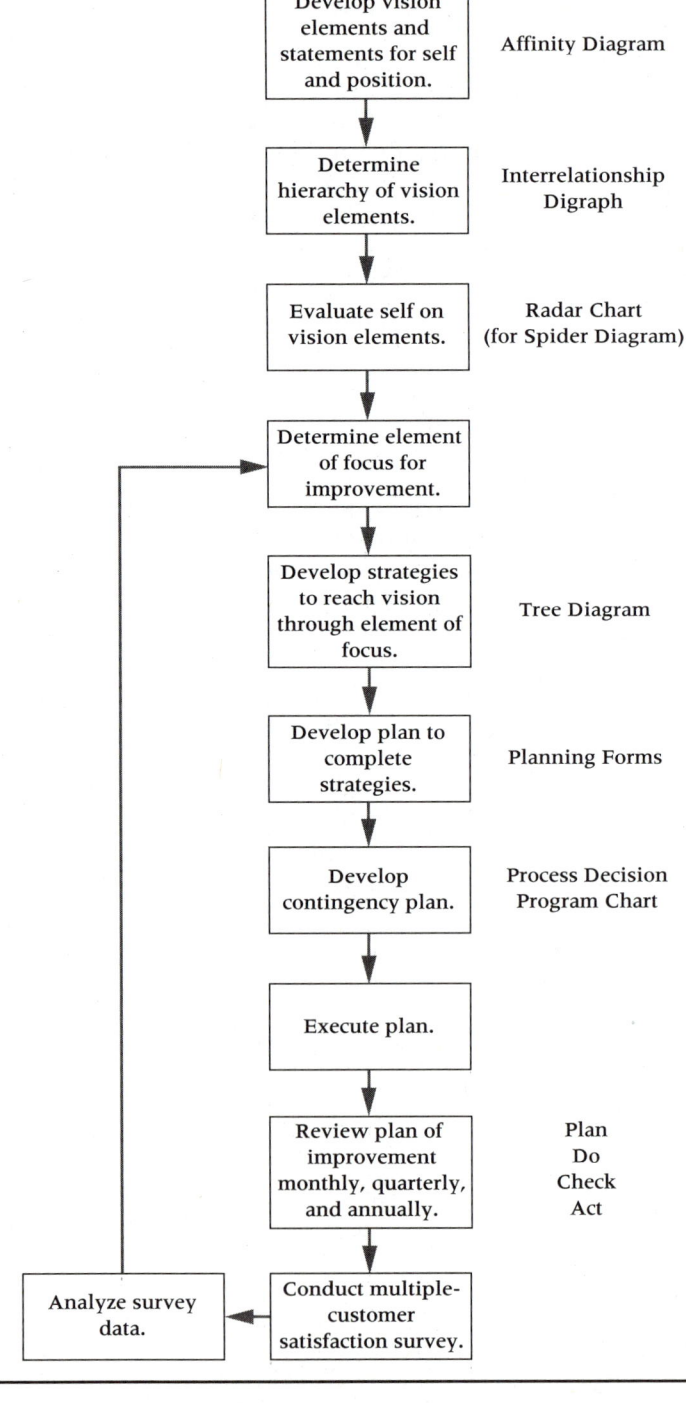

BIBLIOGRAPHY

Brassard, Michael. *Memory Jogger Plus+*. Methuen, MA: GOAL/QPC, 1989.

Collett, Colletti, DeMott, Hoffherr, Moran. *Making Daily Management Work*. Methuen, MA: GOAL/QPC, 1992.

Costin, Harry. *Readings in Total Quality Management*. Orlando: Harcourt Brace & Company, 1994.

Covey, Stephen. *The Seven Habits of Highly Effective People: Restoring the Character Ethic*. New York: Fireside: Simon & Schuster, 1989.

Kauffman, Draper L., Jr. *Systems 1: An Introduction to Systems Thinking*. Cambridge, MA: Pegasus Communications, 1980.

Senge, Peter. *The Fifth Discipline*. New York: Doubleday, 1990.

Wheatley, Margaret. *Leadership and the New Science*. San Francisco: Berrett-Koehler Publishers, 1992.

Total Quality Training for Natural Work Teams and Self-Directed Teams

By Michael J. Brower

INTRODUCTION

American business is moving rapidly to the wide and deep use of teams to organize work, to solve problems, and to improve processes and implement TQM.
The use of teams has been found to improve communications, to provide strong
mechanisms for managerial and employee development, to improve the quality of
decisions, and to raise employee ownership in the directions and decisions of the
organization. Although ideally starting from the top and permeating downward
throughout the organization, in practice teams can begin anywhere and spread
down, sideways, and upwards. There are at least six different kinds and levels of
teams, at three general levels of the organization: top, middle, and bottom.

1. **Senior executive teams.** At the top of the organization, the senior executives can and should operate as a team. This is only possible if the chief executive leads the way, so as yet this occurs in a minority, although a growing
   minority, of businesses.
2. **Top and middle management teams.** Each of the senior executive team
   members can become the leader of a middle management team, including
   all of the managers who directly report to him or her. Similarly, each of these
   middle managers can in turn organize and lead teams of the managers or
   supervisors who report to them. And so on down, for as many levels of management supervisors as there are in the organization.
3. **Project teams.** The third type is that of temporary cross-functional project
   teams, which are roughly mid-level, horizontal teams, although they may
   involve representatives from several different levels of the hierarchy. These
   are not new, but their use has spread dramatically in the last decade with the
   growth of total quality management. These teams are made up of representatives drawn from each of several different departments that "own" a part of

the process being studied by the team. These teams are variously called quality improvement teams (QITs), quality action teams (QATs), process improvement teams (PITs), process action teams (PATs), and more simply, project teams.

4. **Supervisor-led natural work teams.** At the base or front line of the organization, first-line supervisors are increasingly organizing their employees into natural work groups or natural work teams (NWTs). These teams are led by the supervisor; they are permanent, not temporary; and they include everybody who reports to the supervisor, not just a few representatives. The ideal size for such teams is from 5 to 12 people. These teams are most effective when all employees in the unit are included, both for the benefits of diversity in team membership and for the benefits of team membership reaching every single employee. If there are more than 15 people reporting to one supervisor, he or she may divide them into two or three teams, in order to include all employees.

5. **Self-managing teams (SMTs).** When a supervisor retires, transfers, or shifts to other roles and is not replaced, a natural work team can become self-managing. This requires approval and support from middle and even top management, a different form of leadership, and a great deal of training.

6. **Self-directed teams (SDTs).** If a self-managing team is given further training, leadership, and empowerment to set its own *direction*—in alignment with customers and overall organizational direction—it can become a self-directed team (SDT).

This article describes the training and education required for full effectiveness of the last three kinds of teams, all at the base of the organization, involving the people who do the actual production and service work.

In practice there are more similarities than differences between self-managing and self-directed teams. Because of this, and since many companies and authors use the two terms interchangeably, I am combining them under the title of self-directed teams. (For more on the differences between these two versions of empowered teams and on the requirements for full scale empowerment, see Brower, 1994). Furthermore, most of the training required for these teams to be fully successful is the same, regardless of whether they are supervisor-led natural work teams or self-directed teams.

This reading includes the following topics:

- The training and education that is required, in general, for these teams—both natural work groups and self-directed teams—to reach high effectiveness.
- The additional training required for a team to move from supervisor-led to self-directed.
- The additional training required for these teams in unionized organizations.
- The deeper kinds of learning that will be needed if the teams are to move beyond effectiveness to become continuously improving learning organizations.
- The reasons why so much training is necessary for organizations and for the success of the overall economy.

As we consider the sizable quantity and range of training proposed, we should keep in mind that:

1. In most organizations, only some of this training will be provided in a single block. This may be offered in several full days of training, either all at once upon the formation of teams or spread out over several weeks or months. But in most cases, a great deal of the training will come later, spread out in small segments over months and even years.

2. In many organizations it will be very difficult or impossible to release employees from work to train for more than a couple of hours at a time, even though a half or full day of training is usually preferable. Much of this training will be provided "just-in-time," as employees have both a real need and a perceived need for the training, plus an immediate opportunity to apply and test it in practice.

3. Only some of this training will be provided in classrooms and training rooms. Some of it will be done by facilitators and managers during regular team meetings. And some of it will be learned during one-to-one coaching on the production or office floor.

TRAINING FOR NATURAL WORK TEAMS AND SELF-DIRECTED TEAMS

I. CROSS-TRAINING IN WORK SKILLS

The foundation of successful work teams is team members who are knowledgeable and skilled in performing their own basic work and increasingly cross-trained in all the other skills used on the team. A basic level of training supports every member of the team in mastering the knowledge and skills for his or her own job, and in beginning to learn those of one or more other team members. Team members then continue to learn and master the knowledge and skills of at least two and perhaps more jobs on the team. After still more cross-training, team members are fully capable of performing all the jobs on the team. Depending on the complexity of the work of the team and on the difficulty of learning the skills, this may take a few, or many years. Or this may never be completely possible in the case of jobs on the team that require a great deal of outside professional training and/or certification (for example in engineering, legal, and medical work). On the other hand, in some high performance organizations team members do master after several years all of the skills on one team and will then transfer to a different team where they are again challenged to keep learning additional knowledge and skills.

Whether or not it is possible to complete cross-training in work skills, it remains an ideal, a goal to strive for, for several important reasons. Flexibility is the first reason. Team members can move temporarily, with no risk to productivity or quality, to other tasks in the team or even on other teams, as the need arises. They can substitute for ill or absent team members. When there is a vacancy or team expansion, cross-trained members can shift positions to allow newcomers to start with those jobs easiest to learn.

Secondly, team members who master additional jobs in their team understand better the entire work of the team. They are more likely to understand why, how, and where to improve their own work as it affects the work of others on the team.

And they are better prepared to participate in or lead problem-solving and process improvement work with their team, since this usually depends on understanding many or all of the team processes. This is even more true for those employees who have transferred and learned the jobs on second and third teams and therefore understand a broader range of processes and issues.

The third reason for cross-training is that it contributes to the overall growth of the individual. It gives the employee more self-confidence, self-esteem, and self-worth. In other words, this cross-training expands the employee's sense of *identity*. This is of value to everyone: the employee, the team, the organization, and the employee's family and community. If the organization has to drop some activities or products or production while expanding or creating new ones, there will be a ready supply of skilled and flexible employees. Finally, if the worst happens and the organization has to lay off the employee, he or she is more broadly and deeply qualified and self confident to re-enter the job market and find another high-skill, high-productivity, high-wage position.

II. BUSINESS AND ECONOMIC BASICS

Beyond their work skills, team members will need to understand how businesses in general make profits, survive and thrive, and how specifically *our* business does this. In not-for-profit organizations, team members need this training just as much, although their language will be more in terms of "obtaining resources" and "balancing the budget" or "generating a surplus."

Some of the business and economic topics that will need to be addressed are:

- The basics of creating and measuring business performance
- The basics of profit and loss (or surplus and loss)
- The multiple roles of profit in our economy, and in *our* business
- Current, past, and projected future performance of our organization's income/loss
- The basics of cost accounting in our own department and team. Specifically, what are the costs of everything we handle, use, work with, and produce, per unit and/or per hour?
- Trends in our competition (yes, governments and not-for-profits also have competition)

At a more advanced level, some or all of the team members will need to understand:

- Strategic and tactical financial trends and plans for our organization as a whole and for our division or department
- Trends in market and product developments
- In-depth cost accounting for our organization, including fixed versus variable costs
- Seasonality of figures in our business
- New customer groups, new products, new technology development processes
- In-depth understanding of profit and loss statements and balance sheets

Those interested in learning and thinking more about these topics, and both the individual and overall power that can result from developing all employees' understanding of their company as a business, should read *The Great Game of Business* (Stack, 1992).

III. TEAM MEETINGS AND TEAM DECISIONS

Working in teams is probably natural to humans, as we have inherent social capacities. But in the United States, our recent history has not prepared us for team work. Division of U.S. labor and specialization has been pushed to its extreme in the twentieth century, under the general title and rationale of Taylorism, named for the founder of modern industrial engineering and consulting, Frederick W. Taylor. Management used Taylorism to make it easy to quickly train, frequently replace, and firmly control tens of thousands of new entrants into the urban workforce as they arrived from farms and from overseas. Unions embraced Taylorism and built it into labor contracts in all our major industries, as a way of protecting senior workers' rights. Taylorism may have worked well enough for its time and its purposes, but its legacy leaves us with severe problems. As an assistant to the president of the Steelworkers Union told a conference 15 years ago, this very narrow specialization and repetitive work is destroying our people and the productivity and quality of our companies. Furthermore, employees working under Taylorism do not work in teams; they learn individual work, very narrowly defined. (Weisbord, 1990, Ch. 2; Marshall and Tucker, 1992, Ch. 1) Beyond Taylorism, the ideal of competition, so valuable to making markets work, has been carried over in the United States to the internal working of organizations, with the result of setting individuals and departments against one another and undermining teams and teamwork. (Kohn, 1986; Deming, 1982, 1986; Deming, 1994) So our employees currently need training in the reasons for working in teams and in the benefits that occur with team work. They also need training in how to work in teams—not because it is unnatural to work in teams, but because it is contrary to our industrial experience for most of this century.

In addition, most of us have discovered that good meetings do not happen by chance; they require careful planning and skillful leadership. Nor is it self-evident how teams will make decisions. Some alternatives to be considered are: decisions are made by the supervisor (in the case of NWTs), the team leader (in the case of SDTs), or the acknowledged "expert" on a given issue (if there is one), or by majority vote, or by consensus. I have found that many people confuse decision making by consensus with decision making by majority vote. These are, in fact, very different methods. Consensus requires each participant to speak clearly, listen well, seek to understand, and seek reconciling positions, but *not* to vote, and *not* to end up on the winning or losing side, as often happens with voting. So teams need to address early how they will make decisions, by which methods, and in what circumstances. And then teams will need to return to this issue from time to time, sometimes with a trainer's or facilitator's help, as they grow in experience and authority.

Some of the basic topics to be included on team meetings and decision making are:

- The benefits of working, learning, and improving in teams. This can be done both by calling on participants' own experience with successful teams, and by playing problem-solving games that show that more often than not teams come up with better answers than do individuals.
- The requirements for successful teams. This can also be done by calling on participants' own experience with both successful and unsuccessful teams, plus providing information from studies of many successful teams.
- Developing ground rules for teams in general and for *our* team specifically.
- Using defined leadership roles for team meetings, including chairperson, scribe (at a flip chart), and facilitator, and understanding the separate and collective requirements of these roles.
- Understanding and using my Process Diamond model, or some other equivalent, to plan and lead team meetings. The Process Diamond graphically reminds us to plan and lead meetings around the following five basic elements of a successful meeting (or any other value-adding activity): the purpose, the intended specific products, the processes to be used, the inputs needed, and the physical and human ability required to carry out the processes and create the intended products.
- The roles and requirements for team participants. This overlaps with the team's setting of its own ground rules.
- Auditing meetings at the end, and any time as needed, to improve team working.
- The advantages and special rules of brainstorming and awareness of when brainstorming is an appropriate process. Some teams, after learning how to brainstorm, want to use it for everything, all the time!
- Alternative ways teams can make decisions: boss, loudest, expert, majority vote, or consensus. Differences between voting and consensus. Advantages of each method. What consensus requires and how to reach it. How *our* team will make decisions.

IV. COMMUNICATIONS: LISTENING; SENDING/RECEIVING FEEDBACK; PRESENTATIONS; INTERVIEWING

Most of us tend to assume that: (1) communicating is mostly about sending messages clearly; (2) listening is natural and easy; and (3) listening is mostly a passive activity, unlike talking. These assumptions are all false! Listening is the foundation for all communications. Listening is hard work, and it is active work, not passive. Steven Covey (1989) puts it very well when he says: "Seek First to Understand, Then to Be Understood," as his habit five of highly effective people. Besides listening, team members need to understand how to send and receive both critical and positive feedback in a way that helps them improve. Later, they will need to be able to make presentations to small groups, first to their own team, and later to other teams and eventually to teams of managers and teams from suppliers and customers. Also, team members will need training in how to conduct interviews. They will need to interview customers and to handle bad news without becoming reactive. They will also need to know how to interview members of other teams and departments, as well as candidates for vacancies in their team.

An outline of the training needed is:

- Basic listening; listening at several levels, from pretending to empathic
- Asking questions, either closed or open-ended, listing, probing, or reflecting
- Giving and receiving critical feedback
- Giving and receiving positive feedback
- Understanding and dealing with barriers to good communications
- Preparing and delivering a presentation to a small group
- Understanding the differences between dialogue, discussion, and debate or dispute
- Creating the conditions for and supporting dialogue in our team
- Creating a climate for improved communications in any meeting or situation
- Interviewing of customers: purpose, process, handling criticisms/bad news
- Interviewing candidates for team membership: legal, ethical, practical issues

V. Focus on and Understanding of Customers

"Focus on and Understanding of Customers" is the short title of this section. A more explanatory title might be: "Understanding and Satisfying Customers, Delighting Customers, and Building Partnerships with Customers and Suppliers."

Perhaps the most fundamental concept of TQM is that of focusing on customers, understanding customers' needs and desires, and satisfying, or even delighting, customers. External customers are those who select our products and services instead of competitors', those who pay for them, and those who use them—all of whom may be different players. Internal customers are those who receive the results of our work, the next stage in the process from us, the persons or teams or work stations downstream from us. Teams need to understand both internal and external customers and how to meet or exceed their needs and desires, all without spending so much that our organization fails to make a healthy profit. Beyond that, organizations are also learning how to build long-term partnerships with customers, and teams will need to learn how to do this. This includes helping customers to understand and better satisfy *their* customers, working together on finding the best place in the value-adding stream to reduce variation and improve quality and, in general, blurring or opening the boundaries between us.

Likewise, as taught by Dr. Deming and other quality experts, American business is learning to stop buying parts and raw materials on the basis of short-term contracts and initial cost. Instead we are learning to buy on long-term total costs of a purchase (which may be much greater than the short-term costs), and to build long-term partnerships with major suppliers, developing joint designs and quality efforts to maximize long-term profits and other benefits for all parties.

Some of the specifics that teams will need training in are:

- Preparing a complete flow chart and identifying customers, external and internal
- Understanding the three levels of quality (Assumed; Required; Delighting)

- Interviewing first internal and then external customers to increase understanding of their work, their customers, what they require of us, and how well we are doing
- Building regular, multiple, ongoing channels of communications and feedback from customers
- Translating customer requests/requirements/desires into internal specifications
- How to learn what it would take to not only satisfy, but also delight, customers
- Making thoughtful, analytical decisions about what to offer customers in our efforts to delight them
- Applying the PDCA model to insure that what we are attempting is succeeding in delighting customers, at a justifiable cost

Whenever it is time to move toward developing partnerships with customers, the teams will need training in these additional topics:

- How to develop processes to plan with our customers, and then go together with them to interview *their* customers and watch them using our inputs
- Creating a process of continuous improvement in what we provide our customers so that they will continue to be delighted
- Preparing the rationale and process for building customer partnerships
- Pilot testing these new partnerships, making necessary improvements, and sustaining the effort

VI. UNDERSTANDING PROCESSES AND CONTINUOUS IMPROVEMENT

To become high-performing teams by using the concepts and tools of TQM, NWTs and SDTs will need to gain initial learning and then mastery of two of the most fundamental concepts of TQM: continuous improvement and focus on process.

The concept of *Kaizen,* meaning *Continuous Improvement* in English, permeates Japanese society and corporations. Over a decade ago Masaaki Imai wrote a book (Imai, 1986) to inform Americans on how the Japanese have applied this concept to create success in company after company, market after market.

The Shewhart cycle of PDCA—or Plan, Do, Check, Act—is the most simple and basic model for continuous improvement. It has been used by tens of thousands of employees in hundreds of corporations for over 2 decades in Japan. Many American corporations have learned the importance of this cycle and have taught it to their teams. In its most simple application, a team Plans some improvement idea, they Do it, then they Check (audit) what they have done and its results. Finally, they reflect and then Act on their learnings. The Acting may be to Plan another try to create further gains or to take a completely different approach if the first effort did not work at all. Finally, when the Check step shows sufficient success, the Act step leads us to begin a process for standardizing, or for holding the gains. This cycle is named for Walter Shewhart who developed, used, and taught it at Western Electric in the 1930s. One of his disciples was Dr. W. Edwards Deming, who taught it to the Japanese, who now call it the Deming cycle.

We should not be deceived by the apparent simplicity of this model. Recently, Tatsuro Toyoda, Chairman and CEO for many decades of the extremely successful Toyota Motors, said:

Our manufacturing system—and indeed, most everything else at Toyota—is based in PDCA—Plan, Do, Check, Act—problem-solving and *Kaizen* (continuous improvement). Our search for a better way to do things never ends. (Maynard, 1994)

Similarly, U.S. TQM has learned from the Japanese to focus less on improving results directly and more on improving the *processes* that produce the outputs. As Imai put it:

KAIZEN generates process-oriented thinking, since processes must be improved before we get improved results. Further, KAIZEN is people-oriented and is directed at people's efforts. This contrasts sharply with the result-oriented thinking of Western managers... Only the results count in a result-oriented society.

Bridgestone Tire Co's Otsubo maintains that it is process-oriented thinking that has enabled Japanese industry to attain its competitive edge in world markets and that the KAIZEN concept epitomizes Japan's process-oriented thinking. (Imai, 1986, pp. 16–17).

What should teams be taught about these concepts and models? Here is a partial list:

- Understanding the concept of continuous improvement and its importance
- Understanding the PDCA model for continuous improvement
- Understanding processes at work, what and where they are and their importance
- Understanding process flow charting, from very general to very detailed
- Flow charting and understanding the process(es) of *our own* work
- Using flow charting and other tools (see next section) to improve our processes
- Applying flow charting with other teams to the larger processes we are a part of
- Applying the PDCA model to many different kinds of individual and team activities and improvements

VII. FLOW CHARTING, RUN CHARTING, AND OTHER QUALITY CONTROL TOOLS

All these teams, whether supervisor-led, self-managing, or self-directed, will need training in the basic QC tools. These teams are the front line of TQM. They, and their members, will gather information on their processes and outcomes, will chart and study this information, and will apply various tools to analyze this information and help in developing and implementing improvements. The most important of the basic QC tools are:

- Flow charts (see previous section), which allow a team to picture and analyze the flow of products, services, and/or information before, during, and after their own work, as it is now being done and as they propose to do it after improvements.
- Run charts, which allow a single variable to be plotted and observed over time, providing an opportunity for trends or patterns in the variable to emerge.
- Control charts, which are essentially run charts over a large enough set of observations to allow calculations of mean, standard deviation, and upper and lower

control limits. This allows analysis of the variation in a process and the separation of variation into common and special causes. This is the only common QC tool that requires any significant mathematics skills. It is not important that all team members understand this math in detail. It is important that all team members understand the basic concepts and purposes of the control charts and their uses in understanding common and special causes of variation.

- Cause-effect diagrams (also called fishbone diagrams), which allow focused brainstorming on all of the possible causes of a specific problem, or of a desired outcome.
- Pareto charts, which show in a bar diagram of descending sizes the frequency of the major problems, and their categories and causes.
- Histograms, which show in a bar diagram the frequency distribution of observations of a variable.
- Scatter diagrams, which allow plotting of the observations of two variables against each other to give a visual impression of possible or probable correlation.
- Check sheets, which allow recording observations in an organized way to maximize accuracy and comparability of observations recorded in different places, at different times, and/or by different observers.

For more on these tools, see Ishikawa, 1976; Brassard, 1985; Wheeler and Chambers, 1986; Brassard and Ritter, 1994; Montgomery, 1995A and 1995B; and Costin, 1994, Part III.

Beyond these classical QC Tools, there are the so-called "7 New QC Tools" (Mizuno, 1988), which are also called the "Seven Management and Planning Tools" (Brassard, 1989). These tools, after a few revisions, now include the affinity diagram, the interrelationship digraph, the tree diagram, various kinds of matrices, including decision matrices, a contingency diagram called by the awful name of process decision program chart, and a critical path analysis tool named the activity network diagram. Because of their success in assisting with management and planning, these are very useful tools for natural work teams and for self-directed teams. They could and should be built into training for these teams, to aid their work of improvement.

VIII. USING DISCIPLINED MODELS FOR PROBLEM SOLVING AND PROCESS IMPROVEMENT

The PDCA model is very powerful, but in some cases is too general. And we Americans love to Do, Do, Do. When we gather to solve problems, we are prone to leap immediately to the solutions we personally prefer. We end up fixing symptoms, instead of going to root causes. This means that we repeat this activity many times, without making any serious progress. To keep us from this tendency to rush to solutions without proper study and analysis, we and our teams should be guided by a formal, disciplined problem-solving model, of which there are many available.

We also need to shift our attention from problem solving, which is usually focused on fixing things that have gone wrong (fix the "squeaky wheel"), to process improvement, which selects processes to improve not because they are wrong or broken, but because they are important in determining our long-term success with our customers. Our problem-solving mentality is illustrated in our national "If it ain't broke, don't fix it" slogan. Process improvement calls for a different mentality, a different model, and a slogan that might be: "If it ain't broke, improve it anyway." If we were a nation of process improvers instead of problem solvers, our international trade deficit might be half as large as it is.

Most teams will need to learn first a model for problem solving, since most organizations still have many, many problems to solve. But in later years and in some organizations right from the start, the teams will need to learn a model for process improvement, which starts with deciding which are our key or critical processes and what are our customers' needs and requirements of them. For more discussion of these differences and many examples, see "Solving Problems and Improving Processes: Which Model Shall We Use?" (Reading 4 in this book).

In any case, the teams will also need to learn the importance of staying with the model even when some team members are sure they know the cause and the solution, and are vehemently demanding that the team not waste all this time in following some "stupid old model when we know what to do." At the same time, the teams need to learn the importance of "managing with facts"—of using facts, data, information, and analysis before deciding on causes, priorities, and solutions.

IX. "MANAGING WITH DATA"

One of the main tenets of TQM is that we should all "manage with data." What this means is that good planning, implementation, auditing, application of the PDCA cycle, problem solving, and process improvement *all* require that we gather, observe, analyze, and in other ways utilize facts as accurately as possible. "Facts are friendly," as the saying goes.

"Managing with data" is actually a poor slogan, since data alone can be, or is inevitably, disorganized, confused, and confusing. We all know this from our own experience and our immediate recognition of the term "data dump." What we are really talking about is *information* or data organized to be comprehensible and useful.

To manage with data, teams must be given the following kinds of support:

- Access to corporate, divisional, and departmental financial information, current and in trends and cycles, and full training in what this information means and how to interpret it.
- Information from customers on all aspects of product and service quality.
- Real-time information on quantity, cost, quality, delivery, and related information. This will often require computer terminals, or networked personal computers for every team member, or every work station, or at least one or two for each team. It will also require, obviously, full training for team members in how to use these computer terminals or computers, all of the relevant software, and the actual information being utilized.
- Opportunity, and the requisite leadership and training, to discuss and decide what kinds of information the team needs to do its work and to improve its performance.

X. Developing a Team Mission, Vision, and Values

For teams to become highly effective, they will need to develop their own mission, which is focused outward on the service they provide and the value they create for customers and society. They will also need to develop their own vision of what they are doing, of how they will work together, and of how they will become a team. Both their mission and their vision must be aligned with the larger mission and vision of their organization. Both are important vehicles for aligning team members with one another, with customers and suppliers, and with other departments and functions in their organization. Mission and vision are also vitally important in helping teams and individuals in those teams to focus and sustain their energies and to make sound decisions without having to constantly check with higher authority. Implicit in the mission and vision are the values that the team members believe to be important and commit themselves to live and work by. Although different organizations and consultants have slightly different definitions for these three terms, they are describing the same process and requirements. For example, training will be needed in:

- The meaning and importance of clarity of mission, or purpose.
- Examples of missions and purposes of other corporations, divisions, teams.
- Discussion and analysis of the mission/purpose of *our* corporation, division, and so on.
- Processes for developing and developing again mission/purpose.
- Vision: What it is; why it is important; the power of vision.
- Various paths to creating a vision; how we will create, develop, revise *our* vision.
- Values: What they are; why they are important; how *our* team will clarify our values and align ourselves with the values of our organization.

For more on these topics, see Drucker, 1973; Vaill, 1982; Covey, 1989, pp. 65–144, especially pp. 140–143; Senge, 1990, Chapters 11 and 12; and Senge, et al, 1994, pp. 44–51.

XI. Valuing Differences and Diversity: Supporting Development of Individual Identity

Teams will need to understand the importance of differences and diversity. This starts with differences among team members in age, gender, cultural background, religious beliefs, education, training, job background, and expertise. Diversity in all of these is valuable for a team that needs and wishes to grow. Team members will need training and help in appreciating these differences, and in actually seeking them out in selecting people for team vacancies. Beyond this are differences in ways of thinking and in learning styles, which are also valuable to the team, if properly understood and utilized.

The team also has an interest and an obligation to honor and develop the distinct individual identities of team members. Identity is a subtle and complex concept. My identity is who I am; it is my core, my very essence or being. It is how I see and understand myself. High self-esteem and a high sense of self-worth are indicators of a strong identity. With a strong identity, we also have integrity, which is vital for success in teams, in business, and in life. Our identity is developed, at least in part, by how much continuing interaction we have with a complex and challenging environment. Another way to say this is that identity is built by treating ourselves as though we are open systems, which in fact we are, by putting ourselves into new and challenging environments and circumstances. (Wheatley, 1992, Ch. 5).

Perhaps the best proof is that the U.S. plant with the longest track record of creating and managing with highly empowered teams, P&G's Lima detergent plant, was planned and launched with a very strong emphasis on the development of individual identity. *And* it recently completed a process of involving all employees in 4 full days of diversity training. This training was proposed, developed, and led by some team members themselves, over a period of almost 2 years. (Waterman, 1994, p. 54.)

Every organization will have to work out their own version of training in these complex areas. Here are some suggested topics and approaches:

- Practice team decision making on complex issues with an initial limitation of diversity of inputs, that expands to much broader diversity of all kinds
- Understand how and why human beings categorize and classify information and people
- Understand advantages and disadvantages of classification and categorization
- Understand the historical, sociological, economic, psychological, and personal sources of our classifications and prejudices
- Learn to face honestly our own individual biases, fears, and prejudices
- Understand the sources and importance of self-esteem and self-worth
- Learn to know who I am, why I am that way, and who I want to become or remain
- Develop methods and personal contracts with my team to help me value and develop my own identity, and that of others, and to understand and value diversity

XII. PLANNING CHANGE: ANTICIPATING AND RECONCILING RESISTANCE TO CHANGES

Teams will create change in the processes they use in their workplaces and together with people from other departments and from suppliers and customers, they will be planning much broader changes. In order to do this, and as a result of it, teams will also create change in their own knowledge, skills, and attitudes. Also, they will be bringing pressure for changes in the systems and policies of their larger organizations. To do all of this, they will need to learn how to plan and carry out change and to understand the inevitable resistance to change that will occur within themselves and others. Some of the specific training topics are:

- How to make decisions when costs and benefits can be roughly estimated
- How to make decisions when costs and/or benefits cannot be estimated
- Force-field analysis for analyzing forces for and against a change
- Understanding resistance to change within ourselves and others
- Valuing differences, including resistance to change, and finding reconciling paths
- Understanding my own resistance to change, learning to accept and then reconcile these internal resistances

- Developing and following a team action plan: *who does what, and by when?*
- Developing and following a process for auditing our change implementation
- Learning to apply this thinking to our customer and supplier relations

XIII. SYSTEMS UNDERSTANDING

Teams interact with and depend upon corporate systems, such as attendance, pay, performance review, information, discipline, training, and safety. Teams themselves are systems, made up of subsystems called human beings. Teams are part of larger systems, called departments, functions, and divisions. These departments, functions, and divisions are part of larger systems called companies, hospitals, or governments. These companies, hospitals, or governments are part of larger systems called markets, communities, states or nations, which themselves are. . . and so on. These teams, and the departments and organizations they are part of, are also part of larger environmental and ecosystems. For these natural work teams and self-directed teams to succeed, they must understand the nature of systems, understand themselves as a system, and understand the systems they interact with and are a part of.

Some suggestions for specific training topics in systems understanding are:

- Characteristics of systems, such as interdependence and interaction; examples.
- Understanding the functions of immediate supplier and customer departments and of the ways in which our team and department are interdependent with them.
- Understanding the pay, performance, attendance, discipline, quality, customer service, safety, and other internal systems of our organization, including their purpose and how they function.
- Understanding the environmental and ecological systems we are part of and how we both affect and are affected by them. This could include air, water, visual, noise, traffic, and social and political systems.
- Understanding the interdependence between our marketing, sales, engineering, production, quality, finance, training, and other departments, and how they function together to retain or lose existing customers, and to acquire or lose new customers. Only from a systems perspective do employees come to understand that "we are all in quality," "we are all in sales," "we are all in customer service," and so on.

At a later, more advanced level of learning, we might add topics, such as:

- Understanding how and through what channels of formal and informal organization each of our systems (including pay, performance, attendance, discipline, quality, customer service, and safety) is susceptible to change and improvements.
- Understanding the purposes and functioning of major external customers, and how our products/services are used by them and contribute to their success in satisfying or delighting *their* customers, customers of customers, and end users.
- Understanding ourselves as human, thinking, and learning systems.

ADDITIONAL TRAINING FOR SELF-DIRECTED TEAMS

Natural work teams that have worked and improved together for several years, and who have participated together in large parts of the training topics outlined previously are well on their way to functioning like self-directed teams even though they may still have a formally designated supervisor. They are probably ready to operate with more self-direction, including choosing their own leader. In other words, the training described previously has covered most of the training requirements for self-directed teams. Here are some additional training topics they will need to become more fully self-directed:

- What types of authority this team has, and what is the process for taking on more authority, including what are the performance, information, and capability prerequisites for increased authority?
- What it means to accept accountability; what accountability *our* team accepts, for what, and how we will audit ourselves against that accountability.
- Performance measurements for our team that we will initiate and track, in addition to any required by upper management.
- Leadership issues: What does leadership mean and require? What kind of leadership do *we* want? What kind of leader do we want? How will we select/elect our leader? For how long a term will our leaders serve? The need for short terms with rapid rotation versus long or indefinite terms in office.
- The meaning and potentials of distributed leadership. How well does it fit for *our* team? How could or will we adapt it to fit our situation and needs? How will we implement it?
- Team decision making. As we move from supervisor-led to self-directed teams, are we ready to or do we need to expand or modify our decision-making methods and choices?
- Managing conflicts in our team, or with others. As we move out "on our own" without a supervisor, do we need to polish up or deepen our communications skills, or our ability to resolve and reconcile conflicts within the team? Between ourselves and other teams?

ADDITIONAL TRAINING FOR TEAMS IN UNIONIZED ORGANIZATIONS

In unionized organizations, it is important that all supervisors, team leaders, and team members be given some additional training related to the union–management contract and situation. This should include:

- The basic provisions of the union contract.
- The rights of the union members under the contract.
- The grievance procedure.
- The nature, purposes, vision, ground rules and processes of any joint union–management effort, including employee involvement, quality of working

life, work design or redesign, or partnerships to create a "new American work-place," or other kinds of planning or steering committees or efforts.
- How individuals and teams may participate in or contribute to any such joint labor–management processes and any agreed upon limits on this participation.

For an early work on how these joint processes are started and governed, see Brower, 1982. For a very recent official union view of how partnerships should be structured to create a "new American workplace," see AFL-CIO, 1994. For examples of how unions and TQM can interact, see Bernstein, 1994; and, including a bibliography, Waxler and Higginson, 1994. For a case study of how Xerox and the ACTWU got together on a cooperative process, see Cutcher-Gershenfeld, 1988.

ADDITIONAL TRAINING AND LEARNING FOR TEAMS AS LEARNING ORGANIZATIONS

If these teams are to go beyond learning the basic skills and ideas outlined previously, they will need to learn how to become "learning organizations" themselves and to contribute to an overall organizational learning culture. Learning how to learn is a complex matter; what follows is only one way to approach this challenging issue.

We might distinguish five separate levels of learning:

The first is that described in most of the sections of this article in which individuals and teams are being trained and are developing new knowledge and skills to enable them to conduct and improve their work.

At a second level is learning about learning, learning how different people learn, learning how *I* learn best, learning about thinking about learning as a never-ending process.

At a third level, team members learn to be self-aware and self-observing, that is, able to observe their own thinking and actions, while they are right in the middle of the thinking or acting. Or, as Argyris calls it, learning how to utilize "double-loop learning" (Argyris, 1992, especially Part 1), which is about observing and understanding our own "governing variables," which drive and determine our actions. Those who have attempted this will verify that it is easier to learn originally and to practice occasionally, than it is to remember to do it for more than a few moments, especially when the stakes are high and we are personally invested in the results.

At a fourth, more complex level is to develop the knowledge of cognition and the structures which shape the way we think about any given situation. (Senge, 1990, Ch. 10).

A fifth level is that of learning about and studying the meta-paradigms that we grow up with and accept unconsciously. McWhinney calls these "worldviews" and "alternative realities." When team members understand that their thinking is influenced, even determined, by their mental models, which in turn are influenced or determined by their worldview, they are then on the road to being able to make conscious choices and to become truly self-directing and truly empowered. (Senge, 1990, Ch. 12; Senge, et al., 1994; Argyris, 1992; Wheatley, 1992; and especially, McWhinney, 1992).

SOME REFLECTIONS ON THE
IMPORTANCE OF THIS TRAINING

The basic 13 training areas recommended in the major part of this reading add up to a great deal of training. Is this much really necessary? I think so. First, it is important that we stop looking for an easy answer. The benefits of employees working in effective teams are enormous. The payoff is high. But we do not get these benefits for nothing. There must be an up-front investment. Although most organizations provide far less training than this, a few are now beginning to invest in this kind of long and deep team training. A few years ago, the president and CEO of Corning set a corporate goal of investing 5 percent of every employee's time by 1993, on the average, each year, in training. That equals 104 hours per year per employee, or a little over 2 1/2 weeks per year. That much time is enough to cover, in a couple of years, most of the basic and some of the advanced training recommended here. It is not unusual for Procter and Gamble and other companies starting up new team-based plants to have all employees needed for the plant selected, on the payroll, and into training a full 6–8 weeks before the plant must ship any product to market.

Unfortunately, many other companies are setting up teams and expecting high performance from them with very little, or clearly inadequate, training. The result is that for every team that is succeeding in improving continually its performance and its service to customers, there is probably at least one team that is failing, or at least failing to significantly improve itself and its performance. In a survey of major U.S. corporations a few years ago, "insufficient training" was identified as the largest single cause of failure of self-directed teams. (Wellins and George, 1991, p. 29)

How important is this training to out future? Drawing on the work of the Commission on the Future of the American Workforce, and its final report *America's Choice: High Skills or Low Wages,* former Secretary of Labor Ray Marshall and Marc Tucker, President of the National Center on Education and the Economy, have written:

> "We have made a case that the economic future of the United States depends mainly on the skills of the front-line work force, the people whose jobs will not require a baccalaureate degree. Success, then, depends on developing a program to prepare close to three-quarters of our work force to take on tasks in restructured workplaces that, up to now, have been assigned mainly to the college educated. Bank tellers will have to know about the full line of the bank's products, from zero-coupon bonds to tax-deferred annuities and checking-account lines of credit, and be able to steer the customer to the right product. People who work on automobile assembly lines will have to know how to use flexible-automation systems, program computers, use the methods of statistical quality control, and do production scheduling. The salesperson in the carpet store will have to know not only the characteristics of the various synthetic and natural fibers from which carpets are made, the strengths and weaknesses of different fabrication and weaving methods, and the pros and cons of different stain-resisting treatments, but also the fundamentals of retail sales and marketing." (Marshall and Tucker, 1992, p. 155)

The authors' main plea is to enable our educational systems to provide this kind of training and to get the rest of us to restructure the way we work. But in the meantime, given how little of this training is being provided in high school (or even colleges), the burden is falling squarely on industry to provide it. And of course, even when (or if) our educational system completely reforms and begins to provide much more highly qualified personnel, industry will still have to invest a great deal in continuing training if they are to develop and reap the benefits of truly high-performing teams. For many companies, highly developed people (in teams, I would add) may be the only remaining competitive advantage.

We really no longer have any choice. At the organizational level, some businesses still have excessive levels of managers trying to micromanage front line people who are under-trained and underutilized. These businesses, even the giants, are failing at a rapid rate; most will not be here very long into the next century. It is increasingly clear: in almost every marketplace, with almost every product and service, the competition is now worldwide. The survivors and winners are and will be those companies that train their front-line employees, organize them into teams, focus them on serving and delighting customers, align them and the larger organization around common mission and vision, get middle management off their backs, and encourage them to become lifelong learners and to use their minds and creativity—not occasionally, not just as part of a special project team, but all day, every day. At the national level, there is no other way that I know of for us to regain our competitiveness, to close our trade deficit, and to sustain a large number of high productivity, high wage jobs.

BIBLIOGRAPHY

AFL-CIO Committee on the Evolution of Work. *The New American Workplace: A Labor Perspective.* Washington, D.C.: AFL-CIO, 1994.

Argyris, Chris. "Why Individuals and Organizations Have Difficulty in Double-Loop Learning." In *On Organizational Learning.* Cambridge, MA: Blackwell Publishers, 1992.

———. "Teaching Smart People How to Learn." In *On Organizational Learning.* Cambridge, MA: Blackwell Publishers, 1992.

AT&T Quality Steering Committee. *Process Quality Management & Improvement Guidelines.* Indianapolis: AT&T's Customer Information Center, 1987, 1988 (Issue 1.1).

Bernstein, Aaron. "Why America Needs Unions, But Not the Kind It Has Now." *Business Week,* May 23, 1994, pp. 70–82.

Brassard, Michael. *The Memory Jogger.* Methuen, MA: GOAL/QPC, 1985.

———. *The Memory Jogger Plus+*® Methuen, MA: GOAL/QPC, 1989.

Brassard, Michael, and Diane Ritter. *The Memory Jogger* ™*II.* Methuen, MA: GOAL/QPC, 1994.

Brower, Michael. *Starting Labor–Management Quality of Work Life Programs.* Washington, D.C.: U.S. Department of Labor, 1982.

———. "Implementing TQM with Self-Directed Teams." In *Readings in Total Quality Management,* edited by Harry Costin. Fort Worth: The Dryden Press, 1994, pp. 403–420.

Costin, Harry. *Readings in Total Quality Management.* Fort Worth: The Dryden Press, 1994.

Covey, Stephen. *The Seven Habits of Highly Effective People.* New York: Simon & Schuster, 1989.

Cutcher-Gershenfeld, Joel. *Tracing a Transformation in Industrial Relations. The Case of Xerox and the Amalgamated Clothing and Textile Workers Union.* Washington, D.C.: U.S. Department of Labor, Bureau of Labor–Management Relations and Cooperative Programs, 1988.

Deming, W. Edwards. *Out of the Crisis*. Cambridge: M.I.T. Center for Advanced Engineering Study, 1982, 1986.

———. *The New Economics: For Industry, Government, Education*. Cambridge: M.I.T. Center for Advanced Engineering Study, 1994.

Donnell, Augustus, and Margaret Dellinger, for the AT&T Quality Steering Committee. *Analyzing Business Process Data: The Looking Glass*. Indianapolis: AT&T's Customer Information Center, 1990.

Drucker, Peter. "Business Purpose and Business Mission," In *Management: Tasks-Responsibilities-Practices*, edited by Peter Drucker. New York: Harper & Row, 1973.

Imai, Masaaki. *Kaizen. The Key to Japan's Competitive Success*. New York: Random House, 1986.

Ishikawa, Kaoru. *Guide to Quality Control*. Tokyo: Asian Productivity Organization, 1976.

Juran Institute. *Quality Improvement, Team Training Workbook*. Wilton, CT: 1992.

Kohn, Alfie. *No Contest: The Case Against Competition*. Boston: Houghton Mifflin, 1986.

Marshall, Ray, and Marc Tucker. *Thinking for a Living*. New York: Basic Books, 1992.

Maynard, Micheline, "Toyota Dodging 'Big company Disease,' Search Still on for Inefficiencies." (Interview with CEO Tatsuro Toyoda). *USA Today,* May 28, 1994

McWhinney, Will. *Paths of Change*. Newbury Park, CA: Sage, 1992.

Miller, Lawrence M., and Jennifer Howard. *Managing Quality through Teams*. Atlanta: The Miller Consulting Group, 1991.

Mizuno, Shigera. *Management for Quality Improvement: The 7 New QC Tools*. Cambridge, MA.: Productivity Press, 1988.

Montgomery, William L. *Power-Up Teams & Tools for Process Improvement & Problem Solving*. Princeton, N.J.: The Montgomery Group, 1995.

———. *Power-Up Team Guide, Examples of Process Improvement & Problem Solving*. Princeton, N.J.: The Montgomery Group, 1995.

Orsburn, Jack D., Linda Moran, Ed Musselwhite, and John H. Zenger. *Self-Directed Work Teams*. Homewood, IL: Business One Irwin, 1990.

Scholtes, Peter R. *The Team Handbook*. Madison: Joiner Associates, 1988.

Senge, Peter M. *The Fifth Discipline*. New York: Doubleday Currency, 1990.

Senge, Peter M., Charlotte Roberts, Richard B. Ross, Bryan J. Smith, and Art Kleiner, *The Fifth Discipline Fieldbook*. New York: Doubleday Currency, 1994.

Shiba, Dr. Shoji. November 15, 1993 talk jointly sponsored by the Merrimack Valley Chapter of the American Society for Quality Control (ASQC) and the Greater Boston Chapter of the Association for Quality and Participation (AQP).

Stack, Jack. *The Great Game of Business*. New York: Doubleday Currency, 1992.

Vaill, Peter. "The Purposing of High-Performance Systems," *Organizational Dynamics*. (Autumn 1982): 23–39.

Waterman, Bob. *What America Does Right.*, New York: W.W. Norton, 1994.

Waxler, Robert P., and Thomas Higginson. "TQM: Labor-Management Cooperation," in *Readings in Total Quality Management*, edited by Harrry Costin. Fort Worth: The Dryden Press, 1994, pp. 421–429.

Weisbord, Marvin R. *Productive Workplaces*. San Francisco: Jossey-Bass, 1990.

Wellins, Richard and Jill George. "Training for Self-Directed Teams," *Training & Development Journal*. (April 1991) 26–31.

Wheatley, Margaret J. *Leadership and the New Science*. San Francisco: Berrett-Koehler Publishers, Inc., 1992.

Wheeler, Donald J., and David S. Chambers. *Understanding Statistical Process Control*. Knoxville, TN: Statistical Process Controls, Inc., 1986.

By Kate Jones-Randall

The research process, like any process, is one that requires strategic preparation, careful execution, and revision based on feedback from results (not unlike the implementation of a total quality management program).

Total quality management as a concept dates back to the early 1950s and was introduced as "total quality control." TQM, as a true subject heading utilized in indexes and abstracts to literature, did not emerge until the early 1980s. It was frequently used as an "identifier" or an unofficial subject heading in the 1970s. Many print indexes still required the researcher to look under "quality control" or for quality or process control as a part of a particular industry, such as aerospace or automotive. Now, however, TQM is ubiquitous, and the researcher must take care to look for quality initiatives once again in relationship to a particular industry or service area.

A recent glance at the CD-ROM **Business Periodicals Index** published by Wilson Co. listed just over 400 entries under "total quality management" dating from 1983 onward, from a wide variety of industry areas. UMI's Proquest CD-ROM database **ABI/Inform** listed over 3,200 entries under "total quality," from January of 1992 alone. This list could go ever onward; we have not even begun to look at Internet resources yet!

If you wish to refine research strategies to manage optimally information retrieval, there are some key strategies to follow. Clearly, the information is available, and it is now a question of focusing on specific subtopics linked with total quality in order to improve your search results. The researcher must define the area in which he or she wishes to discover the use of total quality management processes as a tool within a particular industry or service area. For example, total quality initiatives have been in place successfully in the U.S. military, various hospital systems, and certain companies in the automotive industry for some time. TQM in higher education has become a major focus of many academic communities, and a number of Internet resources are devoted to this area alone. Frequently, the researcher might also incorporate other terms, such as "benchmarking," or "business process engineering" or "reengineering" with TQM or total quality, in order to further refine a search strategy regardless of industry or service area.

A researcher may begin within the indexes and abstracts to business literature to look for applications of TQM principles in all possible industry and services areas. Two of the most useful of these indexes/abstracts are **ABI/Inform** and **Business Periodicals Index,** as mentioned previously. Both are available in CD-ROM format, as well as through online access via DIALOG and WILSON-LINE. DIALOG offers *One Search* or the capability to search simultaneously many management-oriented databases, such as Management Contents, ABI/Inform, PAIS International, Harvard Business Review, Delphes European Business, and EIU: Business International. This is a boon to researchers, especially from an international perspective. It is not, however, free of charge. While many libraries will typically hold many CD-ROMs that are generally available to the public, online access rarely is, and is usually on a fee-for-service basis. Always consult your local public or academic library professional for the types and costs of resources available.

Business literature is not the only place to search, however. Researchers should consider subject-specific databases, indexes and abstracts, or CD-ROM files in the various areas where they would like to find applications of total quality management principles. For example, the Cumulative Index to Nursing and Allied Health Literature (CINAHL) is available both in print and on CD-ROM, and both the Health Periodicals Database or MEDLINE database are available on DIALOG, among many other medicine related files. Both would offer access to articles or books detailing TQM implementation in hospitals, nursing homes, and so on.

Another excellent source of information on quality in many areas is the **Quality Abstracts,** published by Advanced Personnel Systems, Roseville, CA. It is a companion publication to *Training and Development Alert,* and deals specifically with total quality management issues. It began in November of 1992, and is currently available only in print.

Many publishers specialize in certain areas of quality issues, among them the **American Society of Quality Control Quality Press** (P.O. Box 3005, Milwaukee, WI 53201, 800-952-6587); **Business One Irwin** (1818 Ridge Rd., Homewood, IL 60430, 800-634-3961); **Chapman & Hall** (29 W. 35th St., New York, NY 10001, 212-244-3336); **GOAL/QPC** (13 Branch St., Methuen, MA 01844, 800-643-4316); **Productivity Press** (P.O. Box 13390, Portland OR 97213, 800-394-6868); and **John Wiley & Sons** (605 Third Ave., New York, NY 10158, 800-225-5945). This list is not exclusive, merely representative of publishers currently producing numerous titles related to total quality management. Catalogs are readily available from publishers so that you can keep abreast of the most recent trends, and purchase volumes directly if you so desire.

The Internet is a rich source of information on total quality. In addition to numerous library online catalogs that may be searched for their holdings on quality topics, there are specific TQM listservs dedicated to quality management. One of the best of these is QUALITY - Total Quality Management (TQM) information at Babson College, readily accessible through either Veronica or gopher searching under the terms "total quality," or telnet directly to **vaxvms.babson.edu.** It is extensive, including Babson's quality program initiatives in addition to a long bibliography of Babson College Horn Library holdings in quality. It also mentions various other listservs, among them TQM-L@UKANVM, or TQM in higher education, TQMEDU-L@HUMBER (also education-related), and TQMLIB@WAYNEST1, a list on TQM in libraries. A new server, TQM Bulletin Board from Clemson University (previously only available by modem to the TQMBBS in Washington, D.C.), is accessible by telnet to **deming.eng.clemson.edu** or gopher to **deming.eng.clemson.edu:70,** with comments to **quality@eng.clemson.edu.**

For an introduction to NIST's Quality Award, telnet to **zserve.nist.gov,** for the NIST Malcolm Baldrige Quality Award files.

A quality discussion list, QUALITY@PUCC.PRINCETON.EDU, has been set up as "a forum for the discussion of quality manufacturing and service . . . and to be a clearinghouse of information in the form of 'datafiles' which are stored at PUCC." Researchers may subscribe using the following standard command to the LISTSERV@PUCC.PRINCETON.EDU, with no entry in the subject field, SUBSCRIBE QUALITY firstname lastname.

Other pathways on the Internet, either using Gopher Jewels (a subject collection of Internet files) by keyword, or PEG (a peripatetic, eclectic gopher) using Veronica to search the 'virtual reference desk,' lead the researcher to files detailing books, articles, projects, and a variety of files on total quality. The list is seemingly endless, although Internet browsing, or "surfing," often leads the surfer around in circles, and you can find yourself accessing a file today that disappears tomorrow. This will change, as the Internet becomes more organized, and is cataloged or indexed by information professionals seeking to make access more efficient. In the meantime, enjoy the ride and expect many technical delays.

Researchers now have a wealth of information available to them. As is often the case, an information professional can be the best guide through the forest to the specific trees that will yield the information the researcher is seeking. Always check with your business or other subject-specialist librarian for the sources that can give you the best results.

Increasingly, Internet tools have been developed which greatly aid information seekers. Most useful is the graphical universe of networked information, the World Wide Web, and the numerous "browsers" which have been created to search it. The web is explained in minute detail in the following article by Eric Lease Morgan ("The World-Wide Web and Mosaic: An Overview for Librarians." The Public-Access Computer Systems Review 5, no. 6 (1994): 5-26. To retrieve this file, send the following e-mail message to listserv@uhupvm1.uh.edu: GET MORGAN PRV5N6 F=MAIL. Or, use the journals/uhlibrary/pacsreview/v5/n6/morgan.5n6.)

Searchers with access to Netscape, Mosaic, Lynx, or other "browser" interfaces can make direct queries to multiple data collections about their specific areas of interest, retrieving ranked results which can usually be downloaded or printed in a full-text format, often with accompanying graphics. In addition to these search "engines," lists or "guides" by subject area abound on WWW "Home Pages."

APPENDIX B *Database of Authors*

Michael Brower
Michael Brower & Associates
30 Alpine Street
Cambridge, MA 02138
Tel.: (617) 492-8893
Fax: (617) 492-6441

Terence Burton
The Center for Excellence in
Operations
One Clocktower Place, Suite 415
Nashua, NH 03060
Tel.: (603) 883-3677
Fax: (603) 598-3766

Harry Costin
Harry Costin & Associates
P.O. Box 15619
Boston, MA 02215
Tel.: (617) 738-5059
Fax: (617) 277-9140

Joann DeMott
The J. DeMott Company
31347 Cougar Lane
Philomath, OR 97370
Tel.: (503) 929-6785
Fax: (503) 929-6757

Ellen R. Domb
The PQR Group
190 N. Mountain Ave.
Upland, CA 91786-9764
Tel.: (909) 949-0857
Fax: (909) 949-2968

Glen D. Hoffherr
Markon Inc.
P.O. Box 423
Windham, NH 03087-0423
Tel.: (603) 898-3919
Fax: (603) 894-5770

Kate Jones-Randall
Library Communications Center
University of Massachusetts
Dartmouth
285 Old Westport Road
North Dartmouth, MA 02747
Tel.: (508) 999-8670
Fax: (508) 996-9759

John W. Moran
308 Stow Rd.
Harvard, MA 01451
Tel. & Fax: (508) 456-3881

Paul H. Wang
1012 Hollins College Court
Virginia Beach, VA 23455
Tel.: (804) 552-0491

Norman W. Young
Markon Inc.
P.O. Box 423
Windham, NH 03087-0423
Tel.: (603) 898-3919
Fax: (603) 894-5770

Index